Air Wars

Air Wars

TELEVISION ADVERTISING IN
ELECTION CAMPAIGNS, 1952–1996

SECOND EDITION

Darrell M. West
Brown University

Congressional Quarterly Inc.
Washington, D.C.

Cover design: Paula Anderson

Library of Congress Cataloging-in-Publication Data

West, Darrell M.
   Air wars : television advertising in election campaigns, 1952–1996
/ Darrell M. West.—2nd ed.
      p.   cm.
   Includes bibliographical references and index.
   ISBN 1-56802-347-2 (hard). — ISBN 1-56802-346-4 (paper)
   1. Advertising, Political—United States.   2. Television in politics—United States.
3. Electioneering—United States.   4. Politics and government—1945–1989.
5. United States—Politics and government—1989–
I. Title
JF2112.A4W47   1997
324.7'3'097309045—dc21   97-6405

*To Annie Schmitt, for her
continuing love and affection*

———————————

Contents

Tables and Figures

Tables

Figures

Preface

Since the publication of the first edition of this book in 1993 there have been several new developments in the advertising world: Internet ads for candidates, free television time for one- to two-minute presentations, new technology that allows candidates to manipulate ad images electronically with ease, increasing recognition of the importance of visual messages in ads, changes in the relationship between ads and the news, controversies over the use of ad watches by the media, growing use of issue advocacy ads by independent groups, and computerized ad-buy strategies to target candidate messages. It therefore is timely to have a new edition that addresses each of these developments with new material from the 1996 campaign. Several new chapters on ad buys, voluntary codes, and playing the blame game have been added. In addition, all of the remaining chapters have been thoroughly revised and updated. Chapter 1 discusses how ads are put together. It emphasizes the attention media consultants pay to music, color, editing techniques, audio voice-overs, code words, visual text, and visual images. Chapter 2 shows how candidates buy air time. These decisions—called ad buys—are the most fundamental decisions made in any campaign.

Chapter 3 reviews the messages presented in ads broadcast over the air as well as through the relatively new medium of the Internet. Chapter 4 looks at the relationship between ads and the news, focusing in particular on how reporters cover political ads. Chapter 5 examines controversies over ad watches by the media and other voluntary approaches to policing advertisements.

Chapters 6 through 9 investigate the impact of ads on viewers, looking at what citizens learn about the candidates through ads, the effects of ads on the agenda, candidate efforts through advertising to shift the standards voters use to assess contestants, and the way candidates play the blame game to shift responsibility for negative campaigning to their opponents. Chapter 10 puts advertising within the framework of democratic elections and shows that the risk of voter manipulation remains an important problem in democracies. Several possible remedies for dealing with this problem are discussed.

In each of these chapters, I have undertaken new data collection on the 1996 campaign. This includes interviews with media consultants and political reporters, new material on ad buys, a review of issue-advocacy advertising, content analyses of campaign ads and media coverage of ads, a national survey of local television news directors and newspaper managing editors about ad watches, a review of voluntary approaches to ad oversight, alternative communications avenues such as debates and free television time, a national public opinion survey undertaken during the last week of the 1996 campaign, and the results of focus groups in which voters were shown ads and ad watches.

I would like to thank the Pew Charitable Trusts and the Committee for the Study of the American Electorate for grant support on the 1996 phase of this project. Portions of Chapter 2 appeared earlier in "Ad Buys in Presidential Campaigns," *Political Communication* 12 (July–September 1995), coauthored with Montague Kern, Dean Alger, and Janice Goggin.

I appreciate the helpful comments on the first edition that were made by Dean Alger, Craig Allen, Michael Delli Carpini, Brett Clifton, Robert Dewhirst, Richard Francis, Chris Goodwin, Matthew Kerbel, Diana Mutz, and Michell Wilson. Their suggestions made this edition more readable and comprehensive.

The staff members at Congressional Quarterly deserve a big thank you. I am grateful to executive editor David Tarr and his assistant Gwenda Larsen for their help in making this edition possible. Debbie K. Hardin did a masterful job of copyediting the manuscript. Talia Greenberg made sure production ran smoothly. Gary Hallquist of Prime Time Video produced the still photos for this book from ad videotapes. Jack Combs provided invaluable help on the national public opinion surveys conducted for this book.

I also would like to thank the Department of Political Science and the John Hazen White Sr. Public Opinion Laboratory of the A. Alfred Taubman Center for Public Policy and American Institutions at Brown University for their help on this project.

Preface to the First Edition

Few topics have generated greater interest among observers of the media recently than the widespread use of television advertising in election campaigns. Commercials have become one of the dominant means of communication in contemporary races. Citizens are bombarded with millions of dollars' worth of ads during the political season.[1] Today, it is nearly impossible to imagine campaigns without political commercials.

Air Wars: Television Advertising in Election Campaigns, 1952–1992 addresses two central questions about television advertisements. First, how much influence do ads have on viewers? Much has been made about the presumed ability of campaign commercials to alter public opinion, but there have been few detailed historical studies of this subject.[2] Aside from analyses of ad content, which have addressed changes in the television spots themselves, not many projects have examined the effects of political commercials over several decades. This omission makes it difficult to know whether particular results are limited to the election under consideration or represent a more general feature.

Second, are campaign ads good for democracy? Many observers have voiced complaints about democracy in the United States—for example, that citizens lack knowledge and that the nation's representative institutions are weak.[3] However, few developments have prompted more concern about the overall health of democracy than the reliance by candidates for public office on paid television advertisements. Critics charge that campaign commercials undermine democracy by shortening public discourse to thirty-second segments. Moreover, advertisements are said to distort citizens' assessments of the candidates because of the tendency of individuals to engage in "information grazing." If people only periodically tune in to the campaign, there is a potential danger to decision making.[4]

The research reported in this book adopts a fundamentally different perspective than is found elsewhere in the media studies field. To explore the impact of the media, scholars have used psychological models linked to citizens' exposure to and processing of information provided by the media.[5] The assumption is that individual attributes, such as background qualities and personal orientations, are the primary explanations of viewers' responses. Although these models have been useful for general analysis, they cannot be used for gauging the impact of campaign commercials. Psychological perspectives common in news studies need to be supplemented with material from the broader fabric of campaign politics. Spot advertising is inherently a political phenomenon in which the context of ad development, broadcasting, and response is quite important. The same type of commercial can have remarkably different consequences depending on the electoral setting and behavior of the candidates. Therefore, I have developed a contextual model of advertising that looks at the structure of the campaign system, the strategic behavior of candidates, and coverage by the news media. Paid advertisements cannot be understood without considering these vital features of the political context.

Chapter 1 introduces the framework on which the book rests. Chapter 2 reviews the methodology of advertising research. The analysis of campaign advertisements poses a number of challenges, including how best to study ads, how to measure viewers' reactions, and how to disentangle the effects of advertising from their possible influences on citizens. In Chapter 2 I discuss how I addressed these challenges.

Chapter 3 investigates the strategic aspects of advertising by looking at the content of ads from 1952 to 1992. I demonstrate that candidates' appeals have varied considerably over the years but that the level of specificity increased in the 1980s and 1990s. Commercials have become quite negative in style of presentation, although this trend is not without precedent in the period immediately after World War II.

Chapter 4 studies changes in media coverage of campaign advertisements since 1952. No aspect of political spots has undergone more dramatic development than this one. Journalistic attention to ads has increased substantially over the past forty years. However, much of the coverage of advertising emphasizes strategic rationales behind the commercials and the electoral consequences for candidates, rather than the content of the commercials.

Chapters 5 through 7 investigate voters' reactions to television spots. Chapter 5 relies on models of learning to examine the effects of advertising on views about the candidates. What do citizens learn about the contestants based on exposure to television ads? I show that ads contribute to citizens' impressions of candidates' prospects and images.

Agenda setting is the subject of Chapter 6. How do ads influence voters' feelings regarding public priorities? Using citizens' assessments of the most important problems facing the country and the most significant events of the campaign, I investigate how ads influence and reflect voters' feelings regarding public priorities. Leaders are able to shift citizens' impressions through the ephemeral and media-dominated world of campaign events as well as through public policy.

Chapter 7 examines priming in election campaigns: Can political commercials change the standards by which candidates are evaluated? I distinguish priming from defusing and show that at various times television advertising can either elevate (prime) or weaken (defuse) the importance of particular factors in vote choice. Candidates can have considerable success by defusing matters that are problematic for themselves or by playing the blame game so that their opponent is seen as responsible for turning the tone of the campaign negative.

Chapter 8 discusses the significance for democratic elections of the results obtained in this study. Elections are the lifeblood of democratic political systems. They are a means by which ordinary people acting together determine who leads the country. However, the heavy reliance on television advertising at a time when the political system places great emphasis on personal popularity has raised doubts about the quality of the information presented during election campaigns and about how voters make decisions. Chapter 8 reviews these concerns and assesses the contexts in which ads are most problematic.

Many people deserve thanks for their assistance with this project. Steven Ansolabehere, Richard Brody, Doris A. Graber, Kathleen Jamieson, Dorothy Nesbit, and Michael Traugott gave careful readings to earlier versions of this manuscript. Their comments were quite helpful, and I owe them a lot. In addition, Thomas Anton, Kathleen Dolan, Ellen Hume, Shanto Iyengar, Tom James,

Lynda Lee Kaid, Marvin Kalb, Patrick Kenney, Margaret Latimer, Richard Marshall, Robert McClure, Jonathan Nagler, Eric Nordlinger, Victor Ottati, Thomas Patterson, Nancy Rosenblum, Annie Schmitt, John Zaller, and Alan Zuckerman made valuable comments on papers drawn from this manuscript. Dean Alger, Tim Cook, Ann Crigler, Marion Just, and Montague Kern shared their reactions with me during our collaboration on the 1992 media project.

Outstanding research assistance was provided by a number of undergraduate and graduate students at Brown University: Rima Alaily, Christopher Goodwin, Leslyn Hall, Jonathan Klarfeld, Sara Leppo, Nancy Lublin, Dan Miller, Cristina Muñoz-Fazakes, Martin Sabarsky, Daryl Wiesen, Matthew Woods, and Jonathan Wyche. This book could not have been written without them. I am deeply grateful to the scores of students who have taken my "Campaigns and Elections" and "Politics and the Mass Media" courses in recent years. The chance to bounce preliminary ideas off bright and engaging students was invaluable.

Videotapes of commercials of past races were provided by Julian Kanter of the Political Commercial Archive at the University of Oklahoma. Patrick Devlin of the University of Rhode Island also made available selected ads from previous elections. Marilyn Fancher of the Broadcast Division at the Republican National Committee helped arrange permission to use the 1988 Bush ads in this research. Frank Greer and Alexa Suma provided access to Clinton's and Bush's 1992 ads, respectively. Video Plus provided copies of Perot's thirty-minute infomercials. In addition, I benefited enormously from a number of lengthy interviews conducted with prominent journalists in 1992: Brooks Jackson of the Cable News Network, Elizabeth Kolbert of the *New York Times,* Howard Kurtz of the *Washington Post,* Mara Liasson of National Public Radio, Renee Loth of the *Boston Globe,* and Tom Rosenstiel of the *Los Angeles Times.* My thanks to these individuals for sharing their impressions with me. Conversations over the years with journalists in Rhode Island also have sharpened my understanding of campaigns and elections. Thank you to M. Charles Bakst, Russ Garland, Katherine Gregg, Scott MacKay, John Martin, and Mark Patinkin of the *Providence Journal;* Dyana Koelsch, Jim Taricani, Doug White, and Patrice Wood at WJAR-TV; Sean Daly, David Layman, and Barbara Meagher of WLNE-TV; Walter Cryan of WPRI-TV; Paul Zangari of WSBE-TV; Steve Kass and

Arlene Violet of WHJJ Radio; and Mary Ann Sorrentino of WPRO Radio.

Jeanne Ferris of Congressional Quarterly deserves kudos for her assistance on my manuscript. She made a number of helpful suggestions, which strengthened the arguments developed in this book. Nola Healy Lynch improved the manuscript considerably through a superb job of copyediting, and Laura Carter performed admirably as production editor despite the difficulties of intercontinental communication. Every author should be fortunate enough to have editors like these.

The John Hazen White Sr. Public Opinion Laboratory of the A. Alfred Taubman Center for Public Policy and American Institutions at Brown University, the Institute for Research in Social Science at the University of North Carolina, the Inter-University Consortium for Political and Social Research at the University of Michigan, and the CBS/*New York Times* survey operation facilitated this analysis by making available data from a number of public opinion surveys. Jack Combs, research administrator at the Taubman Center, and Matthew Woods deserve thanks for making sure that our 1992 surveys ran smoothly. A sabbatical leave at Nuffield College of Oxford University provided a stimulating environment as I was wrapping up this project. My thanks to Byron Shafer for helping to arrange the time for writing.

A special debt of gratitude is owed to John Hazen White Sr., president of Taco, Inc., of Cranston, Rhode Island, and his wife, Happy White. At a time of great crisis within the state, the White family provided a generous endowment for the Public Opinion Laboratory at Brown. This timely contribution helped make possible the analysis presented in this book.

Finally, I would like to acknowledge the financial support of the National Science Foundation (SES-9122729), MacArthur Foundation, Ford Foundation, Twentieth Century Fund, Joan Shorenstein Barone Center on Press, Politics and Public Policy at Harvard University, Everett McKinley Dirksen Congressional Leadership Research Center, and the following units at Brown University: the Department of Political Science, the A. Alfred Taubman Center for Public Policy and American Institutions, the Undergraduate Teaching and Research Assistantship program of the Dean of the College, and the Small Grants program of the Graduate School. None of these individuals or organizations bears any responsibility for the interpretations presented here.

Television Advertising in Election Campaigns: A History in Pictures

1964

Johnson's "Daisy" ad shocked viewers in 1964.

1984

Reagan's "Bear in the Woods" ad was the most remembered spot in 1984.

1988

Bush's "Revolving Door" ad was one of the most notorious spots of 1988.

1990

Helms's 1990 spot, "White Hands," helped him win reelection.

1992

Clinton pioneered ads with footnotes to document his claims in 1992.

1992

In 1992, Perot attacked Clinton's job-creation record in Arkansas.

1992

Bush used a desolate landscape in 1992 to argue Clinton was too big of a risk.

1993

"Harry and Louise" helped undermine support for Clinton's health care reform in 1993.

1996

In 1996, Clinton surrounded himself with police officers to buttress his credentials as a leader who is tough on crime.

1996

Democrats turned Dole and Gingrich into Siamese twins in the 1996 campaign.

1996

The Republican National Committee attacked Democrats across the country in 1996 for "being too liberal."

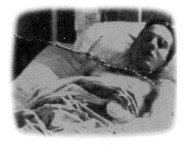

1996

Dole's "American hero" ad documented his war wounds.

Air Wars

Chapter 1

Rethinking Ads

Graphic images of drug use filled television screens across the country in the fall of 1996. Republican nominee Bob Dole was broadcasting an ad criticizing President Bill Clinton for a doubling in drug use by teenagers during his presidency. The commercial replayed a clip from a political forum aired on MTV during the 1992 campaign in which an audience member asked Clinton, "If you had it to do over again, would you inhale?" A goofy-looking Clinton replied, "Sure, if I could. I tried before." Within 24 hours, the president's ad team responded with a spot condemning Dole for having voted against the creation of a drug czar and touting Clinton's strengthening of school anti-drug programs and expansion of the death penalty to drug kingpins. Clinton went on to win reelection by 49 percent to 41 percent, with Reform Party candidate Ross Perot getting 8 percent of the vote.

Meanwhile, in congressional elections that year, the AFL-CIO spent $35 million on ads targeting thirty-two Republican members of the House of Representatives. While ominous music played in the background, one such ad showed an anxious woman sitting at her kitchen table talking about the high cost of a college education: "My husband and I both work. And next year, we'll have two children in college. And it will be very hard to put them through, even with two incomes. But Congressman Frank Riggs [R-Calif.] voted with Newt Gingrich to cut college loans while giving tax breaks to the wealthy." But Riggs fought off his opponent, which helped Republicans keep control of the House. Only one-third of the targeted House Republicans lost their seats.

These competing media constructions of reality illustrate how elections have become a television game. Television ads are the single biggest expenditure in most major campaigns today. They

1

shape citizen impressions and affect news coverage about the candidates. But not all spots produce the same results. Analysts must look at the history of ads, production techniques, ad buys, opposition responses, news coverage, and citizen predispositions to determine which spots will be the most influential. Through detailed studies of ad campaigns over the past 40 years, this book shows how candidates use television advertising to influence voters and win elections.

The History of Ads

From the earliest days of the Republic, communications devices have been essential to political campaigns. In 1828, handbills distributed by Andrew Jackson's supporters portrayed John Quincy Adams as "driving off with a horsewhip a crippled old soldier who dared to speak to him, to ask an alms." A circular distributed by Adams's forces meanwhile attacked Jackson for "ordering other executions, massacring Indians, stabbing a Samuel Jackson in the back, murdering one soldier who disobeyed his commands, and hanging three Indians." [1]

The method, though perhaps not the tone, of communicating with the electorate has changed dramatically since 1828. Handbills have virtually disappeared. Radio became the most popular vehicle in the 1920s and 1930s. But after World War II, television emerged as the advertising medium of choice for political candidates.

The 1952 presidential campaign was the first one that featured television ads. In that year, each party ran television and print ads evoking World War II memories. Republicans, in an effort to support General Dwight Eisenhower and break two decades of Democratic control, reminded voters in a *New York Times* ad that "one party rule made slaves out of the German people until Hitler was conquered by Ike." Not to be outdone, Democratic ads informed voters that "General Hindenburg, the professional soldier and national hero, [was] also ignorant of domestic and political affairs. . . . The net result was his appointment of Adolf Hitler as Chancellor." [2]

In the 1960s, television spots highlighted differences in candidates' personal traits. The 1964 presidential campaign with Lyndon Johnson and Barry Goldwater was one of the most negative races since the advent of television. Johnson's campaign characterized Goldwater as an extremist not to be trusted with America's future.

One five-minute ad, "Confession of a Republican," proclaimed, "This man scares me. . . . So many men with strange ideas are working for Goldwater."[3] Johnson's "Daisy" ad made a similar point in a more graphic manner. Its dramatic visual image of a mushroom cloud rising behind a little girl picking daisies in a meadow helped raise doubts about Goldwater's fitness for office in the nuclear age. A firestorm of protest forced the ad off the air after only one showing, but it helped Johnson win a landslide victory.

Ads in the 1970s and 1980s took advantage of public fear about the economy. When the country started to experience the twin ills of inflation and unemployment, a phenomenon that led experts to coin a new word, "stagflation," campaign commercials emphasized economic themes. In 1980, Republican challenger Ronald Reagan effectively employed ads to criticize economic performance under President Jimmy Carter. When the economy came roaring back in 1984, Reagan's serene "Morning in America" ad communicated the simple message that prosperity abounded and the country was at peace.

The 1988 presidential contest was the zenith of attack politics in the post–World War II period. This campaign illustrated the powerful ability of ads to alter impressions of a candidate who was not well-known nationally. Early in the summer of 1988, Michael Dukakis held a 17-percentage-point lead over his Republican rival, then Vice President George Bush. Women preferred Dukakis over Bush by a large margin, and the governor was doing well among blacks, elderly citizens, and Democrats who previously had supported Reagan.

Meanwhile, Republicans were test marketing some new advertising material. Over Memorial Day weekend in Paramus, New Jersey, Bush aides Jim Baker, Lee Atwater, Roger Ailes, Robert Teeter, and Nicholas Brady stood behind a one-way mirror observing a small group of so-called Reagan Democrats. Information concerning William Horton, a convicted black man who—while on furlough from a Massachusetts prison—brutally raped a white woman, was being presented. The audience seemed quite disturbed. Atwater later boasted to party operatives, "By the time this election is over, Willie Horton will be a household name."[4] The words were eerily prophetic, and Bush went on to beat Dukakis by 53 percent to 46 percent.

The 1992 campaign represented the dangers of overreliance on attack ads and the power of thirty-minute "infomercials" by inde-

pendent candidate Perot. Throughout the race, Bush used ads to
attack Clinton's character and record as governor of Arkansas. But
unlike his 1988 race, Bush did not prevail. Between the poor economy, the backlash that developed against Bush's advertising
attacks, and Clinton's quick responses to criticisms, Clinton beat
Bush by 43 percent to 38 percent. Perot finished in third place with
19 percent, the best showing for a third-party candidate since
Theodore Roosevelt in 1912.

Throughout the elections of the television age, ads were a valuable lens on the inner workings of the campaign. Candidates
revealed in their commercials important aspects of their vision,
leadership style, and substantive positions. As stated by Elizabeth
Kolbert, a news reporter for the *New York Times* who covers campaign air wars, "Every advertising dollar spent represents a clue to
a campaign's deepest hopes and a potential revelation about its
priorities." [5]

How Ads Are Put Together

Production techniques for commercials have improved dramatically over the past forty years. Ads in the 1950s were rudimenta-
ry by contemporary standards. Political spots often took the form
of footage from press conferences or testimonials from prominent
citizens. Many were of the "talking head" variety in which the
candidate (or his or her supporter) looked straight into the camera
and spoke for thirty or sixty seconds without any editing. There
were no colorful graphics and no use of animation.

Contemporary ads, in contrast, are visually exciting. Technological advances allow ad producers to use colorful images and
sophisticated editing techniques to make spots more compelling.
Images can be spliced together to link one visual image with another. Animated images can visually transpose one person into another in a split-second using a technique called "morphing." As we
will see in the sections that follow, there are a variety of ways in
which catchy visuals, music, and color capture viewer attention
and convey particular political messages.

Visual Images

The visual aspect of advertising is the most important part of
commercials. According to the old adage, a picture is worth a

thousand words. Contemporary ads use graphic visual imagery to grab the public's attention and convey a message. Whereas traditional research has focused on the spoken content of ads to determine ways of conveying messages, modern analysts study both the audio and visual aspects of advertising.

Candidates often attempt to undermine political opponents by associating them with unfavorable visual images. A 1990 campaign ad by Louisiana senator Bennett Johnston (D) against his opponent David Duke showed pictures of Duke addressing a Ku Klux Klan rally in the presence of a burning cross to make his point that Duke was an extremist who should not be elected to a seat in the U.S. Senate.

A similar phenomenon happened in 1996. Taking advantage of House Speaker Newt Gingrich's high unpopularity, Democrats across the country broadcast ads showing pictures of Gingrich side-by-side with Dole and House and Senate Republican candidates. The message was clear. A vote for the Republican was a vote for Gingrich. After the election, Gingrich claimed in speeches that 75,000 ads were aired against him, which was an extraordinary 10 percent of all the political spots broadcast in 1996.

Politicians also seek to enhance their positive appeal by associating themselves with images of flag and family. It is common in biographical spots at the beginning of campaigns to see pictures of the candidate with his or her family members or in official meetings surrounded by flags or other symbols of American democracy.

The visual aspect of campaign advertising is crucial because it is the one that is most remembered by viewers. When scholars have ads on videotape, they watch the ad with the sound on and then with the sound off. The reason is simple—people remember visual images longer than they do spoken words. Listening to a campaign message with the sound off lets you see the part of the ad that is most persuasive with voters. Pictures carry an emotional impact that is much more powerful than the spoken word.

CBS news reporter Lesley Stahl tells the story about a hard-hitting evening news piece she did on Reagan's presidency in 1984. The story claimed that Reagan had done certain things, such as cut the budget for the elderly, which were contrary to what he said he had done. Accompanying the story were a series of pleasant visual images of Reagan "basking in a sea of flag-waving supporters, beaming beneath red-white-and-blue balloons floating skyward, sharing concerns with farmers in a field." After the story aired, Stahl was surprised with a favorable telephone call from a top Reagan assistant. Asked why he liked the story given her harsh words, the Reagan advisor explained she had given the White House four and a half minutes of positive pictures of President Reagan: "They don't hear what you are saying if the pictures are saying something different." [6]

Visual Text

Visual text is messages that are printed on the screen, generally in big, bold letters. Printed messages on screen grab the viewer's attention and tell him or her to pay attention to this ad. As an example, Perot's 1992 ads used visual text scrolling up the screen to persuade the American public to vote for him (see Appendix for texts of memorable ads in recent elections). Spots for Clinton in 1996 used big, splashy text on-screen to make the political point that Republicans wanted to "CUT MEDICARE." Advertisers have found that memory of a message is greatly enhanced by combining visual text with spoken words and descriptive images.

Music and Sounds

Music sets the tone for the ad. Just as hosts use upbeat music to accompany a party or educational institutions play "Pomp and Circumstance" to set a graduation scene, campaign ads use music to convey the mood of a particular commercial.

Uplifting ads use cheery music to make people feel good about a candidate. For example, the 1984 campaign featured an independently produced ad called "I'm Proud to Be an American," which used music from country singer Lee Greenwood's song of that same name. The music played over scenes of Reagan, the American flag, and cheerful scenes of happy Americans. It conveyed the message that things were good in America and people should vote for Reagan.

Conversely, somber or ominous music in an ad seeks to undermine support for the opponent. Bush's "Revolving Door" ad in 1988 had dark and threatening music accompany scenes of prisoners walking through a revolving door while an announcer attacked Dukakis's record on crime. The sounds of drums, the footsteps of guards on metal stairs, and threatening voices were integral to the ad's message that voters should reject Dukakis in the November elections because he was soft on crime.

But sometimes, musical accompaniments to campaign events can backfire. At countless rallies across the country in 1996, Dole's campaign used the 1967 Motown hit, "Soul Man" by Isaac Hayes and David Porter, as an introduction to "Dole Man." However, after Rondor Music International accused the campaign of copyright violations, Dole agreed to stop play of the song.[7]

Color

Color communicates vivid messages in ads. Media consultants use bright colors to associate their candidates with a positive image and grayish or black and white colors to associate opponents with a negative image. For example, in the MTV ad Dole's campaign ran in 1996, discussed earlier in the chapter, a color videotape clip in which Clinton said if he had it to do over again, he would inhale marijuana, was broadcast in black and white in order to make Clinton look sinister.

The 1992 Bush campaign developed an ad called "Arkansas Record" that featured a vulture looking out over a dark and barren landscape to make its point that Clinton had poorly governed Arkansas. That year, Bush also used a low quality grayish photographic negative of Clinton from an April 20, 1992, *Time* magazine cover to exhort voters to defeat the Arkansas governor in November. The cover with the photographic negative of Clinton was entitled, "Why Voters Don't Trust Clinton." Bush's ad juxtaposed a nice color image of himself to convey the message that voters should not vote in favor of Clinton.

Editing

Editing determines the sequencing and pacing of an ad. The sequencing of ad images refers to how images in one scene are related to following scenes. For example, the 1984 Reagan ad, "Morning in America," showed images of Reagan interspersed with scenes of Americans at work and a country at peace. The sequencing linked Reagan with the popular themes of peace and prosperity. All of this was accompanied by music that enhanced the emotional impact of the ad.

The pacing of an ad refers to whether the visual images flow smoothly or abruptly from scene to scene. Abrupt cuts from image to image create a jarring look that tells the viewer something bad is appearing before them. It is a common way of conveying negative feelings in attack ads.

Audiotape Voice-Overs

Through an off-screen announcer, audiotape voice-overs provide a roadmap that knits together visual scenes. Campaign ads are composed of different pictures that convey particular points. The announcer guides the viewer through these scenes so that the person is able to understand the message being communicated.

Typically, attack ads use male announcers to deliver blistering criticisms. But Dole made history in 1996 by using a female announcer to condemn Clinton's "failed liberal drug policies."

Code Words

Code words are short-hand communication devices. Even in the limited space of thirty seconds, campaigns can use code words and short messages to communicate broader messages to the public. Many people feel that thirty seconds is too short a period to convey much in the way of substantive themes. But during election campaigns, single words can take on enormous importance.

One illustration of this from recent elections has been the widespread use of the word "liberal." Reliance on this code word has skyrocketed in the past few elections. In 1988, Bush called Democratic candidate Dukakis a liberal thirty-one times and used it in one-third of his speeches. The message got through to voters. Whereas 31 percent in May 1988 believed Dukakis was liberal, the figure rose to 46 percent by September.

In 1992, Bush's use of the term "liberal" rose to sixty-two times. Similar to 1988, the word took on a number of negative meanings, such as being fiscally irresponsible, soft on crime, and dangerously out of touch with the American public. This allowed Bush to condemn Clinton with the single word of "liberal" without having to voice more detailed descriptions of the candidate's positions.[8]

These types of code words are powerful communications devices because they allow voters to associate particular messages with the code word. For example, one voter might associate "liberal" with fiscally irresponsible, whereas another could interpret that word as synonymous with moral laxity. This allows candidates to send different powerful messages to various people in only a few seconds.

By 1996, the country's airwaves were filled with the word. Dole ran ads condemning Clinton as a tax-and-spend liberal and as someone whose failed policies were "liberal." In one speech in September, Dole used the word fourteen times. Republican congressional candidates used the same appeal all over the country. Ads financed by the Republican National Committee criticized Democratic House and Senate candidates as "liberals," "ultra-liberals," "super-liberals," "unbelievably liberal," "embarrassingly liberal," "foolishly liberal," and "taxingly liberal."

But because of the country's changed political climate after the abortive Gingrich Revolution, the use of the "epithet" did not resonate with voters in the same way it had in earlier years. As one voter in a 1996 Brown University focus group put it, "liberal" meant helping people. Others felt that "liberal is having an open mind."

This view was supported in a CBS News/*New York Times* survey asking people what they thought of when they heard someone described as "liberal" and "conservative," respectively. The most common responses for liberal were open minded (14 percent), free spending (8 percent), high degree of government involvement (7 percent), helps people (5 percent), and pro-handouts (5 percent). The most common responses for conservative were fiscally responsible (17 percent), closed minded (10 percent), careful (8 percent), against change (7 percent), and low degree of government involvement (6 percent).[9]

Polls did not find that many more people saw Clinton as liberal in 1996 than had done so in 1992, despite increased use of the code word. According to a September 1996 CBS News/*New York Times* national survey, 43 percent saw Clinton as liberal, 36 percent as moderate, and 12 percent perceived him as conservative. In fall 1992, a CBS News/*New York Times* survey found that 38 percent considered him liberal, 37 percent moderate, and 13 percent conservative.[10]

The Impact of Ads

Ads are fascinating not just because of the manner in which they are put together but also because of their ability to influence voters. People are not equally susceptible to the media, and political observers have tried to find out how media power actually operates.

Consultants judge the effectiveness of ads by the ultimate results—who wins. This type of test, however, is tautological in nature and never possible to complete until after the election. It leads invariably to the immutable law of advertising: Winners have great ads and losers do not.

As an alternative, journalists evaluate ads by asking voters to indicate whether commercials influenced them. When asked directly whether television commercials helped them decide how to vote, most voters say ads did not influence them. For example, the results of a 1996 survey by the Media Studies Center placed ads at the bottom of the heap in terms of possible information sources. Whereas 45 percent of voters felt they learned a lot from debates, 32 percent cited newspaper stories, and 30 percent pointed to television news stories, just 5 percent believed they learned a lot from political ads. When asked directly about ads in a 1996 CBS News/*New York Times* survey, only 11 percent reported that any presidential candidate's ads had helped them decide how to vote.[11]

But this is not a meaningful way of looking at advertising. Such responses undoubtedly reflect an unwillingness to admit that external agents have any effect. Many people firmly believe that they make up their minds independently of the campaign. Much in the same way teenagers do not like to concede parental influence, few voters are willing to admit that they are influenced by television.

Political psychologists determine whether ads work through laboratory experiments. Viewers are generally randomly assigned to groups. One group sees an ad and the other does not (or they may see ads with different messages). Then the opinions of the groups are compared to see how ads might have influenced viewers.

But this approach is unreliable because it removes viewers from the context of their actual political environments. The same ad can have very different consequences depending on the manner in which an opponent responds, the way a journalist reports the ad, the number of times a spot is broadcast, or the predispositions of the viewer.

For these reasons, it is important to emphasize the overall context in which people make decisions. A vivid example is found in

Kathleen Hall Jamieson's study of the 1988 presidential campaign.[12] The effectiveness of Bush's "Revolving Door" ad on Dukakis's crime record was enhanced by the majority culture's fears about black men raping white women and from earlier news stories that had sensationalized Horton's crime spree. Bush did not have to mention Horton in this ad for viewers to make the connection between Dukakis and heinous crimes.

This idea is central to understanding campaign advertisements. Commercials cannot be explored in isolation from candidate behavior and the general flow of media information. As shown in the following sections, the analysis of thirty-second spots requires a keen awareness of the structure of electoral competition, strategic candidate behavior, media coverage, and public opinion.

The Structure of Electoral Competition

The structure of the electoral process defines the general opportunities available to candidates. The most important development at the presidential level has been the dramatic change in how convention delegates are selected. Once controlled by party leaders in small-scale caucus settings thought to be immune from media influence, nominations have become open and lengthy affairs that are significantly shaped by the mass media. The percentage of delegates to national nominating conventions selected through primaries increased significantly after 1968. From the 1920s to the 1960s, about 40 percent of delegates were selected in primaries, with the remainder chosen in caucus settings dominated by party leaders. However, after rules changes set in motion by the McGovern-Fraser Commission of the Democratic party following the 1968 election, about 70 percent of convention delegates in each party were chosen directly by voters in presidential primaries.

Nominating reforms have required candidates to appeal directly to voters for support and in the eyes of many observers have altered the character of the electoral system.[13] No longer are candidates dependent on negotiations with a handful of party leaders. Instead, they must demonstrate public appeal and run campaigns that win media attention. Campaigns have become longer and have come to depend increasingly on television as a means of attracting public support. The heavy emphasis on commercials led Massachusetts senator Paul Tsongas to describe ads as the "nuclear weapon" of the campaign business.[14]

Some campaigns get far more attention than others. Citizens are more interested in and knowledgeable about presidential general election campaigns than nominating contests. Although there is a variation in individual contests depending on the particular candidates involved, nomination races typically generate less citizen interest and less media coverage. It also is more common for candidates who are not well known to run in the primaries.

These differences in the rules of the game, the visibility of the candidates, and the extent of media coverage are important for the study of television advertisements. Because less visible races feature candidates who are not well known, ad effects on citizens' opinion of the candidates often are significant. Past research has demonstrated that television's impact is strongest when viewers have weakly formulated views. It is easier to run ads against candidates who are not well known because there is no preexisting attitudinal profile to shield that individual against critical claims.

Advertising and Strategic Politicians

Early research downplayed the power of ads to mold public images of candidates. The pioneering study was the innovative effort of Thomas Patterson and Robert McClure, *The Unseeing Eye*.[15] Looking at both content and effects, they sought to dispel the concerns of the public and journalists regarding political commercials. Using a model of psychological reasoning based on voters' knowledge about candidates, these researchers examined whether television ads enabled voters to learn more about the policy views or personal qualities of campaigners. Basically, they found that voters learned more about the issues from the candidates' ads than from the news, because ads addressed some issues whereas the news was dominated by coverage of the "horse race"—who is ahead at a given time. The results of Patterson and McClure's study were reprinted in leading textbooks. Popular concerns about the strategic dangers of ads were minimized as uninformed hand-wringing.

The study's results also fit with the general view among election experts of the 1960s and 1970s that political strategies were not very decisive in determining election results. The era following the 1960 publication of the classic work on voting behavior, *The American Voter,* proclaimed long-term forces, such as party identification, as the most important. Although a few scholars disputed this interpretation, many argued that short-term factors related to media coverage, candidates' advertisements, and campaign spending simply were not crucial to vote choice. For example, Harold Mendelsohn and Irving Crespi claimed in 1970 that the "injection of high doses of political information during the frenetic periods of national campaigns does very little to alter the deeply rooted, tightly held political attitudes of most voters." [16] Even the later emergence of pocketbook voting models did little to change this interpretation. Paid ads were thought to have limited capacity to shape citizens' impressions of economic performance.

Recent decades, though, have begun to see changes in previous viewpoints. Candidates have started to use commercials more aggressively, reporters have devoted more attention to paid advertising, and ad techniques have improved dramatically.

It now is recognized that voters' assessments are quite fluid and that candidates have the power to sway voters' opinions of them. Party identifications have declined and evidence from elections around the country suggests that ads are quite successful in helping candidates develop impressions of themselves. [17] This is particularly true in multicandidate nominating contests, because there are more strategic options available with the larger number of candidates involved.

Because paid ads are so important in contemporary campaigns, candidates take the development of advertising strategies quite seriously. Commercials often are pretested through focus groups or public opinion surveys. [18] Themes as well as styles of presentation are tried out before likely voters. What messages are most appealing? When and how often should particular ads be aired? Who should be targeted? How should ads best convey information?

The number of times an ad is broadcast is one of the most important strategic decisions during the campaign. Professional ad buyers specialize in picking time slots and television shows that are advantageous for particular candidates. Whereas a candidate interested in appealing to senior citizens may air ads repeatedly during the television show "Murder She Wrote," youth-oriented politicians may run spots during "The Simpsons" or "Seinfeld."

The content and timing of ads are crucial for candidates because of their link to overall success. Campaigns have become a blitz of competing ads, quick responses, and counter-responses. Ads have become serial in nature, with each ad building thematically on previous spots. Election campaigns feature strategic interactions that are as important as the individual ads themselves.

In the fast-changing dynamics of election campaigns, decisions to advance or delay particular messages can be quite important. Quick-response strategies require candidates to respond immediately when negative ads appear or political conditions are favorable. Candidates often play off each other's ads in an effort to gain the advantage with voters.

Advertising and the News Media

One of the most striking developments of the contemporary period has been the increasing coverage of political advertising by reporters. Network news executive William Small described this as the most important news trend of recent years: "Commercials are now expected as part of news stories." [19] Many news outlets have even launched "ad watch" features. These segments, aired during the news and discussed in newspaper articles, present the ad, along with commentary on its accuracy and effectiveness. The most effective ads are those the basic messages of which are reinforced by the news media.

Scholars traditionally have distinguished the free from the paid media. Free media meant reports from newspapers, magazines, radio, and television that were not billed to candidates. The paid media encompassed commercials purchased by the candidate on behalf of the campaign effort. The two avenues of communication were thought to be independent in terms of effects on viewers because of the way viewers saw them.

But the increase in news coverage of advertising has blurred or even eliminated this earlier division between the free and paid media. People who separate the effects of these communication channels need to recognize how intertwined the free and paid media have become. It is now quite common for network news programs to rebroadcast ads that are entertaining, provocative, or controversial. Journalists have begun to evaluate the effects of campaign commercials. It has become clear that the evening news and the print media are significant audiences for television ads.

Ads that are broadcast for free during the news or discussed in major newspapers have several advantages over those aired purely as commercials. One strength is that viewers traditionally have trusted the news media—far more than paid ads—for fairness and objectivity. William McGuire has shown that the credibility of the source is one determinant of whether the message is believed.[20] The high credibility of the media gives ads aired during the news an important advantage over those seen as plain ads. Ailes explained it this way: "You get a 30 or 40 percent bump out of [an ad] by getting it on the news. You get more viewers, you get credibility, you get it in a framework." [21]

Ads in the news guarantee campaigners a large audience and free air time. Opinion polls have documented that nearly two-thirds of Americans cite television as their primary source of news. This is particularly true for what Michael Robinson refers to as the "inadvertent audience," those who are least interested in politics and also among the most volatile in their opinions.[22]

But there can be disadvantages to having ads aired during newscasts. When ads are described as unfair to the opposition, media coverage undermines the sponsor's message. The advantages of airing the ad during the news can also be lost if reporters challenge the ad's factual accuracy. How reporters cover ads affects how people interpret commercials.

Changes in Public Opinion

Public opinion and voting behavior have undergone significant changes in ways relevant to advertising. Voters are less trusting of government officials today than they were thirty years ago. Whereas 23 percent in 1958 agreed that you cannot trust the government to do what is right most of the time, 84 percent were untrusting in 1996. Citizens are also less likely to identify with one of the major parties. Thirty years ago, about 75 percent identified with either the Republican or Democratic party. Today, less than 60 percent identify with a major party.[23] This means that a much larger number of citizens classify themselves as independents and are likely to swing back and forth between the parties.

The growing independence of American voters and the political volatility in American politics unleashed by corporate downsizing and the end of the Cold War have unrooted citizen attitudes. People's impressions of political events are more fluid, and there can be great changes in the issues or leadership qualities seen as most important at any given time.

Each of these developments has altered the tenor of electoral campaigns and led to extensive efforts to appeal to independent-minded voters. Writing in the 1830s, Alexis de Tocqueville worried that the great masses would make "hasty judgments" based on the "charlatans of every sort [who] so well understand the secret of pleasing them." [24] The prominence today of an open electoral system filled with independent voters and fast-paced ads has done nothing to alleviate this concern.

Chapter 2

Buying Air Time

Candidates do not air all ads with the same frequency. Some spots are repeated over and over, and others are broadcast more selectively. These choices, called *ad buys,* are at the heart of candidate strategies. Because advertising represents the largest single expenditure in most contemporary campaigns, decisions on the purchase of air time are among the most crucial for campaigners. Choices on when and where to place ads as well as the frequency with which particular spots are run determine how candidates are seen by the viewing public. For that reason, ad buys are the most fundamental decisions made in any campaign.

The Case of John Connally

The importance of ad buys is illustrated by the ill-fated presidential campaign of John Connally. Connally's 1980 race for the Republican nomination was one of the biggest flops in recent memory. Connally spent nearly $10 million for a campaign that netted just one delegate.[1] On a per-delegate basis, this made his race the most expensive failure in the history of the nominating process.

Connally was the former Democratic governor of Texas from 1963 to 1969. On November 22, 1963, he was catapulted into national prominence when he was riding in the same Dallas car as President John Kennedy on the day that Kennedy was fatally shot. Connally sustained gunshot wounds himself, but he recovered and went on to build a successful political career.

Unhappy with the liberal drift of the Democratic party, Connally switched parties in 1973 and was named secretary of the Treasury by Richard Nixon. Firmly ensconced in the Republican party, Connally decided to make his own run for the presidency in 1980.

Because he had high name recognition and the ability to raise large sums of money, Connally chose a national strategy for the nomination. Unlike Bush, then a little known Republican who put nearly all his resources into Iowa and New Hampshire owing to their position first in the delegate selection process, Connally spread his financial resources around the country. He tried to build campaign organizations in every state and devoted no more time to Iowa and New Hampshire than to other states.

In terms of advertising buys, his choices reflected a national strategy for the nomination. Rather than focus advertising on Iowa and New Hampshire, the way most of the other Republican contenders were doing, Connally ran print ads in national newsmagazines and bought time on national television. His goal through this strategy was to boost his name recognition across the country and create an overwhelming clamor for his nomination.

But alas, Connally ignored the fundamentals of ad buys. As with any resource decision, candidates have to buy air time based on the dictates of the election calendar. The nominating process is sequential in nature and reporters place disproportionate attention on early contests in Iowa and New Hampshire; therefore, candidates need to orient their ad buys to those locales. Connally violated this dictum and suffered a costly political defeat.

The Strategies of Ad Buying

Time buys center primarily on rating points, defined by Marilyn Roberts as "the percentage of individuals or households exposed to a particular television program at a specific time." [2] Each rating point nationally represents around 931,000 households. The goal of campaigners is to maximize gross ratings points, which is the rating for each spot times the number of times each spot has aired, for the least amount of money.

Candidates face four key choices in their ad buys. First, candidates must decide on how many issues to emphasize. The basic dilemma centers on the many messages/few messages trade-off. The advantage of putting out many messages is that it allows the candidate to appeal to different types of voters and experiment with various alternatives until successful messages are found. The disadvantage lies in the risk that voters and news reporters will be confused by the diverse messages being run and not be able to get a clear view of where the candidate is coming from.

Such a potentially negative outcome leads some aspirants to follow the few-messages model instead. Under this approach, a relatively small number of themes are presented to voters through commercials, and these are repeated over and over. The strength of this strategy is clarity of the themes being presented. But the risk is that candidates will choose the wrong themes and have nothing to fall back on if their designated themes do not connect with likely voters.

Second, in keeping with recent emphasis on attack politics, candidates face decisions on when to air attack ads. Early attacks offer the potential to define a candidate before his or her own message is put out. But as Republican Steve Forbes found in the 1996 primaries, these attacks can backfire if the press or the public conclude the attacker is crossing the line and being unduly negative. Late attacks shield against backlash but may occur too late to define the campaign dialogue.

Third, candidates must choose how often to broadcast certain messages. Unlike other areas of human endeavor, repetition is a virtue in the advertising world. Because people do not pay close attention to politics, messages must be repeated over and over again to be heard and internalized by viewers. Campaigners must decide which of the messages are most crucial and therefore most important to repeat over the course of the race.

Fourth, there are decisions in presidential races about the proper mix of national and local ad buys. This is not much of a dilemma during the nominating process. The state-centered nature of presidential primaries means that the Connally strategy to the contrary, almost all nomination buys are local.

In the general election, though, this strategic decision is quite important. Because the election takes place simultaneously in all fifty states plus the District of Columbia, and the Electoral College is guided by a winner-take-all system in each state, presidential aspirants must decide on an appropriate mix of national and local ad buys. National buys reach a wider audience, but they are very expensive. They also have the disadvantage of hitting all areas equally, regardless of political competitiveness.

For these reasons, presidential candidates have begun to bypass national networks in their ad buys and purchase time directly from selected local stations. Satellite hookups give candidates the technological means to beam spots to local stations around the country in the blink of an eye. This allows candidates to target messages on particular audiences and emphasize geographic areas that are central to their election strategy.

How Ad Buys Go Wrong

Connally's case clearly represents bad judgment in ad buys, but it also demonstrates how easily such ill-fated decisions can be made. Ad buys are risky because air time must be purchased weeks before the election in order to get the most desirable television broadcast slots. Television stations are required by law to sell candidates air time at the cheapest rate available. But federal regulations do not guarantee desirable slots unless the money is paid upfront. For example, the minute before and after the evening news is most desirable because this is when the largest number of viewers interested in public affairs are watching. Therefore, in order to reach the viewers most likely to cast ballots, campaigns must lock up these slots early in the race.

In the rapidly changing world of campaign politics, choices that look good several months before an election may turn out poorly once the active campaign gets under way. Candidates must target the demographics of particular shows in order to build their electoral coalitions. It is not enough to be on television with ads; instead, these ads need to be placed around shows the viewers of which are likely to be persuaded to vote for the candidate. Television shows vary dramatically in the numbers of senior citizens, African Americans, and women watching, and candidates therefore must match their ad buys to time slots that make political sense for them.

These decisions are tricky because advertising is not a one-player game. Rather, it is a contest in which each candidate's ads get assessed in light of what rival candidates are broadcasting. These strategic interactions, not just individual ads, determine how voters see the respective candidates. Campaigners may make ad buys that miss the mark once they see where and how often their opponents are running ads.

The 1992 General Election

It has been difficult in the past to study ad buys because of problems in getting adequate information. Unlike general financial expenditures that are filed with the Federal Election Commission, there is no central clearinghouse for ad-buy data. Instead, information must be compiled directly from candidates, the national networks, or local television affiliates around the country. Television stations are required by the Federal Communications Commission to maintain logs for public inspection of ads that are broadcast on their channels. This information is painstaking to compile, but it is a gold mine regarding electronic forms of electoral persuasion.

In 1992, for the first time in a national presidential race, a research team of Montague Kern, Dean Alger, Janice Goggin, and myself were able to compile detailed ad-buy information.[3] Our research focused on fifteen-, thirty-, and sixty-second spot ad-buy data nationally throughout the general election campaign for Bush, Clinton, and Perot, as well as local ad buys in four diverse communities around the country: Boston; Winston-Salem, North Carolina; Los Angeles; and the twin cities of Fargo, North Dakota, and Moorhead, Minnesota.

These communities were chosen because they represent media markets ranging from small to large in each major geographic region. Clinton ended up carrying Los Angeles and Boston by big margins in the fall; Winston-Salem and Fargo/Moorhead were closer. Bush narrowly won Winston-Salem, whereas Bush carried Fargo and Clinton came out ahead in Moorhead.

For each media market, we compiled local ad buy data from July 1 to November 2, 1992, for Bush, Clinton, and Perot using station log books at the leading television station in each area: WBZ in Boston, WXII in Winston-Salem, KNBC in Los Angeles, and WDAY in Fargo/Moorhead. Our rationale for choosing the leading television station is that presidential candidates generally focus their ad purchases on the station with the largest audience in a given area.

National ad-buy data include spots aired on network television (ABC, CBS, NBC, and Fox) from July 1 to November 2, 1992.[4] Our database contains a wealth of information regarding the timing and placement of specific spots during the general election campaign. For example, the station logs we examined note the candidate running ads on each station, a code for the name of each ad (which we cross-checked with videotapes from each campaign), when the ad was run, and how much the time slot cost. The dollar figure is important because it reflects the station's estimate of the audience size and desirability of specific time slots.

This provides a measure for rating points and the size of the viewing audience.

The national ad buy data provided information on who ran the ad, a code for the name of the ad, and when it was run, but not the cost of the time slot. From this information, we generated a database containing all of the national ad buys for Bush, Clinton, and Perot throughout the campaign as well as local buys for each candidate in the four communities we studied.

National Ad Buys

Presidential candidates face a basic decision in how much of their advertising to broadcast nationally and how much to target on particular local media markets. In the 1992 general election, both Bush and Perot devoted more of an effort than did Clinton to national time buys for their spot commercials. Perot made the most national buys *(N = 205)* in the fall, compared to Bush *(N = 189)* and Clinton *(N = 143)*.

Perot broadcast more ads late in the campaign than did either Bush or Clinton. In the last week of the campaign, for example, Perot broadcast three times as many ads nationally as Bush and 1.5 times as many as Clinton. As is shown later in this chapter, this had important ramifications for the memorability of each candidate's advertisements. Perot's choices were dictated by his late reentry into the campaign in October and the need to get his message out to the widest possible audience.

Bush devoted considerable resources to national buys, though he spread his spending throughout the campaign. Bush's strategy was in reaction to the fact that he lagged terribly in early 1992 polls. Therefore, he needed an early, across-the-board effort that would jump-start his candidacy.

Clinton's limited time buys nationally were in keeping with his organization's decision to target eighteen states for local buys in the fall campaign. He and his staff consciously decided to run no ads in the remaining states either because his lead was secure in that area or because the state had a clear history of going Republican in presidential elections. Clinton did, though, unleash a national ad barrage at the end of the campaign.

There was little lag time in the strategic interactions between Bush and Clinton. In terms of number of ads aired, Clinton's and Bush's daily national buys mirrored one another until the last two weeks, when Clinton began broadcasting twice as many spots as Bush. The rapidity of the strategic interactions was a result in part of technological advances in production that allowed media consultants to develop new ads almost instantly and beam them via satellite to television stations across the country. But after the election, Clinton media advisor Frank Greer confessed his campaign staff had been fast in their counter-responses because they had intercepted the Bush satellite transmission of ads to local television affiliates and thereby had copies of Bush ads *before* they were broadcast.[5]

Of all the national commercials broadcast, Perot ran the largest number of different spots (twenty-nine in all). This was much greater than the seventeen different commercials Clinton broadcast in the fall and the nine ads Bush used. This shows that at least nationally, Bush had the most targeted general election ad-buy strategy and Perot had the most diversified. Bush used a few ads to convey the same type of message over and over. Often, this message was linked to Clinton's character.

Using the national ad-buy data, we tabulated for Bush, Clinton, and Perot their most frequently aired national commercials. Bush's most widely used ad was called "Agenda." This spot started running October 22, two weeks before the election. It ran sixty-four times and featured Bush discussing his agenda for American renewal. Tied to a prominent speech Bush gave in Detroit outlining his plans for reviving the economy, it was a positive presentation of his plan for the future with no attacks on the opposition. The spot started with Bush in the Oval Office discussing the difficult transition from wartime to peacetime and the uncertainties brought about by this change. Without being very specific, he indicated he understood the feelings of Americans and had an agenda to restore economic prosperity. The ad closed with images of George and Barbara Bush surrounded by their grandchildren.

This ad was notable because of its positive thrust. It was in response to widespread criticisms of Bush for his attacks on Clinton's patriotism, integrity, and trustworthiness and polls showing that people blamed Bush much more than Clinton for the negative tone of the campaign. In fact, Bush's second and third most frequently aired ads ("Gray Dot" and "Federal Taxes") were very negative. They ran often in early and middle October, when Bush was trying to regain the offensive. The "Gray Dot" commercial ran 40 times on network television and sought to present an image of Clinton as untrustworthy. It asserted that Clinton could not be trusted because he didn't really believe in anything. According to the commercial, one candidate was in favor of term limitations, and the other opposed them. The ad closed with a gray dot obliterating a picture of Clinton as a tag line said "Too bad they're both Clinton." The spot, "Federal Taxes," was broadcast twenty-five times nationally. It claimed that if elected, Clinton would raise federal taxes.

Clinton's most frequently aired ads included "Remember" (run forty-one times) and "Even" (broadcast twenty-three times). "Remember" built on Pat Buchanan's critique of Bush's economic record during the Republican primaries. It tied the poor economic performance under Bush's administration directly to Bush's 1990 tax flip-flop and the perception of his general insensitivity to the plight of the average person. After enumerating declining family incomes over the past four years, an announcer intoned, "President Bush says, 'If you elect me President, you will be better off four years from now than you are today.' [The announcer asks] 'Well, it's four years later. How're you doing?'" "Even" was a positive ad listing a number of prominent economists who had endorsed Clinton's economic program. It was designed to emphasize the widespread support for the Democrat's economic revitalization plan and the fact that Clinton had a plan of action. Coming near the end of a hard-fought campaign, it furthermore conveyed the idea that, in noticeable contrast with Bush, Clinton had campaigned positively.

Perot's top ads were "Storm" (run twenty-three times), "Purple Heart" (run sixteen times), and "We Can Win" and "How to Vote" (each run fourteen times). "Storm" was an emotional spot that showed storm clouds approaching while an announcer talked about the country's problems being unaddressed. "Purple Heart" was an emotional ad that told the story of a Vietnam veteran who had lent a purple heart to Perot for the campaign as a sign of his trust and confidence in the candidate. "We Can Win" appeared late in the campaign and talked about how Perot could win the race and take action as president to break the logjam in Washington.

In addition to total ads aired, the frequency with which particular ads were run at various points during the contest is important for understanding the strategic thrust of the campaign. Our data show the frequency of Bush airings each day for his top five ads from his first nationally broadcast general election ad on September 23 until the end of the campaign on November 2. In this forty-one-day period, Bush juggled several ad messages. He opened his air campaign with a positive ad, "What Am I Fighting For." But by early October, he shifted to major attacks on Clinton's character, using the "Gray Dot" and "Federal Taxes" ads. These commercials each started running on October 2 and were broadcast through the middle of the month. Unfortunately for Bush, these attacks proved quite controversial. A number of media reports condemned Bush's tactics and public opinion polls showed that twice as many Americans blamed Bush than Clinton for the negative tone of the campaign. Perhaps as a result of this backlash, Bush shifted to more positive advertising. Bush's "Agenda" ad promoting his agenda for American renewal began running October 22 and by far was his most frequently broadcast national ad in the last two weeks of the campaign. However, it still was interspersed with smaller buys on October 22, 28, 30, and 31 for the "Gray Dot" commercial.

These strategic alterations were in noticeable contrast to those for Clinton and Perot, respectively. As the front-runner in preelection polls, Clinton had the luxury of saving his most frequently aired ads for the last two weeks of the campaign. Unlike Bush, who started big national buys in late September, Clinton's biggest buys started on October 22, two weeks before Election Day. His most prominent ad at this time was the attack spot, "Remember." Clinton's "Even" spot started October 28 and ran each day the rest of the campaign. On October 29, Clinton also started buying national time for his "Senator Nunn" ad discussing how he and Al Gore represented new-style Democrats who supported capital punishment and a new way of thinking about social problems.

Perot started his national ad campaign on October 10 with his "Kids" ad noting the buildup of national debt being left to the country's children. He added the "Storm" spot on October 14 and broadcast it heavily until October 26, when it ceased running. Beginning on October 28 and for the rest of the race, Perot emphasized his "We Can Win" and "How to Vote" spots. Perot's spots rarely mentioned his opponents by name but rather emphasized the need for action to solve pressing national problems.

Local Ad Buys

Candidates supplement national ad buys with time purchases in local markets. There were dramatic differences in ad buy strategies in the four communities we studied: Boston, Los Angeles, Winston-Salem, and Fargo/Moorhead. Of these locales, Clinton purchased time only in Winston-Salem; Bush bought television time in Boston, Winston-Salem, and Fargo/Moorhead; and Perot purchased time in Los Angeles and Fargo/Moorhead. These choices obviously reflected strategic decisions within each campaign about targets of opportunity within particular areas.

Bush ran general election ads in Boston, Winston-Salem, and Fargo/Moorhead. His most frequently broadcast commercials in Boston were "Arkansas Record," "Trust," and "Federal Taxes." Overall, he spent $111,390 on twelve different ads. He added "Guess" in Winston-Salem and "Luke" and "Peter" in Fargo/Moorhead. His spending totaled $79,935 in Winston-Salem for twenty different ads and $8,205 in Fargo/Moorhead on nine different ads. All of these ads were hard-hitting attacks on Clinton's trustworthiness and taxing proclivities. The "Arkansas Record" spot was a harsh-reality commercial featuring Clinton's Arkansas as a desolate, wind-swept landscape, presided over by a raven. "Luke" and "Peter" were man-on-the-street spots in which ordinary Americans voiced their doubts about Clinton's character.

Bush ran negative ads more frequently in local than national markets. For example, his "Agenda" spot was Bush's most frequently broadcast commercial nationally, but it did not receive prominent air time in any of the local markets we studied. This reflected a stealth strategy in the closing days of the campaign, whereby Bush went positive nationally but stayed negative locally. The goal was to gain the benefits of attack in selected markets while minimizing the national backlash from an observant press corps.

Perot ran sixteen different ads costing $146,200 in Los Angeles and thirteen various ads costing $5,465 in Fargo/Moorhead. "Storm" was his most frequently aired ad in Los Angeles, running seven times for a total of $17,800. "Purple Heart" was broadcast twice during prime spots for a total cost of $23,800. In Fargo/Moorhead, Perot's most frequently broadcast commercial was "Trickle Down." It ran five times and talked about the failure of Republican economic policies.

The Case of Winston-Salem

Of the four communities in our study, Clinton ran fall ads only in the closely contested site of Winston-Salem. It is noteworthy, though, that he outspent Bush by $175,080 to $79,935 in this area. Clinton ran twenty-two ads here, whereas Bush broadcast twenty. Clinton's top ads were "Billion," "Curtains," and "Promise." Each of these spots emphasized the poor economic performance under Bush and Bush's broken tax promise.

Clinton was able to outspend Bush in North Carolina because it was one of Clinton's targeted states. North Carolina was one of the most competitive states in the country politically during the 1992 campaign. As a sign of its competitiveness, the North Carolina air wars started much earlier than did the national ad buys. Bush began running local ads in Winston-Salem on August 4, much earlier than the September 23 start of his national advertising campaign. Clinton retaliated by starting ads in Winston-Salem on August 31, compared to his national ad kickoff of September 25.

To see how each campaign allocated its Winston-Salem ad buys, we looked at the frequency of Bush and Clinton ad buys for their top commercials at various points during the fall campaign. Among their top ads, Clinton began broadcasting "Curtains" on September 21 and ran it heavily until September 30. At that point, he shifted to "Promise," which ran from September 30 to October 12. Bush responded on September 26 with his "Guess" ad, which was seen on WXII through October 2. From October 14 to 20, Bush saturated the air waves with his "Trust" ad attacking Clinton's character. From October 22 to 26, Clinton ran his "Billion" ad proposing a tax on foreign corporations.

It is interesting to note that none of Clinton's top ads in North Carolina received any buys after October 27. This ceded the field to Bush, who began running "Arkansas Record" on October 28. It aired six times in Winston-Salem on October 28, followed by seven on October 29, eight on October 30, six on October 31, five on November 1, and eight on November 2. Given the wide range of factors that could have been decisive, it is difficult to state definitely that this strategic interaction cost Clinton the state.

Yet it is worth noting that Bush, in a late surge, ended up carrying North Carolina by 43 percent to 42 percent. In a closely contested election, last-minute ads conceivably could move a sufficient number of swing voters to provide the margin of victory. According to Franklin's (1994) analysis of a Wisconsin Senate race, [6] a net television advertising advantage at the end of a campaign is worth a gain of 2 percentage points of the vote. In addition, our detailed interviews and focus groups in Winston-Salem at the end of October revealed grave concerns about Clinton. Several swing voters specifically cited the "Arkansas Record" ad as influential to last-minute votes for Bush.

It is clear, based on our analysis, that there were substantial differences in how presidential aspirants allocated their advertising efforts. Bush and Perot devoted more resources nationally than Clinton did, and Clinton targeted more expenditures on local markets in selected states. There also were important differences in ads aired in different cities, in the timing of attack ads, and in strategic alterations during the campaign.

Strategic moves were linked to state polling results, coverage by the news media, and ads run by opponents. Bush's stealth campaign was especially important in North Carolina, because last-minute attacks on Clinton's Arkansas record helped Bush score a narrow victory.

Perot's ad buys played a key role in his strong finish with 19 percent of the vote. Because Perot reentered the race in early October, he was able to spend nearly all his advertising dollars in the last three weeks of the campaign, thereby far outspending either Bush or Clinton during that crucial period. This saturation of the air waves made his commercials unusually memorable for viewers and helped create positive impressions of Perot's leadership abilities.

The 1996 Primaries

The Republican nominating process featured a crowded field of contenders: Senate Majority Leader Dole, conservative television commentator Pat Buchanan, Senator Phil Gramm, former Tennessee governor Lamar Alexander, and magazine publisher and multimillionaire Forbes, among others. By dint of his organization, fund-raising, and endorsements from a multitude of party leaders and elected officials around the country, Dole was the clear front-runner. Throughout 1995, he led in the polls by more than 40 percentage points.

Early in this campaign, Dole and his advisors targeted Gramm as their most serious opponent. With a strong organization in Iowa and New Hampshire and a strong fund-raising base nationally, Gramm seemingly had all the ingredients of a successful challenger. He was a sitting senator with strong support in the South. He also drew support from conservatives and religious fundamentalists who were increasing their grip on the GOP.

But that was before Forbes launched his multimillion-dollar campaign. Featuring saturation buys in early states and attack ads against Dole and other candidates, Forbes upset many of the early expectations. Julie Campasano, who was in charge of selling political advertising for television station WMUR in Manchester, New Hampshire, explained that right before Forbes announced his candidacy in September 1995, a group of his campaign advisors came to visit her: "They wanted to do a megabulk buy. . . . They wanted tonnage [and] frequency. . . . They wanted to buy every stitch of advertising they could get." [7]

In each of the early states, Forbes set a record for spending on television advertising, with more than two-thirds of his spots being attack ads. At WHO-TV in Des Moines, Iowa, for example, he bought $190,149 of time, compared to $119,228 for Dole and $109,771 for Indiana senator Richard Lugar. Overall, Republican ad expenditures at this station totaled $630,169, which was more than three times the $183,873 spent in the 1988 Republican and Democratic caucuses. [8]

The same thing happened in New Hampshire. A CNN survey of TV stations in the area showed that Forbes spent $1,515,360 on ads, compared to $1,095,723 for Dole, $693,021 for Alexander, and $329,895 for Buchanan. [9] His television buy in New Hampshire totaled about 2,000 gross ratings points, meaning that the average viewer would have seen a single Forbes ad twenty times, roughly double what either Dole and Alexander bought. [10]

For the primaries as a whole, Forbes spent around $36 million, which was close to the $33 million that Dole spent. But figures released after the primaries showed how Dole's early strategic decisions almost cost him the nomination. [11] Whereas Forbes put $24 million (67 percent of his budget) into television ads and almost no money into organization, Dole only spent $6 million on ads (20 percent of his overall budget). Of that amount, $1 million went to produce ads. Nearly one-third of his money ($10 million) went into raising more money and another third ($12 million) went into overhead for his organization, such as staff salaries, rent, and travel.

In the short run, it looked like the Forbes air war would succeed. With ads attacking Dole for raising taxes, increasing his congressional pension, and being a Washington insider, Forbes rose in the polls while Dole fell precipitously from his Iowa, May 1995 poll support of 57 percent. In September 1995, Dole led Forbes by 35 percent to 6 percent. By January 1996, after months of advertising attacks, Iowa polls put the race at 26 percent for Dole and 18 percent for Forbes. Forbes ended the month of January on the covers of *Time* ("Does a Flat Tax Make Sense?") and *Newsweek* ("Rip!: Steve Forbes Wants a Flat Tax. Do You?"). The following week, the *Newsweek* cover pictured a dark, unsmiling image of Dole with the headline, "Doubts about Dole."

Yet the unrelentingly negative tone of Forbes's ads created a backlash against his candidacy. Rather than being the beneficiary of Dole's weakness, Forbes began to sink. Dole barely won Iowa on February 12 by 3 percentage points over Buchanan and Alexander, and Forbes finished in fourth place.

Right after the Iowa caucuses, Dole's advisors held a telephone conference call to assess the damage.[12] Private tracking polls in the upcoming February 20 New Hampshire primary revealed that Dole was about to blow the nomination to Alexander, who had finished a strong third in Iowa. Dole was seen as having no new ideas and being a creature of Washington. In the three days from February 12 to 15, Alexander had jumped from 8 percent to 18 percent. Alexander also was viewed more positively (57 percent to 10 percent) among undecided voters than any of the other candidates. His ads proclaimed him the candidate of new ideas and a former governor who was from outside of Washington.

Dole's advisors concluded that the real threat was not Buchanan, who was too far out of the party mainstream with his controversial views on protectionism and immigration. Nor was it Forbes, whose support had slipped badly as he bore the blame for the negative tone of the Republican campaign.

The Dole campaign decided to open a last-minute television advertising blitz against Alexander the weekend before the New Hampshire primary. Alexander was a tax-and-spend liberal who was not what he pretended to be, the attack argued. The script for the Dole ad asked, "Is Lamar Alexander too liberal? As Governor, he raised taxes and fees fifty-eight times and doubled state spending. He even signed a bill allowing violent criminals to be eligible for parole after serving less than half their prison sentence. He's just too liberal. We need a proven conservative leader. The choice for conservatives: Bob Dole."

The charge about early release for prison inmates was especially deceptive in light of the fact that Tennessee had released inmates because it was under a court order for overcrowding. But Dole spent hundreds of thousands of dollars on ad buys to make sure

New Hampshire voters saw this attack ad repeatedly over the weekend. Alexander had no time or money to respond.

The results were devastating to Alexander. On February 15, before the ads were broadcast, 44 percent of voters believed Alexander was conservative. Five days later, after saturation advertising with "liberal Lamar" spots, only 22 percent thought Alexander was conservative and 54 percent thought he was moderate or liberal. The final vote in New Hampshire was 28 percent for Buchanan, 27 percent for Dole, and 23 percent for Alexander. Alexander commented on hearing the results on election night: "They decided to beat me in New Hampshire and get Buchanan later." Shortly thereafter, Alexander was out of the race and Dole swept the remaining primaries over Buchanan and Forbes to become the Republican nominee.

The 1996 General Election

The 1996 campaign featured new technology designed to track ad buys nationally. Unlike previous systems that were dependent on personal checks with ad buyers or local station managers, the GOP media buying firm National Media, Inc., relied on a new system called POLARIS, short for Political Advertising, Reporting and Intelligence System. This technology used "sound pattern recognition technology originally developed by the Pentagon to monitor, track, and report client schedules of buys, as well as those of the opponent." [13]

Under this system, computers monitor satellite transmissions by broadcast and cable networks and tape commercials aired in each of the top 75 of the 216 media markets across the nation. This covers about 80 percent of the country as well as twenty-five major cable networks. In 1996, this system found that 57 million commercials aired from April 1 to November 4, of which 752,891 were political spots. Twenty percent (167,714 ads) were broadcast in the presidential campaign by the two major candidates and their respective national parties.[14]

These tapes give campaign strategists the ability to see who was running ads, where they were running, how much was being spent, and an audiotape and selected videotape snapshots from each ad. They also give reporters a new tool for ad monitoring. For example, Brooks Jackson of CNN has used this ad detector on the show "Inside Politics." This tool allowed Jackson to spot commercials politicians were testing in small markets before they were broadcast nationally and a sense of how big an ad buy was being used.

The results reveal how candidates allocated their ad dollars in the campaign. While Republicans were lobbing video grenades at one another in the spring, Clinton was luxuriating in an uncontested renomination. But this did not mean that Clinton ceded the television field to Republicans. Through ads sponsored by the Democratic National Committee, Clinton was the beneficiary of $15 million in ads promoting his candidacy in 1995 alone. These spots argued that Clinton was the remaining safeguard against Republican extremism in the areas of Medicare, Medicaid, and the environment.

As Republicans settled their nomination on Dole, the DNC launched another torrent of campaign ads for Clinton in mid-March. From March 7 to 18, Democrats made 2,500 ad buys in forty-two cities. This was two and a half times the number of ad buys for Dole during this period.[15] From March 1 through June 14, the DNC and Clinton's reelection committee ran more than 17,000 ads. The ads targeted shows from "CBS Sunday Morning" to daytime talk shows like "Live with Regis & Kathie Lee." [16]

In keeping with Clinton's general election strategy in 1996 of targeting medium-sized markets in key swing states, Democrats ran ads in twenty-four states. In the Northeast, they emphasized Maine and Connecticut. In the South, ads were broadcast in Florida, Georgia, North Carolina, Tennessee, Kentucky, Arkansas, and Louisiana. In the Midwest, spots appeared in Ohio, Pennsylvania, Michigan, Wisconsin, Illinois, Minnesota, Iowa, Kansas, and Missouri. Western states included California, Washington, Oregon, Nevada, New Mexico, and Colorado. This list was similar to the states Clinton had targeted in 1992.

One DNC ad opened with Dole proclaiming "We sent him the first balanced budget in a generation. He vetoed it. We're going to veto Bill Clinton." An announcer then replied: "The facts? The President proposes a balanced budget protecting Medicare, education, the environment. But Dole is voting no. The President cuts taxes for 40 million Americans. Dole votes no. The President bans assault weapons; demands work for welfare while protecting kids. Dole says no to the Clinton plans. It's time to say yes to the Clinton plans—yes to America's families."

Dole's campaign lambasted Clinton on the tax issue. One GOP ad showed Clinton saying in 1992 that he would "not raise taxes on the middle class" and then accusing him of the nation's biggest tax increase six months later. All in all, the ad claimed, federal taxes rose $1,500 for the typical American family, "a big price to pay for his broken promise." The next day, Clinton's team responded with an ad showing a 1984 Newt Gingrich quote saying Dole was the "tax collector for the welfare state," and a man who was responsible for "35 years of higher taxes."

By the summer of 1996, the Clinton campaign was saturating the airwaves. Whereas Dole in July was out of money as a result of the spring nomination struggle and the $37 million ceiling on primary spending, Clinton went on an advertising spending spree with his unspent primary money. The campaign spent $6.5 million in July, with two-thirds of it ($4 million) going to advertising. This was almost as much as the Clinton campaign had spent in the preceding fifteen months. At the beginning of August, they had about $10 million left, which they spent by the convention. According to Clinton campaign manager Peter S. Knight, "We felt that August was a very important month in the campaign and it's just prudent to hold your resources as close to Election Day as possible." [17]

This produced a dramatic imbalance in money spent airing ads. For the period of the nominating process, Dole spent $7 million on advertising, compared to $13 million for Clinton. Dole was also outspent at the level of the national committees. The Republican National Committee spent $28 million airing ads on behalf of Dole and fellow Republicans by the time of the conventions, whereas the Democratic National Committee spent $40 million.

In the direct run against Dole in the fall campaign, the president switched from attacks on Republican extremism to attempts to co-opt popular Republican issues, such as welfare reform and crime. With the president having signed a compromise welfare reform bill approved by the Republican Congress, it became more difficult to criticize the GOP as extremist.

Dole went through a three-stage strategy of attack ads against Clinton. The first stage, starting at the Republican convention and continuing through the early part of September, emphasized an economic message based on Dole's 15-percent income tax cut proposal and Clinton's signature on what the Dole camp claimed using numbers not adjusted for inflation was the largest tax increase in American history. In mid-September, Dole shifted to the "drugs and crime" phase in which he criticized the president for rising drug use and crime rates during his presidency. By early

October, Dole went to his end game, focusing attention on character issues and scandals, such as Whitewater, Travelgate, and the acceptance of campaign funds from foreign sources.

The Dole ad in mid-September talking about Clinton's MTV admission of wanting to inhale marijuana and having liberal drug policies aired 7,300 times on local television stations from September 16 to 25, with nearly 15 percent (949 airings) in Florida alone. The Dole campaign targeted shows aimed at women and senior citizens on the grounds that these people would be most upset at rising teenage drug usage. The ad buys were heavily concentrated in fourteen states: Florida, Arizona, Nebraska, Ohio, Michigan, Kentucky, Tennessee, Georgia, Iowa, Pennsylvania, Connecticut, New Mexico, Colorado, and California.

Clinton's response ad on this issue ran 4,600 times from September 16 to 25, which represented double the ad buy of earlier ads. Clinton's ad buyers also paired their drug response with another ad claiming Dole was against Medicare, student loans, and a higher minimum wage.

By the end of this time period, the CNN/*USA Today* daily tracking poll showed Dole had closed the margin to 10 points (49 percent for Clinton and 39 percent for Dole), which was the smallest Clinton lead in the fall. Before this ad volley had started, Clinton held a 17-point lead with him getting 53 percent of the vote, compared to 36 percent for Dole.[18] But this tightening did not hold up. By the following week, all of Dole's gains had proven to be short-term.

Overall, there were interesting differences in the geographic areas targeted by Clinton and Dole. As shown in Table 2-1, Clinton's top area for ad buys in the period from April 1 to November 4, 1996, was Albuquerque, New Mexico (3,079 spots aired), followed by Lexington, Kentucky (2,681 spots) and Sacramento, California (2,535 spots). Dole's top areas were Los Angeles (3,543 spots), Denver (2,727 spots), and Sacramento (2,635 spots).

Perot meanwhile saved about 75 percent of his $29 million in public monies for the last three weeks of the campaign. This meant that he was buying around $1.1 million of ads and infomercials each day. The night before the election, Perot bought thirty-minute infomercials on CBS and NBC and an hour on ABC, at a total cost of $2 million. In conjunction with his attacks on Clinton's character and exhortations to reform the campaign finance system, this raised Perot's support in the last week of the

TABLE 2-1
Presidential Ad Buys by Geographic Area: 1996

Clinton and the Democrats		Dole and the Republicans	
Market	Number of Spots	Market	Number of Spots
Albuquerque	3,079	Los Angeles	3,543
Lexington, Ky.	2,681	Denver	2,727
Sacramento	2,535	Sacramento	2,635
Tampa	2,446	Cleveland	2,284
Denver	2,397	Nashville	2,244
Louisville	2,392	Albuquerque	2,216
Flint, Mich.	2,384	Tampa	2,161
Cincinnati	2,381	Cincinnati	2,131
Cleveland	2,345	Atlanta	2,097
Detroit	2,316	San Diego	2,056

Source: New York Times, November 13, 1996, A16.

Note: These entries reflect the number of television spots broadcast in the nation's seventy-five largest markets from April 1 to November 4, 1996.

campaign from 5 percent to 8 percent.[19] But it was too late to salvage his candidacy.

With his own presidential bid down 20 percentage points and Republican control of Congress at risk, Dole decided in the closing weeks to allocate his time and ad dollars protecting party control of the House and Senate. He made campaign visits to states such as Kansas, Virginia, and New Hampshire that typically are sure Republican states for presidential candidates but where there were Republican senatorial candidates who needed a boost. Dole also allocated $7 million to a last-minute ad blitz in California, pulling money out of New Jersey and Pennsylvania in the process. But this did not stem the Clinton tide. In the last week of the race, Clinton was outspending Dole by a significant margin. Whereas Clinton averaged $1.2 million a day in ads, Dole was broadcasting about $900,000 a day. This ensured that in targeted media markets, the average television viewer would see twenty Clinton commercials the week before the election.[20]

The 1996 presidential contest demonstrates the value of early ad spending to set the agenda of the campaign. Political communications experts long have argued that such expenditures were wasted money. No one pays attention to campaigns fifteen months before the election. The only people who decide how they are going to vote that early are strong partisans with well-defined political views. These are not the type of voters one would predict to be very susceptible to advertising.

But through early spending and a clear Democratic advantage in ad expenditures throughout winter 1995 and the spring and summer of 1996, Clinton framed the election as a referendum on the Republican Revolution, not himself. This may have been the first presidential election in this century to serve as a referendum on a sitting Speaker of the House of Representatives.

Chapter 3

Ad Messages

Candidates do not choose their advertising messages lightly. Most campaigners develop commercials based on game plans that guide organizational decision making. These documents outline the desired targets of the campaign as well as the themes and issues to be addressed. Candidates often test basic messages through polls and focus groups. Reagan manager Ed Rollins said in reference to the 1984 campaign against Walter Mondale: "We made some fundamental decisions . . . to take [Mondale] on the tax issue . . . to try to drive [his] negatives back up. . . . The decision was to go with two negative commercials for every one positive commercial. . . . Let me say the commercials clearly worked, we drove [Mondale's] negatives back up again, the tax thing became the dominant issue at least in our polling, and it helped us get ready for the final week of the campaign." [1]

Different models have been developed to explain the choice of campaign strategies. Anthony Downs's model suggests that candidates are political free agents who look for the midpoint of public opinion and direct their appeals to that place on the spectrum. [2] The reasoning is simple: Because winning an election requires the development of a broad-based coalition, it makes sense for politicians to aim for the most votes.

Increasingly, though, Downs's theory of democracy has been supplanted by party cleavage models, which posit the importance of party arenas to electoral appeals. As described by Benjamin Page, proponents of party-cleavage models argue that candidates' positions are affected by party settings and the views of primary electorates. Candidates of opposing parties often take systematically different positions. [3] According to this perspective, candidates are not ideological neuters with complete freedom to roam the political spectrum. Instead, they bring political views and strategic reasoning to bear on their campaign decisions.

As campaigns have opened up and nominating battles have become common, the strategic aspect of electoral appeals has emerged as a major determinant. Candidates face more choices than at any previous point in American history. A system of presidential selection based on popular support places a premium on these decisions. Campaigners who pursue the wrong constituencies, go on the attack prematurely, or address nonsalient issues end up in political oblivion.

For these reasons, it is instructive to look at ad content and style of presentation with an eye toward strategic behavior. Do ad messages vary by party? How have candidates' presentations changed over time? Are there differences in electronic appeals in different stages of a campaign? What messages are communicated via the newly emerging Internet ads on candidate home pages?

The Content of Ads

The classic criticism of American ads was written by Joe McGinniss following Nixon's 1968 presidential campaign. Nixon entered that race with a serious image problem. His previous loss in 1960 and public impressions of him during a long career in public service led many to believe he was a sour, nasty, and mean-spirited politician. His advisers therefore devised an advertising strategy meant to create a "new" Nixon. As described by McGinniss, who had unlimited access to the inner workings of Nixon's advertising campaign: "America still saw him as the 1960 Nixon. If he were to come at the people again, as candidate, it would have to be as something new; not this scarred, discarded figure from their past. . . . This would be Richard Nixon, the leader, returning from exile. Perhaps not beloved, but respected. Firm but not harsh; just but compassionate. With flashes of warmth spaced evenly throughout."[4]

The power of this portrait and the anecdotes McGinniss was able to gather during the course of the campaign helped create a negative impression of political ads that has endured to this day. For example, Robert Spero describes the "duping" of the American voter in his book analyzing "dishonesty and deception in presidential television advertising."[5] Others have criticized ads for being intentionally vague and overly personalistic in their appeals.

Political commercials do not have a great reputation among contemporary viewers either. An October CBS News/*New York Times* survey during the 1988 presidential general election asked those exposed to ads how truthful they considered commercials for each candidate. The Bush ads and Dukakis ads scored the same: only 37 percent felt they were mostly truthful. The remainder believed that campaign commercials were either generally false or had some element of falsehood.

Even more interesting were overall beliefs about the impact of television ads. People felt the strongest effects of ads were to influence general feelings about the candidates and the weakest were in the communication of substantive information. Fifty percent said ads made them feel good about their candidate, whereas only 25 percent said ads had given them new information about the candidates during the fall campaign.

Citizens also believe that contemporary campaigns are more negative than in the past. When asked whether the 1988 race had been more positive, more negative, or about the same as past presidential campaigns, 48 percent of the respondents said it had been more negative. But 1988 was the high point in terms of voter views about negativity. In 1992, 36 percent felt that the presidential race was more negative than past contests. In 1996, just 11 percent believed that the race had been more negative than in the past.[6]

Studies of the effects of ads have rarely paid much attention to the dimensions of evaluation. Many criticisms of commercials have failed to define the elusive notion of substance or distinguish it from image-oriented considerations. One exception is a study by Leonard Shyles, who draws a distinction between image, which he defines as "character attributes of candidates," and issues, which he defines as "current topics and civic concerns linked to the national interest."[7] There can be no clear distinction between image and issues, because many ads are based on a combination of substantive matters and character attributes. In fact, a number of commercials use discussions of substantive points to create an impression of knowledge, experience, or competence; this mixture further complicates assessments of ad content.

This problem notwithstanding, there have been several efforts to investigate the content of ads. Such research generally has attempted to assess the quality of the information presented to viewers. In keeping with the interest in issue-based voting during the 1970s and recognizing the centrality of policy matters to democratic elections, much of the work on ad content focused on the treatment of issues. It is surprising to note that in light of popular beliefs about the subject, most of the research has found that ads present more substantive information than viewers and journalists generally believe.

Richard Joslyn has undertaken one of the most thorough and systematic efforts in his 1980 study of 156 television spot ads aired during contested general election campaigns. He measured whether political issues were mentioned during the ad. His research revealed that 79.6 percent of presidential ads mentioned issues. Based on this work, he argued that "political spot ads may not be as poor a source of information as many observers have claimed." [8]

Others have reached similar conclusions. Richard Hofstetter and Cliff Zukin discovered in their analysis of the 1972 presidential race that about 85 percent of the candidates' ads included some reference to issues. In comparison, only 59 percent of the news coverage of George McGovern and 76 percent of the news coverage of Nixon had issue content. Likewise, Patterson and McClure demonstrated, in a content analysis of the 1972 race, that issues received more frequent coverage in commercials than in network news coverage. Robinson and Sheehan report in regard to 1980 CBS news coverage that 41 percent of the lines of news transcript contained at least one issue mention. [9]

These projects have attracted considerable attention because they run contrary to much of the popular thinking and press criticism about media and politics. At the normative level, the findings are reassuring because they challenge conventional wisdom warning of the dangers of commercials. Rather than accepting the common view, which emphasizes the noneducational nature of ads, these researchers claim that commercials offer relevant information to voters.

But there has been little follow-up work on these important analyses. Few studies have extended the investigation to recent elections. Because much of this past research has focused on single elections, without considering how to generalize the results, it remains to be seen whether the results stand up over time. In addition, past research has ignored the variety of ways in which substantive messages can be delivered, beyond direct policy mentions. [10] For example, character and personal qualities are increasingly seen as vital to presidential performance. It is therefore important to assess the full range of the content of ads in order to reach more general conclusions about the rhetoric of candidates.

Prominent Ads

The study of ad content poses several problems. Foremost is the dilemma of how to come up with a representative sample when the full universe of ads from 1952 to 1996 is not available. One approach, which was common in the past, is to use convenience samples based on ads the scholar is able to obtain. However, it is difficult to establish how representative the ads in a convenience sample are. Thus, it is impossible to generalize and account for the results.

Research is complicated because not all ads are equally important. A random sample has the unfortunate tendency to weight important, frequently aired ads the same as less important ads. The failure to distinguish prominent from less important commercials is troubling, because in each presidential year certain ads attract more viewer and media attention than others. As pointed out in Chapter 2 on ad buys, some ads are broadcast much more frequently than others. These ads are the most central to the candidates. In addition to being aired most frequently, prominent ads are discussed and rebroadcast by the media. Owing to the general noteworthiness of these ads and their heightened exposure through the free media, they are the most likely to be influential with voters. It makes sense to investigate commercials generally regarded as the crucial ones in particular campaigns.[11]

I studied prominent ads as defined by Kathleen Jamieson, the leading historian of political advertisements. For every presidential campaign since 1952, Jamieson, on an election-by-election basis, has described the presidential campaign ads that were newsworthy, entertaining, flamboyant, or effective. I used her detailed histories to compile a list of prominent spot ads from 1952 to 1988. For 1992 and 1996, prominent ads were defined as those broadcast in "CBS Evening News" stories. In all, 379 prominent ads were studied.[12]

This set is a complete enumeration of all the spot ads cited by Jamieson and for the last two elections aired during the "CBS Evening News," but it is not designed to be a random sample of all ads from this period. Rather, it is a listing of all the commercials judged by one ad historian to have been among the most visible and important ones in given years. Using a common source facilitates comparability over time; Jamieson presumably employed consistent criteria for selecting prominent commercials. Reliance on a single historian, of course, does not ensure a full list of prominent ads.[13] Every historian has to make choices, given the limits of time and space, about which commercials to include in a listing. But a perusal of *New York Times* and *Washington Post* coverage reveals that Jamieson was generally successful at identifying the commercials that attracted media attention. Most of the spots mentioned in stories are included among the prominent commercials described by her.

Appendix Table A-1 lists the party, candidate, campaign stage, and chronological breakdowns for the prominent ads from 1952 to 1996. It is obvious that not all candidates who ran for president during the period are represented in this set, nor should they be. For example, there are no ads in this sample for Phil Crane, Connally, and others who were also-rans. There is a much better representation, however, of prominent ads each year for the party nominees and major challengers. The commercials included in this analysis come from both the presidential nominating process *(N* = 94) and the presidential general election *(N* = 270), and ten dealt with congressional races and five dealt with ballot measures. Overall, there were 192 Republican ads, 166 Democratic ads, and 21 independent candidate or referenda ads. The period from 1960 to 1976, when there were a number of competitive Democratic primaries, slightly overrepresents Democratic ads, whereas the time from 1980 to 1996 slightly overrepresents Republican spots. Intercoder reliability scores were computed for the content categories. In general, the scores were well within the range of acceptability, as about 85 percent of the content codes were consistent between reviewers.

For these ads, codes were compiled for each commercial based on the year of the election, type of election (presidential general election or nominating stage), sponsoring party (Republican, Democrat, or other), and content of the ad. Ad messages were classified into the areas of domestic concerns, international affairs, personal qualities of the candidates, specific policy statements, party appeals, or campaign process. Specific policy appeals involved clear declarations of past positions or expectations about future actions. General categories were subdivided into more detailed types of appeals. Domestic concerns included the economy; social welfare; social issues; crime, violence, and drugs; race and civil rights; taxes and budgets; corruption and government performance; and energy and the environment. International affairs consisted of war and peace, foreign relations, national security and defense, and trade matters. Personal qualities included leadership, trust and honesty, experience and competence, compassion, independence, and extremism. Party appeals were based on explicit partisan messages (such as the need to elect more Republicans) and references to party labels. Campaign appeals included references to strategies, personnel matters within the campaign, electoral prospects, or organizational dynamics.

The Paucity of Policy Appeals

Issue information in advertising can be assessed either as action statements or as policy mentions. The former refers to specific policy statements—that is, clear statements of past positions or expectations about future actions. For example, Reagan's 1980 ad promising a "30% federal tax cut" that would benefit every group and offer the government an actual gain in revenue was an action statement. Johnson's criticism of Goldwater for past statements proposing that Social Security become a voluntary retirement option was a specific policy mention, although Johnson never made clear whether Goldwater still supported this proposal. (One of the ads supplied the dates of Goldwater's statements.)

Few discussions of domestic or international matters reach this level of detail, however. The more common approach is the policy mention, in which general problems of the economy, foreign relations, or government performance are discussed, but no specific proposals to deal with the matter are made. For example, an Eisenhower ad about the economy in 1952 showed a woman holding a bag of groceries and complaining, "I paid $24 for these groceries—look, for this little." Eisenhower then said, "A few years ago, those same groceries cost you $10, now $24, next year $30. That's what will happen unless we have a change."[14] This commercial obviously does not suggest a plan for combating inflation, although it does portray the painfulness of price increases.

Prominent ads were more likely to emphasize personal qualities (32 percent) and domestic performance (31 percent) than specific domestic or foreign policy appeals (23 percent) (see Table 3-1). Ads for Republicans included more specific pledges (24 percent) than Democrats (19 percent). Those for Republicans were more

TABLE 3-1
Content of Prominent Ads: 1952–1996

Appeal	Percentage of Ads
Personal qualities	32%
Domestic performance	31
Specific domestic policy	19
Specific foreign policy	4
International affairs	7
Campaign	5
Party	2
N	(379)

Sources: Kathleen Jamieson, *Packaging the Presidency,* 2d ed. (New York: Oxford University Press, 1992) for campaigns 1952–1988, and "CBS Evening News" tapes for 1992 and 1996 campaigns.

likely to emphasize international affairs (10 percent) than for Democrats (4 percent). In contrast, ads for Democrats were much more likely to emphasize personal qualities (39 percent) than were those for Republicans (29 percent).

The party differences reflect interests within each party and have consequences for how each party is viewed by the public. The greater attention paid by Republicans to international affairs and by Democrats to domestic areas is consistent with party coalitions. It also helps to explain why Democrats are viewed as weak on foreign policy and Republicans are seen as inattentive to domestic matters. The public and the media take cues about party priorities from the visibility of issues in political advertising.

These results offer little encouragement regarding substance in campaigns. Even if one follows the lead of other scholars and uses the less demanding standard of policy mentions regardless of specificity, the overall level of substantive information is not impressive. Joslyn, as well as Hofstetter and Zukin, combined specific policy statements with more general discussions of domestic performance and international affairs to form a broader measure of substantive appeals.[15] According to this more general standard, 61 percent of prominent ads contained policy mentions. These figures are considerably lower than the 85 percent found by Hofstetter and Zukin for 1972 and the 79.6 percent uncovered by Joslyn for his sample of races.

The unwillingness of candidates to discuss policy or to propose plans of action creates obvious difficulties for models of issue-based voting. If candidates do not make statements about how they would deal with policy problems, then voters who might cast ballots based on the issues face barriers. Most commercials are not very specific, and they fail almost completely as policy blueprints.

Of course, even mentioning issues allows voters to incorporate broader notions of accountability into their choices. If candidates mention unemployment in an ad but do not say what they will do about the problem, the ad can serve an agenda-setting function. The mention may increase the importance of employment policy in voters' priorities or in campaign coverage by the media. Scholars may turn to performance-based models, such as pocketbook-voting models, under which voters do not require detailed policy information to hold leaders accountable. Because the field of voting studies has evolved in recent years from issue- to performance-based models, it is important to recognize that ads may be influential even if their specific policy content is limited.

Shifts over Time

There is little reason to treat all elections the same or to assume that every contest engenders the same type of advertising appeals. Based on obvious differences in strategic goals among presidential aspirants and shifts in voters' priorities over the years, one would expect extensive fluctuations in commercials from election to election. To see exactly how advertising messages have changed, it is necessary to study ads from a series of elections.

Some believe that ads have become less policy oriented and more personality based in recent years. When one looks at changes in policy appeals, it is obvious that prominent ads in the 1980s and 1990s were more substantive than those of earlier periods (Figure 3-1). Twenty-six percent of commercials in 1984, 45 percent in 1988, and 41 percent in 1992 included specific statements about public policy. In 1996, 28 percent of ads featured policy-specific statements, down from the preceding two elections.

The only other period when specific policy messages were common was the 1960s (23 percent in 1964 and 31 percent in 1968). However, as has been found in other areas of research, the 1960s were an anomaly in terms of specific policy mentions. The more

Figure 3-1   Prominent Ad Content by Election Year: 1952–1996

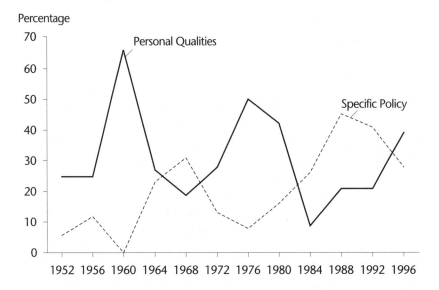

Sources: For 1952–1988, Kathleen Jamieson, *Packaging the Presidency,* 2d ed. (New York: Oxford University Press, 1992); and for 1992–1996, "CBS Evening News" tapes.

common pattern in earlier historical periods was a relatively low level of specificity.

Ads based on personal qualities reached their high points in 1960 (69 percent of all appeals), 1976 (50 percent), and 1980 (42 percent), but dropped back to lower levels of 9 percent in 1984, 21 percent in 1988, and 21 percent in 1992. In 1996, there were nearly twice as many appeals based on personal qualities (39 percent) than in 1988 or 1992. This reflects attacks during the nominating process on Dole's experience, Buchanan's extremism, and Alexander's trustworthiness in light of his past business dealings, and criticisms during the general election of Clinton's character and honesty.

Races having the greatest emphasis on personal qualities involved challengers who were either unknown or inexperienced. For example, in 1960 many questions were raised about the qualifications and experience of John F. Kennedy. In a similar way, ads during the Gerald Ford–Carter contest in 1976, the Reagan–Carter–John Anderson campaign in 1980, and the Bush–Clinton–Perot race of 1992 devoted a great deal of attention to personal characteristics, such as leadership, trustworthiness, and experience. But these emphases were more a matter of defusing or highlighting personal qualities important in a particular race than a manifestation of any general trend toward personalistic politics.

It is interesting to examine variations in ad categories over time. Table 3-2 presents the breakdowns of prominent ads for the broad categories of domestic matters (specific domestic policy appeals combined with general domestic performance), international affairs (both specific and general mentions), personal qualities, party appeals, and campaign-related messages. Party appeals were stronger in the 1950s than in any period since then. Twelve percent of prominent ads in 1956 emphasized appeals to party, the highest of any election in this study. In fact, for many elections from 1960 through 1996, there were no prominent ads that featured direct party pitches.

The 1956 election may have been a high point in terms of the strength of party appeals in the post–World War II era. The classic study of voting behavior, *The American Voter,* argued that party identification was the dominant structuring principle of public opinion.[16] It may be no accident that most of the authors' data came from the 1950s. In that decade, it made sense for candidates to incorporate partisan pitches in their television advertising: Partisanship allowed them to win votes from the electorate. Hence, we see Republican Eisenhower and other members of his cabinet exhorting viewers to give them a "Republican Congress."[17]

However, after the 1950s, party loyalties in the American public began to decline. In their research, reported in *The Changing American Voter,* Norman Nie, Sidney Verba, and John Petrocik show how party identification and party-based voting ebbed in strength.[18] Independents began to rise as a percentage of the overall electorate, and candidates rarely made advertising appeals based on party.

Advertising shifted toward other topics. Not surprisingly, given the nature of the times, war and peace issues rose during the Vietnam period. Fifteen percent of ads in 1964 and 25 percent in 1968 discussed war and peace topics. For example, in 1964 some of the Johnson advertising effort against Goldwater emphasized the danger of war and Johnson's record of preserving the peace. In the 1968 Democratic nominating race, print ads for Eugene McCarthy attacked Robert Kennedy for John Kennedy's decision to send troops to Vietnam: "There is only one candidate who has no oblig-

TABLE 3-2
Detailed Breakdowns of Prominent Ads: 1952–1996

	1952	1956	1960	1964	1968	1972	1976	1980	1984	1988	1992	1996
Domestic matters	62%	62%	24%	39%	30%	46%	38%	44%	68%	58%	68%	59%
Economy	50	25	0	0	0	8	17	31	30	7	8	4
Social welfare	6	25	12	31	12	18	3	6	4	3	11	9
Social issue	0	0	0	0	6	0	0	2	4	0	19	4
Crime, violence, drugs	0	0	0	4	12	3	6	0	0	41	11	16
Race, civil rights	0	0	12	0	0	0	0	0	0	0	0	4
Taxes, budget	0	0	0	0	0	12	6	5	26	0	17	20
Corruption, government performance	6	12	0	4	0	5	6	0	0	0	2	2
Energy, environment	0	0	0	0	0	0	0	0	4	7	0	0
International affairs	6	0	6	19	37	21	3	11	17	10	6	0
War and peace	6	0	0	15	25	8	3	3	4	0	2	0
Foreign relations	0	0	6	4	12	5	0	2	9	3	2	0
National security, defense	0	0	0	0	0	8	0	6	0	7	0	0
Trade	0	0	0	0	0	0	0	0	0	0	2	0
Personal qualities	24	24	69	27	18	29	50	41	8	20	21	39
Leadership	0	0	25	0	0	5	3	8	0	0	2	13
Trustworthiness, honesty	6	0	0	0	6	0	31	6	0	10	11	6
Experience, competence	0	12	25	4	6	8	8	18	0	3	2	7
Compassion	0	12	0	0	0	13	8	6	4	7	6	2
Independence	12	0	19	0	0	0	0	0	4	0	0	7
Extremism	6	0	0	23	6	3	0	3	0	0	0	4
Party	6	12	0	0	0	3	3	3	0	0	0	0
Campaign	0	0	0	16	12	3	9	0	4	10	6	3
N	(16)	(8)	(16)	(26)	(16)	(39)	(36)	(62)	(23)	(29)	(53)	(55)

Sources: Kathleen Jamieson, Packaging the Presidency, 2d ed. (New York: Oxford University Press, 1992) for 1952–1988, and "CBS Evening News" tapes for 1992 and 1996 campaigns.

ations to the present policies in Vietnam and who is under no pressure to defend old mistakes there." Another noted that "Kennedy was part of the original commitment. . . . He must bear part of the responsibility for our original—and fundamentally erroneous—decision to interfere in Vietnam." In the general election, both Nixon and Hubert Humphrey ran spots emphasizing Vietnam. For example, Nixon tried to tie his Democratic opponent to the unpopular war. In contrast, a voice-over in a Humphrey ad criticized Nixon's refusal to discuss Vietnam: "Mr. Nixon's silence on the issue of Vietnam has become an issue in itself. He talks of an honorable peace but says nothing about how he would attain it. He says the war must be waged more effectively but says nothing about how he would wage it." [19]

Meanwhile, domestic economy and tax and budget matters attracted considerable attention in the late 1970s and the 1980s. In 1976, 17 percent of ads addressed economic concerns, whereas 31 percent in 1980 and 30 percent in 1984 touched on the economy. One has to harken back to the 1950s to find elections with as much emphasis on the economy. Tax and budget matters were also particularly popular during this period. Republicans have repeatedly run ads challenging past Democratic performance, and Democrats have criticized Republican failures to deal with federal deficits.

There have been some interesting nonissues on the advertising front. Until 1992, advertisements on social issues, such as abortion, busing, and the Equal Rights Amendment, were not very common.[20] With the exception of a George Wallace ad against school busing in 1968 and a 1980 Carter commercial in which actress Mary Tyler Moore told viewers Carter had "been consistently in favor of any legislation that would give women equal rights," [21] political spots generally have avoided these subjects. Social issues undoubtedly are seen by candidates as very divisive, and campaigners appear reluctant to take clear stands in their ads on these matters. In fact, a 1989 decision by Virginia gubernatorial candidate Douglas Wilder to incorporate abortion rights advertising in his campaign attracted considerable attention precisely because of the novelty.

But a change of tactics in 1992 altered this situation. Along with other challengers around the country, Indiana congressional candidate Michael Bailey used graphic antiabortion footage during his race to unseat pro-choice representative Lee Hamilton. The goal obviously was to attract media attention and raise public awareness. Yet there is little evidence in overall results that this effort worked. Of the thirteen congressional candidates in 1992 who relied on this tactic during the nominating process, only two won their primaries and none won in the general elections.[22]

In 1996, there was more extensive use of television advertising on abortion. Johnny Isakson, the leading Republican candidate for the U.S. Senate in Georgia, highlighted his support for abortion rights through an ad in order to distinguish himself from the other five Republicans in the primary. With his wife Dianne and their nineteen-year-old daughter Julie by his side, Isakson's spot took the unusual step of using a female announcer to attack his Republican opponents on the grounds that they would "vote to ban abortions, making criminals out of women and their doctors." Isakson then went on to proclaim: "I don't believe our Government should fund, teach or promote abortion. But I will not vote to amend the Constitution to make criminals of women and their doctors. I trust my wife, my daughter and the women of Georgia to make the right choice." But this appeal was not successful. Isakson lost the Republican primary by 53 percent to 47 percent.[23]

The Impact of Campaign Stage

Television ads used to be the near-exclusive purview of presidential general elections. As noted earlier, the nominating process was an elite-based activity in which party leaders exercised dominant control over delegate selection. Because voters were not central to the process, candidates made little use of television advertising. Much greater emphasis was placed on personal bargaining and negotiations with political leaders.

However, in recent years, advertising has become a prominent part of presidential nominating campaigns. Candidates spend a considerable amount of their overall campaign budget on advertising. Commercials have become a major strategic tool in the nominating process. Candidates use ads to convey major themes, make comments about the opposition, and discuss each other's personal qualities.

As pointed out previously, there are substantial differences between stages of the campaign, and one might expect to find different appeals in the nominating and general election campaigns. In nominating contests, candidates of the same party compete for

TABLE 3-3

Ad Content by Campaign Stage: 1952–1996

Appeal	Percentage of Ads	
	General Election	Nominating
Personal qualities	31%	39%
Domestic performance	36	22
Specific domestic policy	14	26
Specific foreign policy	3	5
International affairs	8	4
Campaign	6	3
Party	2	0
N	(269)	(94)

Sources: Kathleen Jamieson, *Packaging the Presidency,* 2d ed. (New York: Oxford University Press, 1992) for campaigns 1952–1988, and "CBS Evening News" tapes for 1992 and 1996 campaigns.

their party's nomination. There are often a number of candidates on the ballot. In contrast, general elections typically are two-person battles between major party nominees. One can expect political commercials to emphasize different points in different stages.

Table 3-3 lists the distribution of prominent ad appeals from 1952 to 1996 by campaign stage. Personal qualities were used more often in the nominating campaign than in the general election campaign. For example, in 1980 Carter employed so-called character ads to highlight the contrast between his own family life and that of his Democratic opponent, Sen. Edward Kennedy: "I don't think there's any way you can separate the responsibilities of a husband and father and a basic human being from that of the president. What I do in the White House is to maintain a good family life, which I consider to be crucial to being a good president." Personal qualities also played a major role in Carter's 1976 nominating campaign effort. Taking advantage of public mistrust and skepticism following Watergate disclosures, Carter pledged he would never lie to the public: "If I ever do any of those things, don't support me." [24]

Structural and strategic differences between the nominating and general election stages of the campaign help to explain the use of personal appeals in the primary season. The nominating stage often generates more personal appeals because, by the nature of intraparty battles, personality and background more often than substantive matters divide candidates. With Democrats competing against Democrats and Republicans against Republicans, there are at this time usually as many agreements as disagreements on policy issues and general political philosophies. Politicians therefore use personal qualities to distinguish themselves from the field and point out the limitations of their fellow candidates.

Domestic performance appeals in prominent ads were less common in the nominating process than in the general election campaign. One standard appeal concerned credit claiming on economic matters. A 1976 Ford ad showed a woman with bags of groceries meeting a friend who was working for the Ford campaign. The Ford supporter asked the shopper whether she knew that President Ford had cut inflation in half. "In half?" responded the shopper. "Wow!" In a 1980 ad, Democratic contender Kennedy had the actor Carroll O'Connor say that Carter may "give us a Depression which may make Hoover's look like prosperity." [25]

The attention devoted to domestic matters is important, and several articles have addressed issue-based voting by primary voters. [26] But few of these projects address the role of candidates in providing substantive cues. For there to be extensive issue-based voting, candidates must emphasize substantive matters and provide issue-based cues. Although a fair amount of attention is paid to domestic affairs in the nominating process, for prominent ads these types of appeals occupy a smaller percentage in the spring than in the fall.

International relations are emphasized on prominent ads about the same in the two stages. Trying to capitalize on a United Nations vote seen as harming Israel, Kennedy in 1980 ran an ad saying Carter "betrayed Israel at the U.N., his latest foreign policy blunder." Meanwhile, on the Republican side in 1980, a Reagan ad noted, "Our foreign policy has been based on the fear of not being liked. Well, it's nice to be liked. But it's more important to be respected." A 1976 Ford ad aimed at Reagan said, "Last Wednesday, Ronald Reagan said he would send American troops to Rhodesia. On Thursday he clarified that. He said they would be observers or advisers. What does he think happened in Vietnam?" The ad then concluded with the tagline, "Governor Reagan couldn't start a war. President Reagan could." [27]

Internet Ads

The 1996 elections were historic in introducing a new type of political communication: ads delivered via candidate home pages on the Internet. Perhaps no technology has developed as rapidly as this one. It is not surprising that candidates for office have attempted to use this increasingly popular technology for their own advantage. Much like they did with the introduction of radio, television, fax machines, and cell phones, campaigners put their creative energy to harnessing the Internet. Each of the candidates in 1996 created home pages filled with information about their candidacies.

Early returns on this experiment reveal that the Internet is more an example of "narrowcasting" than "broadcasting." Only 19 million Americans, less than 10 percent of the population, had access to the Internet in 1996. This compares to the 87 percent of American households who owned a television set in 1960, when television emerged as a major political force. Internet users are mostly white, male, middle-class, and well-educated, hardly a representative group of news consumers. Around 10 percent of those with Internet access report that they surf political pages.[28]

But despite the relatively low numbers of political surfers, the Internet is revolutionary in the type of information that it makes available. Interested browsers can read full-text speeches, detailed biographies, discussions of policy positions, and copies of press releases on-line. On more advanced home pages, they can view video clips and listen to audio tapes about the candidates.

Unlike broadcast ads, almost all of the material presented on the home pages in 1996 were positive portrayals of each candidate's positions, organization, or background. Except for the occasional press release buried several screens into the home page, there were no attacks on the opposition. Instead, World Wide Web visitors could browse Forbes's family pictures and read his announcement speech. Buchanan's home page was filled with speeches and position papers on everything from immigration to trade policy. Dole's site featured video snippets of the Kansan discussing his beliefs.

Much like television commercials, press releases presented on the Internet provide important clues about how each candidate saw their respective strengths. For example, a perusal of Dole's early press releases in the spring nominating contest revealed that 77 percent of them emphasized political endorsements the candidate was receiving across the country. In contrast, a number of Forbes's press releases announced the latest ad the candidate was broadcasting. In this regard, the Internet did capture the essence of each contender's basic strategy. In general, the messages conveyed via the Internet were consistent with each candidate's general campaign message. Alexander's home page had the familiar box touting "Lamar!" and a giant graphic backdrop showing his trademark red and black flannel shirt. The candidate described his message saying, "Our purpose is as great as the country itself; To restore America's sense of confidence through growth, freedom and personal responsibility." Buchanan's home page showed a picture of the candidate draped in American flags and a golden eagle. Visitors were greeted with the message, "Welcome 1996! The Year of Our Second American Revolution." Dole's page bragged about the 4 million home page visits through March 11, 1996, in an obvious effort to boost the inevitability of Dole's nomination.

The most novel feature of any of the home pages was Forbes's Flat Tax Calculator. With this segment, visitors entered their wage and salary income, checked a box for their personal exemption ($25,600 for joint married returns), and their number of dependents. After clicking the calculate box, the home page would automatically calculate the viewer's income tax under Forbes's 17-percent flat-tax proposal. It also would produce a table showing the tax savings for five different income levels between the current and flat tax. The demonstration concluded with the tag line: "It's simple. It's honest. And that's a big change for Washington." No other candidate in the spring had any interactive demonstrations regarding the impact of their policy proposals.

Alexander had the most video-oriented site. His page presented six different clips showing his inauguration as governor and the candidate working in communities across the country and participating in presidential forums. This compares to four video clips for Dole ("What You Believe In," "Faith and Values," "Bob's #1 Way to Balance the Budget," and "An American Hero"), two for Buchanan (covering foreign aid and the command of U.S. troops, respectively), and none for Forbes.

But most of these clips were rather unimaginative by contemporary standards. In the vast majority of them, the candidate was a talking head speaking on each respective subject. Those clips resembled ads from the 1950s that used footage from speeches and interviews without any graphics or fast-paced edits. In that respect, Internet ads are completely unlike broadcast spots of the 1990s.

Buchanan won the prize for being most verbose. His home page featured 113 separate audio clips, including everything from his debate statements and appearances on network interview shows to his speeches. This compares to seventeen sound clips for Dole, seven for Alexander, and none for Forbes.

The page featuring the easiest access to issue information was Buchanan's. Unlike the other candidates, who would put their position papers and speeches one or two screens into the home page, making them less prominent visually, Buchanan gave four issues (the economy, right to life, immigration, and NAFTA) prominent places near the top of his home page. With most of the other candidates, it took more of an effort to find out where the candidate stood on major issues.

In terms of style of presentation, Buchanan also had the most emotional tone. His opening screen listed provocative quotes from the candidate ("Don't wait for orders from headquarters! Mount up! And rise to the sound of the guns!") and alerts for his volunteer group, the "Buchanan Brigade" ("How long are we gonna fight? Til hell freezes over! And then we're gonna fight on the ice!"). There also were quotes from military personnel proclaiming "Real Americans Don't Wear UN Blue." None of the other candidates came close to Buchanan in the emotional intensity of their Internet messages. For most, it was a cool medium with low-key content.

In the general election, candidates also made extensive use of the Internet. Clinton, Dole, and Perot each had home pages emphasizing their general themes: "Building a Bridge to the 21st Century" for Clinton, "More opportunities. Smaller government. Stronger and safer families" for Dole, and "For Our Children and Our Grandchildren" for Perot. There were sections outlining the candidates' policy positions, speeches, biographies, and press releases, among other things. Perot was alone in not featuring a picture of his running mate, Pat Choate, at the front of his home page.

Dole offered an interactive feature on his fall general election page clearly modeled after Forbes's Flat Tax Calculator. This was the Dole-Kemp Interactive Tax Calculator, which gave visitors the opportunity to estimate the "value and magnitude of the Dole-Kemp tax cuts for a person or family at your income level." After inquiring about marital status, number of dependent children under the age of 18, and income level in 1996, the page automatically calculated one's current tax costs, what the person's tax would be under Dole-Kemp tax cuts, and the value of the estimated savings.

However, the calculator only took account of the 15 percent across-the-board tax cut and the $500 per-child tax credit. It did not include the impact of the earned income tax credit, the capital gains tax cut, the education and training deduction, or the charitable contribution tax credit. Taxes were calculated as if the plan were fully phased in, even though that would not take place until the year 2000.

Clinton meanwhile featured his own interactive segment called the Electoral College Computer. Under this feature, visitors chose a candidate, predicted which candidate would win the various states, and then the computer automatically tabulated the first candidate to reach the required 270 Electoral College votes.

In terms of videotape clips, Dole featured a wide array of commercials: Elizabeth Dole—"Honesty," "Doing What's Right," "Living Up to His Word"; Bob Dole—"The Better Man for a Better America," "Economics and Furthering America," and "Economic Plan to Help Every American." Completely absent from the ad offerings on his home page were spots on drugs and crime (which Dole emphasized in his broadcast commercials), character attacks, or attack ads on other topics. Clinton's commercials online were, "President Clinton Works to Strengthen the Values of Family and Work" and "President Clinton to Move America Ahead." Both were positive recitals of his program and agenda with few attacks on the opposition. Perot's ad offerings included the text of his infomercials and clips from his short spots.

Unlike the nominating stage, when Dole's press releases were primarily oriented to endorsements and organizational moves, more of his fall releases were substantive. Fifty percent of his general election releases dealt with substantive issues such as Dole's economic program, partial-birth abortions, Clinton's Indonesian connection, teenage drug use, workplace flexibility, and the Bosnian elections.

This compared to 25 percent of releases devoted to substantive issues for Clinton. The president devoted more attention in his press releases to announcing his latest ads or announcing group endorsements of his campaign than substantive pronouncements.

The candidate featuring the lowest number of press releases devoted to the issues was Perot. Only 10 percent of the Texan's releases involved substantive issues. By and large, his press statements were heavily oriented to Perot's exclusion from the presidential debates and the various suits and complaints Perot had filed about that decision.

The Rise of Negative Advertising

Critics have widely condemned the advertising style in recent elections for being among the dirtiest and most negative in the nation's history.[29] The tone of the 1988 presidential campaign was so appalling that in an unprecedented action, one candidate actually broadcast an ad complaining about the tenor of the race and attempting to blame his opponent for that situation. The ad by Dukakis, "Counterpunch," proclaimed, "I'm fed up with it . . . [I] never have seen anything like this in twenty-five years of public life. . . . George Bush's negative TV ads [are] distorting my record." [30] The 1992 and 1996 campaigns also featured sharp attacks through campaign commercials. One reporter, Eric Engberg of CBS, described the primary contest as a "political food fight." [31]

Despite the widespread consternation regarding these attacks, few have defined what they mean by *negativity*. Observers often define negativity as anything they do not like about campaigns. Defined in this way, the term is so all-encompassing it becomes almost meaningless. The broadness of the definition brings to mind former justice Potter Stewart's famous line about pornographic material. When asked how he identified pornography, Stewart conceded that he could not define it. But, the justice asserted, "I know it when I see it." [32]

To research campaign negativity in historic context, William Riker undertook an imaginative study of negative campaigning during the constitutional ratification effort of 1787–1788.[33] In his research of the campaign, Riker distinguished direct criticism; charges of threats to civil liberties, governmental structure, and state power; and other types of appeals. Relying on contemporaneous documents employed by each side in the ratification campaign, Riker was able to define negativity more clearly as unflattering or pejorative comments and show that the modern period has no monopoly on negative campaigning.

Following Riker's definition of negativity, I examined the 379 prominent ads for the period from 1952 through 1996 to determine the tone and object of attack. For example, if a candidate challenged an opposing campaigner in terms of policy positions or personal qualities, the ad was described as negative. If the ad included unflattering or pejorative comments made about the opponent's domestic performance, it was labeled negative. Overall, negative comments were classified into the categories of discussions about personal qualities, domestic performance, specific policy statements, international affairs, the campaign, and the political party affiliation in general. Fifty-four percent of prominent ads during this period were negative, with ads in the general election stage being slightly less negative (53 percent) than those in the nominating stage (57 percent). Republicans (60 percent) were more negative in their prominent ads than Democrats (48 percent).[34]

Campaigns through 1960 were not particularly negative in their advertising (Figure 3-2). Twenty-five percent of prominent ads in 1952 were negative, and 38 percent were negative in 1956. In 1960, only 12 percent of the prominent ads featured critical statements. However, starting in the Johnson-Goldwater race of 1964, advertising turned more negative. Fifty percent of the prominent ads in 1964 and 69 percent of the prominent ads in 1968 were negative. The 1964 campaign produced a successful effort on Johnson's part to portray his opponent as a political extremist and threat to world peace. This race, as mentioned previously, featured the "Daisy" ad and others that damaged Goldwater's political prospects. One of the most visible ads of that campaign showed someone cutting off the eastern seaboard of the United States with a saw to make the point that Goldwater was extreme in his perspective. An ad that never aired linked Goldwater to the Ku Klux Klan. Although the ad was produced and given the go-ahead for regional airing, it was pulled at the last minute, according to one Johnson aide, because it "strained the available evidence, it was going too far." [35]

The effectiveness of Johnson's television ad campaign undoubtedly encouraged candidates in 1968 to use negative advertising. The race that year, between Nixon, Humphrey, and Wallace, was quite negative. The presence of Wallace in the race threatened both Nixon and Humphrey, and each responded with ads attacking the Alabama governor. Humphrey ran an ad showing a large

Figure 3-2   Negative Ads as a Percentage of Total: 1952–1996

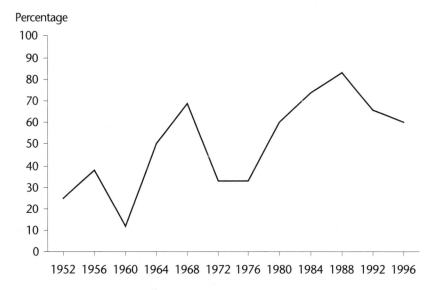

Percentage

Sources: For 1952–1988, Kathleen Jamieson, *Packaging the Presidency,* 2d ed. (New York: Oxford University Press, 1992); and for 1992–1996, "CBS Evening News" tapes.

picture of Wallace while actor E. G. Marshall explained, "When I see this man, I think of feelings of my own which I don't like but I have anyway. They're called prejudices. . . . Wallace is devoted now to his single strongest prejudice. He would take that prejudice and make it into national law."[36] Democrats also sought to take advantage of popular displeasure over the vice presidential qualifications of Spiro Agnew. One of their ads opened with a poster of "Spiro Agnew for Vice President," while in the background a man looking at the picture gradually collapsed in laughter.[37]

Republicans sought to capitalize on the bloody riots that occurred during the 1968 Democratic convention in Chicago by running an ad linking the street disorder with Humphrey. In one of the campaign's most controversial ads, Nixon contrasted footage of the bloody riots with pictures of a smiling Humphrey accepting the nomination. With music from the song "Hot Time in the Old Town Tonight" playing in the background, the ad ended with the tagline, "This time vote like your whole world depended on it."[38]

The elections of 1972 and 1976 were not nearly as negative in tone. In both races only about one-third of prominent ads were negative. Campaigners may have become more reluctant to air negative commercials because of the backlash that followed the highly emotional ads of the 1964 and 1968 races. McGinniss's exposé of the electronic merchandising of Nixon in the 1968 campaign created a climate of skepticism among reporters that increased the risks of negative campaigning. Moral outrage against attack ads dominated the 1976 elections, which followed the "dirty tricks" associated with Watergate.

These sentiments, though, dissipated with time. As the memory of Watergate receded, the outrage associated with it also began to decline. Voters no longer associated attacks on the opposition with unfair dirty tricks. The result was that presidential contests in the 1980s reached extraordinary high levels of negativity. In 1980, 60 percent of prominent ads were negative; 74 percent were negative in 1984; and 83 percent were negative in 1988. For example, the 1980 campaign featured efforts, albeit ultimately unsuccessful, to portray Reagan as a dangerous extremist, in the mold of Goldwater. Carter employed "person-in-the-street" ads in an effort to portray Reagan as dangerous: "I just don't think he's well enough informed. . . . We really have to keep our heads cool and I don't think that Reagan is cool. . . . That scares me about Ronald Reagan."[39] Another ad sought to characterize the Californian as trigger happy by listing cases in which Reagan had backed military force, including the time he said a destroyer should be sent to Equador to resolve a fishing controversy.

Mondale used a similar strategy in 1984 when he ran an anti-Reagan ad showing missiles shooting out of underground silos, accompanied by the musical track of David Crosby, Stephen Stills, Graham Nash, and Neil Young singing lyrics from their song, "Teach Your Children."[40] Mondale also sought to play on concerns about Gary Hart's leadership ability in the nominating process by running an ad featuring a ringing red phone to raise doubts about Hart's readiness to assume the duties of commander-in-chief.

The 1988 campaign attracted great attention because of numerous negative ads like the "Revolving Door." As has been discussed previously, this Bush commercial sought to portray Dukakis as soft on crime by saying the Massachusetts governor had vetoed the death penalty and given weekend furloughs to first-degree murderers not eligible for parole. Although Willie Horton was never mentioned in this ad, the not-so-veiled reference to him generated considerable coverage from the news media, with numerous stories reviewing the details of Horton's crime of kidnapping and rape while on furlough from a Massachusetts prison. The Bush team, headed by Roger Ailes, also hammered Dukakis for his failure to clean up Boston Harbor. Dukakis meanwhile ran ads that reminded viewers of concern about Bush's most important personnel decision, the choice of Dan Quayle as the Republican vice presidential nominee. Widespread doubts about Quayle's ability gave Dukakis a perfect opportunity to run an ad criticizing this selection. The ad closed with the line, "Hopefully, we will never know how great a lapse of judgment that really was."[41]

The 1992 race featured sharp attacks from Clinton and Perot on Bush's economic performance and from Bush on Clinton's past record and trustworthiness, but throughout there was a lower level of negativity than in 1988. Overall, 66 percent of prominent ads were negative. One memorable spot for Clinton tabulated the number of people who had lost jobs during Bush's administration. Bush meanwhile portrayed Clinton as just another "tax-and-spend" liberal who had a weak record as governor of Arkansas and who was shifty in his political stances. Perot ran a generally positive campaign, with commercials and infomercials that addressed the national debt, job creation, and the need for change. However, in the closing days of the campaign, Perot ran the infomercial titled, "Deep Voodoo, Chicken Feathers, and the American Dream," which attacked both Bush and Clinton. One of the most memorable segments of this program featured a map of Arkansas with a big chicken in the middle to convey the message that job growth during Clinton's governorship had occurred mainly through low-paying jobs in the chicken industry.

The 1996 campaign showed a slight drop in the level of negativity, as 60 percent of the ads attacked the opponent. In the nominating process, Forbes ran a series of attacks first on Dole and then on Buchanan and Alexander. In the general election, Dole attacked Clinton's character, record on fighting drugs, and overall liberalism. The Clinton campaign meanwhile linked Dole with unpopular House Speaker Newt Gingrich and accused the duo of slashing popular programs in the areas of Medicare, education, and the environment.[42]

The Objects of Negativity

Attack ads are viewed by many as the electronic equivalent of the plague. Few aspects of contemporary politics have been as widely despised. Many observers have complained that negative campaign spots are among the least constructive developments in politics of recent years. Furthermore, they are thought to contribute little to the education of voters.

But in reviewing the objects of attack ads, it is somewhat surprising to discover that the most substantive appeals actually came in negative spots. For example, the most critical prominent commercials during the period from 1952 to 1996 appeared on foreign policy (86 percent of which were negative) and domestic policy (63 percent), followed by international affairs (56 percent), domestic performance (55 percent), personal qualities (48 percent), campaign appeals (42 percent), and mentions of political party (17 percent).

There were some differences in the objects of negativity based on the stage of the campaign. Negative prominent ads were more likely to appear on international affairs during the nominating stage (75 percent) than during the general election campaign (52 percent). But personal qualities attracted about the same level of negativity during the general election campaign (48 percent) as during the nominating stage (46 percent). The same was true for domestic performance (55 percent in the general election campaign and 52 percent in the nominating stage).

If one charts the percentage of negative ads from 1952 to 1996 by type of message contained in the commercials, it is apparent that in recent years domestic performance and specific policy statements more than personal qualities have been the object of the negative prominent ads. In 1980, 95 percent of ads dealing with domestic matters were negative, as were 73 percent of those in 1984 and 83 percent in 1988. In a similar way, 100 percent of the ads dealing with specific policy appeals in 1984 and 1988 were negative. In contrast, fewer of the prominent negative ads in 1984 and 1988 dealt with personal qualities (50 percent and 67 percent, respectively). This demonstrates that attack ads are more likely to occur on substantive issues than on personality aspects of presidential campaigns.

Candidates often employ attack commercials to challenge the performance of the government or to question the handling of particular policy problems. Despite the obvious emotional qualities of the commercial, Bush's infamous "Revolving Door" ad was quite specific in attacking Dukakis's record: "As governor, Michael Dukakis vetoed mandatory sentences for drug dealers. He vetoed the death penalty. His revolving-door prison policy gave weekend furloughs to first-degree murderers not eligible for parole."[43]

Negative commercials are more likely to have policy-oriented content because campaigners need a clear reason to attack the opponent. Specificity helps focus viewers' attention on the message being delivered. Issue-oriented ads often attract public attention and are likely to be remembered. Political strategists need to be clear about the facts in case of challenges from the media. Reporters often dissect negative ads and demand evidence to support specific claims.

In addition, campaigners are reluctant to criticize candidates personally for fear that it would make themselves look mean spirited. Carter in 1980 ran ads challenging Reagan's experience and qualifications, and he was roundly criticized for being nasty. Results of research by Johnson-Cartee and Copeland demonstrate that voters are more likely to tolerate negative commercials that focus on policy than on personality. Voters' reactions help to reinforce the patterns noted previously.[44]

Critics often condemn attack ads for disrupting democratic elections and polarizing the electorate. Steven Ansolabehere and Shanto Iyengar argue based on experimental research that attack ads lower turnout.[45] However, the 1996 experience does not bear this out. Despite a Republican primary battle that was the nastiest in modern history and the complete absence of a Democratic primary contest, turnout in 1996 rose over 1988 and 1992 in every state primary or caucus except five.[46] And in the 1996 general election, the percentage of attack ads dropped from 1992, but the number of nonvoters rose, which is contrary to the prediction of Ansolabehere and Iyengar.

Indeed, if one examines the 12 presidential elections from 1952 to 1996 on turnout and ad negativity, the correlation between the two is −.59 and the relationship is statistically significant, indicating that the more negative ads are, the lower overall turnout is. This is exactly what Ansolabehere and Iyengar argued.

However, a regression of ad negativity on voter turnout controlling for levels of mistrust toward government produces a result that is contrary to Ansolabehere and Iyengar. Individual-level studies have shown that one of the strongest predictors of turnout is how people feel toward the political system. If individuals feel the government is run by people who do what is right, they feel better about the system and are much more likely to vote. Conversely, if they are alienated and mistrusting, they are less likely to cast ballots.

Testing this idea produces a model in which ad negativity and levels of mistrust toward the government explain 81 percent of the variation in presidential election turnout. But contrary to the expectation of Ansolabehere and Iyengar, turnout is much more dependent on the level of mistrust than the negativity of ads. The relationship between mistrust and turnout is strong and statistically significant in the expected direction; the higher the mistrust, the lower the turnout.[47] In that model, there is no statistically significant relationship between turnout and ad negativity. In fact, the model suggests that each percentage point increase in ad negativity reduces turnout by only 0.03 percent. Or to put it differently, a 30-percentage-point increase in ad negativity would drop turnout by less than 1 percentage point.

There is little reason to expect a strong relationship between ads and turnout. The most powerful predictor of turnout is mistrust and the general sense of political efficacy—in other words, whether people feel their vote will make a difference. Negative ads are as likely as positive ones to make individuals feel their vote matters and that they should care about the electoral outcome. Attack ads can convince viewers that a race is competitive, there are differences between the candidates, and that the substantive stakes are high. In this situation, attacks are as likely to stimulate as depress voter turnout.

From the standpoint of substantive content, therefore, negative ads contribute to public education when they are accurate. They do not necessarily lower voter interest. Observers interested in increasing the amount of substantive information in commercials should realize that negative ads are more informative than is commonly believed.

Chapter 4

Media Coverage of Ads

Reporters used to be governed by the norms of old-style journalism—the "who, what, where, when, and how" approach
to news gathering. Candidates' statements were reported more or
less at face value; behind-the-scenes machinations fell outside the
news; and, by implicit agreement, the private behavior of political
leaders was pretty much ignored. If a leader's personal life included excesses in the areas of drinking, philandering, or gambling, for
example, it was kept quiet on the assumption that these activities
would not affect performance in office. Or leaders who were subject to temper tantrums and uncontrollable emotional outbursts in
private, for example, were not questioned publicly regarding
whether they would be able to withstand the pressures of high
office.

However, Johnson's deception in the Vietnam War and Nixon's
lying in the face of the deepening Watergate scandal led reporters
to take more interpretive and investigative approaches to news-
gathering. Rather than sticking to hard news, journalists today see
a responsibility to put "the facts" in broader context. Reporters
want to enable readers and viewers to see the real picture of political events, not just the version public officials place before them.
Why do leaders act the way they do? What hidden motives govern
leadership behavior? How can outsiders make sense of the ups and
downs of daily political events?

This new-style journalism also led reporters to a different
approach to campaigns. Once content to cover candidate speeches
and travel, reporters began to emphasize behind-the-scenes activities. What strategies were candidates pursuing? What blocs of voters were seen as most critical to electoral success? What clues did
campaigns provide about underlying beliefs and preferences? Fol-

lowing the lead of Theodore White, who revolutionized coverage of presidential campaigns, reporters began to devote greater attention to analysis.[1]

Changes in the nature of presidential selection following the 1968 election created new opportunities for reporters.[2] The decline in the power of party leaders, rise in the number of primaries, and extension of races over a number of months made it dramatically easier for reporters to explore behind-the-scenes maneuvering. In fact, the entry into open nominating contests of little-known candidates made it mandatory that reporters cover the backgrounds and goals of candidates. Who were these new candidates and why were they running for president? Journalists rightly saw their mission as informing the public about these people as well as describing how they were running their campaigns.

The open electoral process made it easier to investigate campaign events. This system brought candidates out of the back rooms into public view. Disclosure requirements associated with campaign finance reforms brought an avalanche of background material out into the open. Reporters gained access to information that allowed them to probe further than ever before.

But according to many observers, the media have not fulfilled their responsibility. There have been a number of critical analyses of how the media cover campaigns. The most common approach has been to distinguish coverage based on policy content from reports regarding the campaign and the personal qualities of the candidates. The assumption is that policy reporting is the type of coverage most relevant to voters. This assumption ignores the fact that knowledge about personal qualities of candidates is equally important to those interested in how well particular individuals will cope with the office or deliver on promised commitments.

Nevertheless, research generally has found that the media devote little space to policy matters. A thorough study by Henry Brady and Richard Johnston of every United Press International story on the Democratic candidates from January 1 through July 31, 1984, revealed that press coverage devoted only 16 percent of lines to policy positions. The more common topic included discussions of the campaign (50 percent overall, which included 21 percent devoted to prospects of election, 20 percent devoted to campaign appearances, and 9 percent devoted to sources of support), personal qualities of the candidates (23 percent), and comments about the opposition (11 percent). These figures are comparable to what Doris Graber found in her study of *Chicago Tribune* coverage of the 1983 mayoral election. In that race, 42 percent of the lines dealt with the campaign, 20 percent were devoted to policy matters, 19 percent dealt with personal qualities, and 20 percent involved other matters, such as ethics or party affairs.[3]

These findings have been disappointing to those who believe the media should play a central role in educating the electorate. In past eras, a variety of institutions assumed the role of civic educator. Political parties helped to define voters' choices, and voluntary associations and interest groups tried to instruct their members in the issues of the day. Today, however, parties engender little respect and group leaders have difficulty representing their followers. This situation has created an information vacuum, which reporters are attempting to fill.

But rather than devoting space to matters that would facilitate public education, the press focuses most often on who is ahead and who is behind. Robinson and Sheehan show in their study of the 1980 presidential campaign that once the nominating season gets under way, "horse race" coverage far outpaces coverage of issues and candidates. They found that in March 76 percent of the campaign coverage time on CBS was devoted to the horse race, compared with 18 percent to the issues and 6 percent to candidate characteristics. In a similar way, in September 62 percent of the news time emphasized the horse race, whereas 25 percent dealt with policy matters and 12 percent involved personal qualities.[4] Just at the point when voters start to pay attention to politics, reporters devote relatively little coverage to the candidates' stances on issues and devote substantial attention to the contest.

This pattern of reporting has affected voters. In their pathbreaking survey research on the 1948 presidential campaign, Berelson, Lazarsfeld, and McPhee discovered that 67 percent of voters' conversations with one another dealt with the policy positions and personal qualifications of candidates, whereas about 25 percent involved questions of winnability.[5] But by 1976, these numbers had reversed in public opinion surveys. According to Patterson, the "game was the major topic of conversation in 1976."[6] In June of that year, near the end of the nominating cycle, 69 percent of conversations involved the game and only 18 percent dealt with substantive matters.

The horse race has become a popular object of press attention because it often involves drama and suspense. Nothing attracts the

attention of the media more than a surprise showing that surpass-
es their expectations. Candidates who have come out of nowhere
and do well in early caucuses and primaries attract a disproportionate share of media coverage.[7] Carter was the classic case: His
campaign's momentum was fueled by media coverage. In the
months before the 1976 Iowa caucuses, Governor Carter of Georgia was a virtual unknown. Public opinion polls a year before the
election had put him on the list of "asterisk" candidates, those
individuals who fell in the "others" category because their public
preference ratings fell under 5 percent. When Carter did better
than expected in Iowa, he received an extraordinary amount of
news coverage, much of which dealt with his success in the horse
race. He then skyrocketed in the polls, was able to raise much
more money, and eventually became the nominee of the Democratic party.

The Increasing Coverage of Ads

Although there has been great interest in media coverage of
presidential campaigns, limited attention has been paid to how
journalists cover television ads. As noted earlier, candidates
devote considerable effort to the messages presented in their ads.
They also use strategy in choosing where and when to show their
ads.

To see how advertising is covered, I made a tabulation of the
number of *New York Times* articles from 1952 to 1996, *Washington Post* articles from 1972 to 1996, and "CBS Evening News"
stories from 1972 to 1996 that covered political advertising.[8] As a
reflection of differences in time periods and scope of coverage,
there were 467 articles about political commercials in the *New
York Times*, 381 articles in the *Washington Post*, and 209 stories
on the "CBS Evening News."[9] For the *New York Times*, 214 articles (46 percent) dealt with the nominating stage, whereas 253
involved the general election. In the case of the *Washington Post*,
205 (54 percent) involved nominations and 176 dealt with the general election. For CBS, 127 (61 percent) of the stories covered the
nominating stage and 82 involved the general election.

There were some differences between the news outlets, but the
general trend has been a substantial increase in coverage of advertisements in the 1980s and 1990s.[10] For both nominating and general election contests, the 1970s did not generate many television

Figure 4-1   Media Coverage of Nomination Campaign Ads: 1952–1996

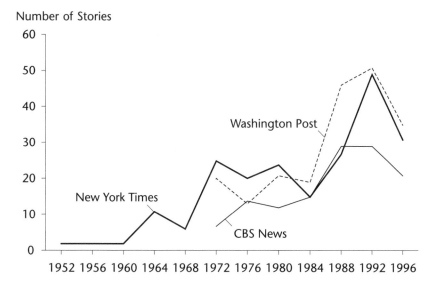

Number of Stories

Sources: *New York Times,* 1952–1996; "CBS Evening News," 1972–1996; *Washington Post,* 1972–1996.

stories about political spot ads (see Figures 4-1 and 4-2, respectively, for the stages). For example, in 1972 only seven CBS stories about ads appeared during the nominating process and four during the general election campaign. In 1976, there were fourteen stories on CBS in the spring and five in the fall. However, the numbers started to rise in 1980 and have continued to rise in recent elections. The 1988 race produced five times the number of ad stories (twenty-nine in the nominating process campaign and twenty-one in the general election campaign) than had the elections of the 1970s. Meanwhile, the 1992 contest generated twenty-nine nomination and twenty-four general election campaign stories. The 1996 campaign had fewer stories (twenty-one in the nomination stage and fourteen in the general election) than 1988 or 1992 because there was a contested nomination only among Republicans and the general election was one-sided in the polls.

This increase in television attention to advertising has had major consequences for candidates and voters. People today are about as likely to see ads through the news as they are to see them directly. This means ads are seen along with comments provided

Figure 4-2   Media Coverage of General Election Campaign Ads: 1952–1996

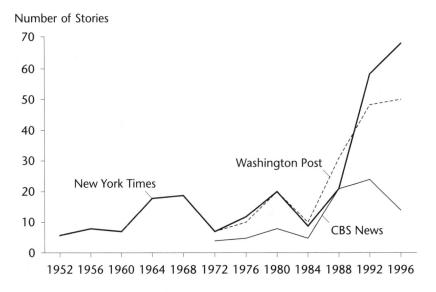

Number of Stories

Sources: New York Times, 1952–1996; "CBS Evening News," 1972–1996; Washington Post, 1972–1996.

by the media. Thus, journalists have gained great influence in shaping public interpretations of the objectives and impact of ads.

In regard to the *New York Times,* the critical turning point in ad coverage for the nominating process occurred in 1972. Before then, there were few stories about political advertising. In 1952, 1956, and 1960, there were two *New York Times* articles about ads each year in the presidential nominating period from January to June. A March 26, 1960, article, for example, described Stuart Symington's decision not to launch a preconvention television drive against Nixon. In 1968, for the same period, six stories appeared. An article on May 8 recounted Robert Kennedy's decision to spend heavily on television in Indiana because of Gov. Roger Branigan's control of the party organization. Most of the other articles dealt with the content of or strategies behind ads.

However, after Democratic reforms and the rise in the number of primaries, the number of stories on ads during the nominating process rose dramatically. The 1972 campaign was the first election conducted under the new nomination reforms, which added more primaries and therefore gave citizens a more direct voice in delegate selection. It is not surprising that press coverage of ads during the nominating period increased considerably. Twenty stories appeared in the *Washington Post* in 1972, compared to thirteen in 1976, twenty-one in 1980, nineteen in 1984, forty-six in 1988, fifty-one in 1992, and thirty-five in 1996. Twenty-five articles about campaign commercials appeared in the *New York Times* between January and June of 1972, twenty in 1976, twenty-four in 1980, fifteen in 1984, twenty-seven in 1988, forty-nine in 1992, and thirty-one in 1996.

A May 22, 1976, *New York Times* story reported Frank Church's (Idaho) accusations that Gov. Edmund Brown, Jr. (Calif.) was trying to "buy" votes in the Oregon primary by spending large sums of money on television advertising. Earlier that spring, on March 28, the *New York Times* had printed a long article by Joseph Lelyveld on Carter's media adviser, Gerald Rafshoon, and his use of television ads in crucial primary states.

Newspaper coverage of general election advertising has changed as well. In general, the number of stories has fluctuated considerably, depending on the closeness of the race. Campaigns that were seen as competitive (1968, 1976, 1980, 1988, and 1992) generated many more stories than those with a clear front-runner (1972 and 1984). This was particularly true in 1992, as the three-way battle between Bush, Clinton, and Perot prompted a dramatic increase in news stories. In close elections, the media devote more coverage to campaign phenomena, such as television advertising, that are thought to make a difference in voters' choices.[11]

Particular attention has been paid in recent years to how television advertising shapes the dynamics of a race. An October 10, 1988, *New York Times* story described how both Bush and Dukakis ran commercials that attacked the opposition, with little positive reference to platforms or promises. Dukakis's inability to produce timely, effective ads was cited in an October 19 article as an indicator of larger failings within his campaign organization.

In 1992 news coverage emphasized the backlash against Bush's attack ads and the big audiences Perot was attracting to his thirty-minute infomercials. Special attention was paid to new media formats that emerged that year: the morning shows, "Larry King Live," the "Arsenio Hall Show," and the new "town meeting" style of debates in the fall. Reporters discussed the major changes that were taking place in the communications industry and the way in which the new outlets were taking attention away from the traditional media.

The 1996 campaign featured discussions about Dole's character attacks on Clinton, the president's lead in public opinion polls, and Perot's relevance as a presidential candidate. Free television time provided by the networks was a new feature in the contest with candidates receiving one- and two-minute chances to make a direct pitch to voters uninterrupted by reporters.

Horse Race Coverage of Ads

The increase in the coverage of ads highlights the blurring of free and paid media, but the raw figures do not reveal what reporters actually said. There has been widespread criticism about media attention to horse race considerations and the limited time spent on policy matters. Because television is the major news source for most Americans, I examined in detail all the stories about campaign advertising that appeared on the "CBS Evening News" from 1972 through 1996. Two features were analyzed: (1) the content of the ad reference and (2) the general topic of the news story in which the ad was discussed. Several categories were developed to assess the quality of coverage and to facilitate comparison with the results for ads themselves, as discussed previously.

There were interesting differences between the descriptions of ads in news stories and the content of the news stories. As shown in Table 4-1, the major contrast concerned the tendency of reporters fascinated with the horse race to convert substantive ad messages into news stories about campaign prospects or strategies. More ads that were reported on in the news were specific (30 percent) than the news stories themselves (15 percent).

CBS often rebroadcast ad segments that were particularly pointed in their charges about opponents' policy positions. For example, a Nixon ad featured in the "CBS Evening News" on October 30, 1972, lambasted McGovern's defense posture and noted which specific weapons programs the Democrat would oppose. In the same vein, CBS showed a Jack Kemp ad on January 19, 1988, which attacked Bush and Dole for being willing to reduce Social Security benefits. Spring campaign coverage tended to be more specific about policy (32 percent) than coverage of the general election campaign (20 percent).

TABLE 4-1

Content and Tone of CBS News Coverage: 1972–1996

Appeal	Percentage of Stories Devoted to Each Appeal	
	Descriptions of Ads	News Stories about Ads
Personal qualities	27%	9%
Domestic performance	31	10
Specific policy statements	30	15
International affairs	6	1
Campaign	6	66
Party	1	0
N	(209)	(209)
Negativity Level	65%	52%

Sources: Vanderbilt Television News Index and Abstracts for campaigns 1972–1988, and "CBS Evening News" tapes for 1992 and 1996 campaigns.

In contrast, most of the news stories about ads dealt with the campaign (66 percent), a figure just below the 76 percent reported by Robinson and Sheehan for general coverage in 1980.[12] Many of these stories included discussions of how particular ads fit strategic goals of the campaign (34 percent), affected the electoral prospects of the candidate (19 percent), or had been produced and financed within the campaign organization (12 percent).

For example, CBS broadcast a story on January 29, 1980, describing an Edward Kennedy ad that addressed the Chappaquiddick incident. The ad itself dealt with personal qualities, such as Kennedy's honesty, but the story emphasized the change in the candidate's strategy, which had been designed to reassure voters about the senator's conduct. Another example appeared February 12, 1988, when a Dukakis ad on the economy was analyzed in terms of its contribution to the candidate's campaign strategy.

The news media were more likely to report specific ad claims for Republicans (39 percent) than for Democrats (19 percent). They also were more likely to cover ads based on international affairs for Republicans (9 percent) than for Democrats (5 percent). In contrast, Democrats earned more news coverage for ads on domestic performance (38 percent) than Republicans (22 percent). There were no partisan differences on personal qualities (26 percent for Democrats and 27 percent for Republicans).

News reports generally placed much less emphasis on personal qualities, domestic performance, or specific policy statements than did the ads themselves. Reporters often blame candidates for not discussing the issues, but it appears that fascination with the horse race leads journalists to turn substantive messages into campaign stories.

In addition, ads broadcast as part of news stories tended to be more negative than the news stories were. Sixty-five percent of ads described in the news were negative in orientation, compared with 52 percent of the news stories themselves. As noted previously, negative ads have become more common. Negative commercials tend to be more controversial, which produces greater coverage than otherwise would be the case. But the media devote considerable time to rebroadcasting negative ads, which reinforces the widespread public view about the negativity of television ads. In fact, it is well known in political circles that one of the easiest ways to attract press coverage is to run negative commercials. Media adviser Ailes explained it this way: "There are three things that the media are interested in: pictures, mistakes, and attacks. . . . If you need coverage, you attack, and you will get coverage." [13]

Shifts over Time in Ad Coverage

An intensive study of *New York Times* ad coverage since 1952 shows exactly how press coverage of commercials has shifted over the past four decades. In the 1950s, consistent with the old-style journalism practiced at that time, considerable attention was devoted to the use of celebrity endorsements in the presidential campaign. For example, Eleanor Roosevelt filmed an endorsement of Adlai Stevenson that generated press attention simply because of her celebrity status. In 1960 an April 20 story discussed a New York telethon plan to raise money for fall advertising time, and a March 26 article recounted Symington's decision not to spend $400,000 in a preconvention television drive against Nixon.

Both of the 1960 articles are noteworthy because of their emphasis on factual events. Each clearly illustrates the "who, what, where" approach to news gathering. Hard facts were emphasized and announcements from campaign officials taken at face value. There was little discussion of how the decision fit broader strategic goals. There was no analysis of campaign maneuvering or how candidates actually reached particular decisions. Furthermore, there was no attention paid to the motivations of campaign decision makers. Reporters did not examine the true motives or goals of Symington or the telethon planners to determine what they really were trying to accomplish or who was winning organizational battles.

A similar example of hard news coverage occurred in 1968. On May 27 the *New York Times* reported that Humphrey had hired the firm Doyle Dane Bernbach as his advertising agency. This seemingly bland news item is noteworthy because of what it did not say. The article more or less stayed on the surface. It did not delve into strategic considerations. It furthermore did not address the consequences of the decision for the power balance within the Humphrey organization. There was no speculation about who won and who lost in this decision or what it revealed about the type of campaign Humphrey might run.

However, the *New York Times* began to cover political advertising in a different sort of way during the 1970s and 1980s. A January 14, 1972, article describing Sen. Edmund Muskie's use of television in his bid for the Democratic nomination illustrates the new tendency to put the campaign in context and tell the story behind the event. The article noted that television would be the dominant element in Muskie's campaign. Muskie's strategy was described as contrasting himself to Nixon's weak credibility. Muskie also planned to stress his own position on sensitive issues and avoid staged scenes characteristic of most political commercials. The newspaper's approach was clearly a departure. The story emphasized strategic considerations—how advertising furthered vote getting. This story also illustrated the effort to report the behind-the-scenes story. Why was Muskie employing particular ads? What was he really trying to accomplish? The attention to the candidate's motivations and goals reflects the new direction in the coverage of political ads.

Later years saw further development of this style of coverage. For example, a March 28, 1976, article discussed the crucial importance of television ads to presidential candidates. It described the dramatic impact Rafshoon had in Carter's primary victories. The article described how Rafshoon put together ads and how polls by Pat Caddell helped Carter officials decide where to place their television commercials. The story analyzed the implications of this approach for Carter's success.

This is not to imply that strategic considerations were the reporters' only focus. Journalists also devoted attention to the substance of television ads. A March 21, 1984, article covering Democratic party ads focused on the "ethical and moral" violations of the Reagan administration. Rep. Tony Coelho (Calif.) was quoted as criticizing President Reagan's willingness to blast welfare cheats but not those who violate the public trust.

There were stories in 1988 that discussed Rep. Richard Gephardt's trade ads in Iowa. The Democratic representative from Missouri used highly effective commercials blasting Far East trading partners for closing their markets to American products while flooding the United States with cheaper imports. These ads noted the threat to American jobs and described Gephardt's legislative plans to force Japan and other countries to open their markets to U.S. goods. A September 1, 1988, story described how Dukakis planned to run commercials that featured the slogan "Bringing Prosperity Home." According to the article, the point of this slogan was to appeal to the economic anxiety of the middle class and help Dukakis regain his lead over Bush.

But even this type of coverage often incorporated considerations of candidates' strategic thinking. A number of stories describing the content of ads showed how particular messages were designed to appeal to particular constituencies. For example, the Coelho articles noted that these commercials were meant to call attention to the nomination of Edwin Meese III as attorney general. Democratic officials hoped that the sleaze factor associated with Meese's questionable private dealings would damage Republican prospects in 1984 and win Democrats the support of voters cynical about American politics. Likewise, the Gephardt ads were described in substantive terms but were used to illustrate the strategic goals of his campaign. His protectionism ads were designed to win labor support and votes from workers worried about losing their jobs. These ads furthermore helped to make Gephardt distinctive from his Democratic rivals, some of whom played down their protectionist sentiments. Therefore, this form of press coverage used substantive messages presented in ads to describe strategic plans within campaign organizations.

"Daisy" and the "Revolving Door"

Nothing illustrates the change in media orientation better than the subject of attack commercials. Although there were many stories condemning the rise of negative ads in 1988, journalists have become over the years quite tolerant of these ads. A simple comparison of reactions to two of the most notorious negative ads—"Daisy" in 1964 and the "Revolving Door" in 1988—illustrates the change. Both commercials dealt with emotional subjects and generated criticisms about playing on citizens' fears—of nuclear war in 1964 and of crime in 1988.

The "Daisy" commercial was probably the most infamous ad in television history. This ad opens with a young girl standing in a meadow plucking petals from a daisy. After she counts "1, 2, 3, 4, 5, 6, 7, 8, 9," a solemn voice begins its own countdown: "10, 9, 8, 7, 6, 5, 4, 3, 2, 1, 0." At zero, the picture of the child dissolves and a mushroom cloud fills the screen. Johnson closes the ad by warning, "These are the stakes. To make a world in which all of God's children can live, or to go into the dark. We must either love each other or we must die." [14]

This ad aired only once, during NBC's "Monday Night at the Movies" showing of "David and Bathsheeba" on September 7, 1964. But condemnation came almost immediately. As recalled by Bill Moyers, then Johnson's press secretary, "The president called me and said `Holy shit. I'm getting calls from all over the country.' Most of them said that it was an effective ad. Others said they didn't like it." Press reaction was swift. According to Lloyd Wright, an advertising strategist for Johnson, "The first night it aired, it created such a media flap that the next night it was used in its entirety on the newscasts on all three networks." Johnson pulled the ad. [15]

Bush's "Revolving Door" ad received quite a different reception. CBS covered this commercial in its broadcast on October 7, 1988. (News stories about Horton had been broadcast September 22.) The story described the commercial as a crime ad that would highlight the prison furlough policy of Governor Dukakis. Clifford Barnes and Donna Cuomo, joint victims of an assault by a convict who had been released on a weekend furlough, were reported to be participating in a speaking tour with a pro-Bush group. Bush meanwhile was shown campaigning with police officers. This was followed on October 20 with another story, this time showing in great detail Horton's crime record and supplying background on the Bush ad. Bush was shown campaigning in New York City at a police union rally. It was not until October 24 and 25—almost three weeks after the commercial appeared—that opponents appeared on the news to claim that the "Revolving Door" ad had racist undertones. But in keeping with the horse-race mentality of the media, a second story on October 25 also quoted media consultant Tony Schwartz as saying that Bush's ads were successful and that the "Revolving Door" was particularly effective.

The contrast with the coverage of the "Daisy" ad could not have been more stark. Whereas the 1964 ad was immediately condemned and removed from the airwaves, reporters in 1988 treated the furlough ad as a typical news story. Its airing was reported. It was described as being quite effective. Criticisms came late and were never solidly addressed; the spot was not pulled off the air.

This subdued and delayed reaction was in keeping with the general tenor of news coverage about attack ads in 1988. A number of CBS stories and *New York Times* articles during the general election campaign emphasized the overall effectiveness of negative political commercials. A September 18 *New York Times* article, for example, discussed the role of advertising in contemporary campaigns. Former governor Brown was quoted, saying that media and professional campaign advisers think negative commercials work better. A number of politicians and consultants were cited as saying that Bush and Dukakis would be foolish to delve deeply into policy issues. This was followed on October 10 with an article that cited campaign officials who believed that the electorate had become accustomed to sharp-elbow tactics.

In addition, political professionals quoted on October 19 derided Dukakis's advertising effort. Several experts complained about the ever-shifting focus of his ad campaign and the fact that his commercials were not well timed. An October 13 story noted that 1988 was the first time candidates used more ads to criticize opponents than to promote themselves. A number of analysts even attributed Bush's lead in the polls to the success of his negative commercials and the lack of an appropriate response by Dukakis.

This tolerance of negativity, combined with the grudging respect reporters had for the effectiveness of the GOP ads, created a pattern of coverage that benefited Bush. Rather than condemning the ad, as reporters had in 1964 with the "Daisy" ad, the reporters of 1988 did not complain when the "Revolving Door" commercial stayed on the air. They even rebroadcast the ad repeatedly throughout the last month of the campaign.[16] This behavior effectively erased the traditional difference between the free and paid media. It gave Bush more air time and therefore lent him more credibility than any campaign organization alone could have managed. This style of news coverage helped make Bush's 1988 advertising campaign one of the most effective of the past twenty years.

Buchanan's "Freedom Abused" Ad

In 1992, some journalists repeated the very same mistakes from the 1988 campaign. The clearest example of this followed Buchanan's airing of his controversial Georgia spot, "Freedom Abused." This spot criticized Bush for supporting public subsidies of homoerotic art.

The video footage for this commercial was taken from a Public Broadcasting Service documentary, *Tongues Untied,* which had been subsidized by the National Endowment for the Arts (NEA). The ad blasted Bush for spending tax dollars on pornographic art that glorified homosexuality and clearly was designed to appeal to traditional voters in the South.

As scenes of partially dressed, dancing, gay men filled the screen, an announcer intoned,

In the last three years, the Bush Administration has invested our tax dollars in pornographic and blasphemous art too shocking to show. This so-called art has glorified homosexuality, exploited children, and perverted the image of Jesus Christ. Even after good people protested, Bush continued to fund this kind of art. Send Bush a message. We need a leader who will fight for what we believe in.

This spot generated widespread press attention and prompted direct comparisons with Bush's 1988 "Revolving Door" commercial. Newspaper accounts were quite critical of Buchanan's airing of this ad. On February 27, almost immediately after the commercial started running, the *Washington Post* printed an article by E. J. Dionne Jr., reporting the ad's airing and reactions from the Bush campaign calling the ad a "blatant distortion of truth." [17]

Buchanan's response was that the ad "has nothing to do with anti-gay prejudice. It has to do with not spending people's tax dollars on values that insult them." Ad watches followed on February 28 by Howard Kurtz in the *Washington Post* and by Renee Loth in the *Boston Globe.* [18] The *New York Times* did not run an ad watch feature but had detailed stories by Robin Toner and Elizabeth Kolbert on that day, with critical comments from campaign strategists and by Alessandra Stanley on March 8 giving the reactions of gay groups. [19]

The *Washington Post* ad watch noted that Bush was not personally responsible for the decision to subsidize the film. The filmmaker, Marlon Riggs, had been given $5,000 by the Rocky Mountain Film Institute, which received the money from the American Film Institute, which got it from the NEA.[20]

In her *Boston Globe* ad watch, Loth was even more critical. She pointed out the limited political control of the White House over the NEA and wrote, "For sheer appeal to intolerance and shock value, this ad pushes all the right buttons. It features a slow-motion film clip from "Tongues Untied," a frank documentary on black gay life. While the ad may galvanize the religious right in Georgia, it also reveals what many could see as an unattractive side of Buchanan."[21]

Others, however, were not nearly as critical. Almost completely unfazed by this commercial was Eric Engberg in a February 28 "CBS Evening News" report dealing with negative ads (specifically, Bush's "General Kelley" ad questioning Buchanan's position on the Persian Gulf War and Buchanan's quota and antipornography ads). Engberg gave a remarkably upbeat interpretation of the anti-NEA ad and stressed its general effectiveness: "By staking a claim to the racially sensitive quotas issue and by coming on as a strong supporter of traditional values, Buchanan is cutting into Mr. Bush's base, something of a surprise for a president who was able to make effective use of Willie Horton just four years ago."

No mention was made of the antihomosexual overtones of the ad or the factual inaccuracies noted by Kurtz and Loth in attributing responsibility to Bush for NEA funding decisions. This story, of course, was not a formal ad watch, and its tone reflected the general tendency of reporters to focus on strategy.

A second feature by Engberg that discussed Buchanan's ad appeared March 2 on the "CBS Evening News." There again was no critique of the commercial, although Engberg was more circumspect in describing the candidate's political fortunes. In his story, Engberg said that Buchanan's advertisements were "turning Georgia into a political mud-wrestling contest that will determine whether Pat Buchanan has political legs or is just a one-time wonder."

Lisa Myers of NBC was more critical in a February 28 story. After she aired a Buchanan segment promising no discrimination and then discussed the new television ad, she raised questions about whether Buchanan was guilty of racism. Buchanan's past statements regarding Martin Luther King Jr. and women serving in the Persian Gulf War were outlined, as were previous comments on David Duke and on Israel.

Chris Bury of ABC was not personally critical of Buchanan in a February 28 story, but statements from White House spokesperson Marlin Fitzwater and Vice President Quayle attacking Buchanan were used in the segment.[22]

All of this reveals the difficulty television has in evaluating emotionally charged ads. The most controversial ads almost always involve graphic visuals. The backdrop of "Freedom Abused" included apparently gay men in chains dancing around a stage. Similar difficulties arose in the case of the "Revolving Door" ad, which featured slow-motion frames of prisoners streaming through a revolving door, while an armed guard watched over them. Television is a powerful medium because of its combination of audio and visual communications. This makes it quite difficult to shield voters from the candidate's message when rebroadcasting advertisements.

Chapter 5

Ad Watches and Voluntary Codes

Dissatisfaction with paid campaign advertisements in recent elections has generated heartfelt pleas for fundamental change in the way elections are conducted. Following the example of Australia and, until recently Germany, some critics in this country have called for an outright ban on television campaign ads in the United States. Others more worried about the effect on last-minute deciders have suggested the application of the French model, where ads are banned altogether during the closing weeks of the campaign.

These calls undoubtedly reflect the deep frustration felt by viewers over the tone and quality of political communications in the United States. Many campaign ads are negative in tone, simplistic in presentation, and deceptive in content. The widespread use of television has dramatically increased the costs of American elections. Fewer resources are available for traditional campaign activities that engage citizens and boost voter turnout.

Complaints about ads have led to a number of different proposed remedies. One approach involves voluntary limits on the part of media consultants and journalists through codes of conduct. A second perspective entails public information services provided by nonpartisan groups such as the League of Women Voters and Operation Vote Smart designed to offset the deleterious effects of ads. A third approach is civic journalism, in which newsrooms directly gear press coverage to improving political discourse, such as through town meetings, debates, and community forums. A fourth view is free television time for the candidates. A fifth perspective is media ad watches that review the content of prominent commercials and discuss their accuracy and effectiveness. This chapter looks at these approaches to determine how well each serves the public.

Codes of Conduct

Self-regulation is the easiest but least viable way to police deceptive ads. The reason is simple. There are no effective enforcement mechanisms when regulation is left to the industry. In the heat of election contests, voluntary self-restraints often are dropped by campaigners. With millions of dollars of consulting contracts on the line, few consultants let voluntary codes dictate their conduct.

Over the years, a variety of good government organizations and industry associations have promulgated codes of conduct. For example, in 1992, the League of Women Voters organized a national effort called "Take Back the System," the purpose of which was to disseminate a voluntary code of conduct. Most state organizations affiliated with the League took part in this effort. Several states, such as New York, Ohio, Oregon, Wyoming, and Texas, developed their own model codes. League affiliates in New York, Oregon, and Washington organized efforts to censure politicians who used racial epithets in political campaigns.

In 1996, the Rochester, New York, League of Women Voters developed a program called Project Positive Campaign, which urged candidates to refrain from negative campaigns. Through flyers, brochures, and public service announcements, the project encouraged voters to "let your candidates know you will vote, financially support and work only for those who run positive, informative campaigns."

In Nashville, Tennessee, a consortium of forty churches and synagogues united behind a Tying Nashville Together program designed to get local candidates to sign a no-negative campaigning pledge. Thirty-three of the forty candidates elected to the county council signed the pledge.[1]

In terms of industry associations, the American Association of Advertising Agencies urged broadcast and print media to assume a watchdog role in the 1996 election. Called the Political Advertising Repair, this initiative encouraged the media to judge candidate claims on the basis of fairness and truthfulness. In the past, this association had called on political consultants to use more positive tactics. However, association leader Hal Shoup says this kind of self-regulation has not been successful because political consultants "turn around and attack the advertising industry" on the veracity of claims in product advertising.[2]

The American Association of Political Consultants (AAPC) has a professional code of ethics for its 850 individual members. The association represents about 70 percent of all political consultants, and AAPC bylaws require that all members sign a copy of the code as a condition of membership.

The code outlines the following principles for running campaigns:

- Do not indulge in any activity that would corrupt or degrade the practice of political campaigning.
- Treat colleagues and clients with respect.
- Respect the confidentiality of clients.
- Use no appeal to voters based on racism, sexism, religious intolerance, or any form of unlawful discrimination.
- Refrain from false or misleading attacks on an opponent.
- Document accurately and fully any criticism of an opponent.
- Be honest in relationships with the news media.
- Use funds received from clients only for those purposes invoiced in writing.

As is usual with industry groups, the association relies on outside complaints for its enforcement mechanism. If someone has an ethics complaint, that person can file an official complaint with the association. But in the first eight months of 1996, no formal complaints were filed.

It is more common for the association to receive calls from reporters, who describe particular practices and who inquire about whether those behaviors comply with the association's ethics code. According to Gary Nordlinger, chair of the association's ethics committee and himself a media consultant with Nordlinger and Associates, "The most effective enforcement is publicity. The last thing a candidate wants right before an election is an ethics complaint." The number one inquiry from reporters in 1996 involved push-polls, a controversial practice of planting unfavorable information about opponents in polls. The association has characterized this as an unethical practice.

More detailed guidelines come from the National Fair Campaign Practices Committee made up of consultants and practitioners. According to its Code of Fair Campaign Practices, candidates for public office have an obligation to uphold basic principles of decency, honesty, and fair play. This includes condemnation of personal vilification and avoidance of character defamation, whispering campaigns, libel, slander, or scurrilous attacks.

The code condemns the use of campaign material that misrepresents, distorts, or otherwise falsifies the facts regarding any candidate as well as malicious or unfounded accusations aimed at creating doubts about loyalty to country and patriotism. Appeals to prejudice based on race, creed, gender, or national origin are to be avoided. Candidates are asked to repudiate any individuals or groups who resort to improper methods or tactics. Anyone who feels those rules have been violated can file a complaint that gets publicized in the consulting industry.

Nine states (California, Hawaii, Illinois, Kansas, Maine, Montana, Nevada, Washington, and West Virginia) have statutes modeled after the National Fair Campaign Practices Committee code. But there are differences in how prejudiced appeals are defined. Unlike the one of the National Fair Campaign Practices Committee, the California statute includes in the categories that are not to be discriminated against physical health and age, in addition to the categories from the model code. The West Virginia statute has a provision condemning prejudice based on physical disability and age. Most of the other states define prejudice in regard to race, creed, gender, or national origin.

The Leroy Collins Center at Florida State University has a model code that goes much further than the National Fair Campaign Practices Committee in evaluating conduct. In it the purpose of elections is defined as the provision to voters of a clear look at the personal values that motivate candidates and the political issues that define them. The code asks candidates to address valid issues, shun demagoguery, and avoid last-minute charges made without giving opponents reasonable time to respond before election day. Journalists are asked to report fairly, ensure equitable access to coverage, emphasize coverage of the issues, and monitor misrepresentations or untruths that may appear in campaign advertisements. The public is asked to participate in self-government, demand the cleansing of politics, and care about the political process. Campaign ads are required to identify the person or organization buying the ad to appear in the ad and to state in the case of attack ads whether the candidate approves or disapproves of the attack.

Based on these types of self-regulations, there have been efforts in individual states to restrain campaign conduct. One of the most ambitious examples of a voluntary compliance code in 1996 came in Minnesota. Put together by reform organizations upset with the tenor of past campaigns, this code, called the Minnesota Compact, set ten standards of clean campaign ads to which it asked candidates to adhere.

The Minnesota Compact

1. The candidate will take full and personal responsibility for all advertising created and placed on behalf of his/her campaign by its staff or related committees.
2. In television advertising, either the candidate's visual likeness, voice, or both will be in the ad at least 50% of the time.
3. In radio advertising, the candidate's voice will be in the ad at least 50% of the time.
4. The candidate will publicly renounce any independently financed ad that violates the standards set forth in this agreement.
5. The candidate will use no appeal to discrimination based on race, gender, or religious belief and will condemn those who do.
6. The candidate will refrain from false and misleading attacks on an opponent, staffer, or member of his/her family and shall do everything in her/his power to prevent others from using such tactics for his/her electoral benefit. ("Misleading attacks" include taking votes or actions significantly out of context and/or distorting the opponent's record by the use of demonstrably unrepresentative votes or actions.")
7. The candidate will document fully any criticism of an opponent or his/her record (including as much of that material as possible in the ad itself).
8. The candidate will refrain from using any still photos, film, or video of the opponent that are designed to make him/her look personally unpleasant or contorted or that are taken significantly out of context.
9. The candidate will acknowledge that the principles detailed above apply to other sorts of campaign communications in addition to ads in the media (e.g., speeches, billboards, direct mail, etc.).
10. The candidate will acknowledge that the principles detailed above also apply to campaign communications from his/her party.

As a voluntary code, the enforcement mechanism was left to candidates, the media, and citizens. According to compact associate director Janna Haug, organizers relied on compact participants to provide "the moral suasion and political climate needed to bring about this changed behavior." As part of the effort, Compact organizers initiated "citizens' conversation groups" consisting of at least ten friends, coworkers, book club members, neighbors, and relatives who would watch ads and debates. Hosts attended a training session on how to lead a discussion and received a conversation starter kit made up of readings, essays, discussion guidelines, and material on how to watch a debate. Following their discussions, hosts submitted a report evaluating each group's experiences.

Minnesota also had a separate advertising code developed by ad executive Lee Lynch. This effort, called the Citizens Campaign Advertising Code (CCAC), took a more aggressive approach than the Compact. It asked candidates to sign a pledge to abide by the code and citizens to sign a petition stating that they would not vote for or contribute to the campaign of any candidates who did not sign the pledge.

The pledge consisted of five specific principles: (1) that candidates be accountable for their advertising, (2) that candidates link themselves to their message, (3) that candidates display the logo of the CCAC to let people know that they have signed the Code, (4) that candidates do not demean each other with distorted, retouched, or morphed photographs, and (5) that candidates publicly rebuke independent expenditures on their behalf that are not in keeping with the spirit of the general principles of the Code.

According to Debbie Drinkwater, assistant executive director of CCAC, the goal was to get 100,000 Minnesotans to sign petitions saying they would not vote for candidates who did not sign the pledge. But this ambitious goal fell far short. Interviews with political observers in Minnesota who followed the campaign found that only a few candidates signed this agreement.

Despite extensive group efforts, there were no noticeable improvements in the civility of campaign discourse during the Minnesota U.S. Senate race. The Republican national party ran hundreds of thousands of dollars in independent ads attacking Sen. Paul Wellstone as an unrepentant liberal. One such ad started with a cartoon figure presenting the distorted face of Wellstone. As clown music played in the background, a cartoon arm popped out holding a sign saying, "LIBERAL." The announcer said: "Since he's been in Washington, Paul Wellstone has cast one liberal vote after another. He voted against the balanced-budget amendment. He voted against the death penalty for murderers, terrorists, and drug kingpins. And he's voted against workfare time and again. Paul Wellstone voted for higher taxes 48 times. He even voted to raise taxes on some Social Security benefits. And he's rated the No. 1 spender in the entire Senate. Paul Wellstone: embarrassingly liberal and out of touch."[3]

With no clear enforcement mechanism in either the Minnesota Compact or the Code, self-restraint was negligible on the part of campaign consultants. Ads on both sides of this race included several appeals prohibited by the code: a failure to renounce independent ads, the candidate's visual absence from attack ads, using still photos designed to make the opponent look unpleasant, and taking votes and comments out of context. From all apparent sources, these voluntary codes did not make a substantial difference in how the Senate television campaign was conducted.

The only thing the attack ads did was to make voters angry about the campaign and the tone of the negative ads. According to a statewide survey conducted by the *Minneapolis Star Tribune* and WCCO-TV, 44 percent of the people said the advertisements made them more likely to vote for Wellstone. Only 30 percent said the ads made them more likely to vote for Rudy Boschwitz. Wellstone won his bid for reelection.

Public Information Services

For years, the League of Women Voters have mailed information to voters about candidates' issue positions and referenda ballot language in conjunction with newspapers around the country. But this service is on the decline. According to League officials, declining membership as more women enter the workforce has led fewer local chapters to provide these circulars. Those that do increasingly have faced fiscal pressure to charge for the service.

For this reason, several states such as California, Oregon, Texas, and Washington have underwritten the costs of publishing and distributing voter pamphlets that provide citizens with candidate biographies and descriptions of issue positions. Other League affiliates print guides in conjunction with local newspapers, who then take responsibility for distributing the guides to their readers.

A telephone survey of state League organizations in 1996 found that most state affiliates had not been very active in the past or did not plan to be active in 1996.[4] Only sixteen state leagues said they had been active in the past and just thirteen indicated they would be active in 1996. Among the more active affiliates, the Florida Pinellas County Fair Campaign Practices Committee had open hearings in 1994, where they asked candidates for office to sign a pledge about fair campaigns. Ninety-six percent of candidates signed the pledge, which was modeled after the national League code.

The Maryland League has written a position paper providing guidelines for televised political advertising. The Minnesota League conducts efforts to aid persons demeaned in the media.

That League also approached media representatives to develop a media self-policing effort, but this was rejected by the local media. The Lincoln, Nebraska League, in conjunction with local political scientists, developed forums to encourage people to think about what they were looking at in political advertisements, especially in regard to negative ads. The New Hampshire League worked with a nonprofit organization to hold a conference on television advertising.

One of the most active League affiliates around the country is the Rochester, New York, League. It has a county fair campaign practices committee that publicizes candidate complaints about unfair practices. It also has run a positive campaigning project in which candidates are told via pamphlets, radio public service announcements, and audiotapes that voters expect campaigns that are issue-oriented, relevant to the office at hand, informative, and constructive in tone. The Ohio League conducted a Meet the Candidates forum during which the candidates were encouraged to sign a campaign practices pledge and remain positive in their campaigns. The Dayton chapter succeeded in getting all the local candidates to sign their local campaign practices pledge. The Oregon League created an 800-number hotline for citizen complaints about candidate conduct in 1994. The Pennsylvania League is working with local academics to produce a detailed research paper on televised advertising in the 1996 campaign. The South Carolina chapter has hosted candidate debates. The South Dakota chapter has put together a local group to monitor campaign ads each week. The Utah League conducted a survey of political scientists in 1992 and 1993 on the subject of campaign advertising. The Washington League eliminated its request that candidates "solemnly pledge" adherence to a campaign practices code after concerns from the Christian Right candidates that God would not approve of them taking such an oath.

As part of its public information efforts, the League of Women Voters Education Fund sponsored a study by Susan Lederman and Gerald Pomper of 1992 U.S. Senate campaigns in New York, North Carolina, and Oregon.[5] Each state developed a fair campaign practices committee to monitor the Senate race, and there was a massive citizen education effort, which included distributing brochures describing fair campaign standards, broadcasting public service announcements about campaign practices, holding information forums, conducting media interviews, and providing a toll-free Citizen Information Service hotline for citizens to register complaints about unfair practices.

Yet according to the study, these activities did little to improve the tenor of the campaign. The New York Senate race was "the nastiest and most expensive campaign in the nation in 1992." Seventy-seven percent of voters said the senatorial candidates spent the majority of their time attacking the opponent, not addressing the issues. Sixty-one percent felt there had been an increase in the use of negative advertisements. Even more ominously, 10 percent of New Yorkers who voted for president did not vote for a senator, a 50-percent increase over the 1988 voter drop-off. In North Carolina, 150 voters called the toll-free hotline to complain about campaign tactics. One academic observer condemned appeals to "racial fears and religious bias, distortions of candidates' records and little if any focus on issues." Alone among the three states, Oregon had a "comparatively fair" statewide campaign. The success of the campaign-watch effort in this state was attributed to strong state League leadership and effective use of political and academic contacts.

Other organizations also provide voter information services. The National Center for Independence in Politics is a national nonpartisan, tax-exempt organization located at Oregon State University in Corvallis, Oregon. It provides citizens with information about the political system, issues, candidates, and elected officials. Its databases are accessible by calling a free 800 telephone number or by an Internet site called Operation Vote Smart located at a World Wide Web address: http://www.vote-smart.org.

Its services include campaign finance data, voting records, performance evaluations by special interest organizations, campaign issue positions, biographical background, and other information on members of Congress and candidates for office. During the 1992 election, more than 200,000 calls came in, 34,000 on election day alone. Many citizens requested copies of the Voter's Self-Defense Manual, which contained printed information from center databases. In 1994, 500,000 manuals were distributed free of charge during the election. According to official documents on its home page, the entire effort "is aimed at providing tools to ensure public accountability by elected officials to those they represent."

The Center's self-evaluation projects have investigated who is using its data in terms of numbers and characteristics. In general, people who use its services are interested in and knowledgeable about politics. The number of people who have relied on its information has grown dramatically over the past three election cycles. It is clear that this type of nonpartisan information service is becoming more popular with voters.

Civic Journalism

There has been a growing effort within the media community to engage journalists in the nation's civic life. In an effort to move beyond ads as the dominant information source, these activities attempt to define issues independent of the campaigns and give the public a more reasoned basis for judging candidates. To aid voter understanding, media outlets sponsor town meetings and candidate debates or conduct focus groups and public opinion polls. According to one estimate, about 40 daily newspapers around the country in 1996 (up from 12 in 1994) used these types of efforts to improve the political dialogue.

One example came in Minnesota, where the *Duluth News-Tribune* ran an article in September 1995 about a local meeting organized by the newspaper to discuss ways of curbing the rising incidence of domestic abuse, murder, and school violence.[6] The goal was to get beyond the usual horse-race journalism in which reporters emphasized who was ahead and behind and draw public attention to serious issues of public policy.

Another came in Wisconsin, when the *Wisconsin State Journal* teamed with a local television station for a "We the People" project. This series sponsored meetings, solicited public comment on issues important to voters, and instructed viewers on how to watch debates and dissect political advertising. A 1995 study of the project, sponsored by the Pew Center for Civic Journalism, used polls taken before and after the 1994 elections to investigate the impact.[7]

In general, the study found that about half the respondents had heard of the project, although 20 percent attributed the effort to a newspaper or television station that had not taken part. Seventy percent felt the program did not increase their interest in politics. The number of people who said their knowledge of important issues had increased went from 51 percent before the election to 56 percent afterward.

In 1996, a number of news organizations sponsored projects with catchy titles, such as "We the People," "Voices of Florida," and "Front Porch Forum." *The Boston Globe* ran a series of town meetings, focus groups, and polling in Derry, New Hampshire. The *Minneapolis Star Tribune* convened 400 people for a citizens' conference on the family, which attracted a visit from First Lady Hillary Clinton. The *Akron Beacon Journal* persuaded 22,000 citizens to mail in coupons pledging to work for improved race relations. *The Charlotte Observer* held a "Taking Back Our Neighborhoods" town meeting that led to the opening of new parks and recreation halls.[8]

One novel experiment took place in North Carolina when several of the state's major newspapers and leading broadcast stations banded together to get candidates to address issues identified by voters as their most important concerns. Called the "Your Voice, Your Vote" coalition and consisting of six newspapers, five television stations, public television, and three public radio stations, journalists surveyed state residents regarding issues facing the state and then ran virtually identical stories each week outlining the positions of state and national contenders. The goal of this coalition was to break out of the normal journalistic tendency in political campaigns to cover the horse race, strategies, and game rather than the issues.

Candidates complained that they were not able to address the issues they wanted to talk about as opposed to the issues identified in public opinion polls that voters cared about. Jim Andrews, campaign manager to U.S. Senate candidate Harvey Gantt, explained that "This philosophy says, it is up to the poll to determine what should be covered and what should not be covered. Part of the job of the candidate is to talk about something he feels is important."[9]

Journalists openly worried that "public journalism" meant campaign agendas were being dictated by reporters, not voters. In a column for the *Washington Post,* Jonathan Yardley wrote, "If 'public journalism' is an attempt to orchestrate the public agenda, it is also both self-serving and an abrogation of basic journalistic obligations."[10]

But based on the numbers of ordinary people who show up for town meetings and community forums and requests for information that newspapers receive, this experiment appears successful in one crucial way. It guarantees at least some substantive information about major issues facing the state. It is hard to determine whether these efforts have stimulated voter interest in politics. It may be beyond the ability of civic journalism to revive public interest and restore citizen confidence in government, given long-term trends in those areas. But they can help voters hear substantive information about issues identified by citizens as important for the future.

Debates

Debates are one of the most visible ways of providing information to voters outside the realm of paid political commercials. In the past, debates have been the Super Bowl of American elections. Typically at the presidential level, the viewing audience for television debates has numbered between 75 million and 90 million, which is practically the size of the entire voting electorate. Voters like these types of formats because they represent a valuable opportunity to see the candidates questioned side-by-side in detail for an extended period of time. Not only do debates provide substantive information, they also allow voters to see how the candidates think and how they respond to various types of questions.

In 1996, there were two presidential debates, a vice presidential debate, and a number of debates in elections for U.S. Senate, House, and governor. In general, viewership levels were down 30 percent to 40 percent from 1992. Part of the problem was that the presidential race did not generate the same level of interest as in previous years and the campaign was seen as one-sided by voters. There also was a sharp drop in general media coverage of the 1996 campaign. Network television coverage was down 40 percent from 1992 and the number of front-page campaign stories in the *Washington Post* was down by 50 percent.[11]

Debates clearly provide valuable information for voters beyond that made available in candidate advertising. When they are broadcast live, featured in media coverage, and watched by large numbers of Americans, they serve a crucial substantive function for voters.

But it is not clear if debates perform the same function below the presidential level. In state elections, for example, debates are not always carried live by television and typically do not receive the same level of attention as at the presidential level. This limits the ability of subpresidential debates to supplement candidate communications in American elections.

Free Television Time

One of the perennial proposals to improve civic discourse in American political life is free television time for the candidates. Put forward in its latest incarnation in 1996 by Paul Taylor of the Free TV for Straight Talk Coalition, this approach was simple. As expressed in a full-page *New York Times* ad on October 1, the coalition proposed that "from October 17 through November 1, all of the major networks carve out two and a half minutes in prime time to allow the presidential candidates to deliver mini-speeches on alternating nights. . . . Whatever President Clinton says one night at, say, 8:58 P.M., Senator Dole can respond to the next night—same time, same vast audience. In the intervening 24 hours, the news media can scrutinize each candidate's presentations and build suspense about the opponent's rebuttal." [12]

The goal of this proposal was to provide unfiltered time for the major candidates to explain their positions outside seven-second sound bytes and the half-truths and false inferences of paid negative ads. In the abstract, if the networks blocked out the same time period every night, these segments could become a "running debate."

But the problem in 1996 was that the major networks refused to adopt a standardized format or schedule. The Fox network agreed to broadcast ten 1-minute campaign statements from Clinton and Dole during prime time in the weeks leading up to the election. Under the plan, each candidate would deliver a one-minute speech in response to each of ten questions that Fox had posed based on questions citizens had indicated were important to them in a national public opinion survey. CBS also agreed to two-minute segments from Clinton and Dole titled "Where I Stand" on each of four consecutive nights starting October 21 based on topics (education, taxes, Social Security and Medicare, and health care) defined as important by voters in a CBS News Poll. However, ABC was willing to give Dole and Clinton a single shot, extended interview in prime time the week before the election, CNN set aside time during "Inside Politics" for candidate segments entitled "Addressing America," and NBC was willing to set aside time during its "Dateline" news magazine program. [13]

The first videotape clip aired by Fox on September 17 was a segment about keeping kids off drugs. The remaining issues were health care, foreign aid, economic anxiety, the candidates' top priority for the next four years, balancing the budget without cutting entitlements, improving public schools, preserving Social Security, and the questions "What do you feel is the most critical problem facing our nation today?" and "Why should we trust you?"[14] No voice-overs were allowed or production assistance, just the candidate speaking directly into the camera. The audience for this segment was tiny as a result of the lack of press attention and the lack of a standardized schedule that could be publicized.

Even more problematic was the unwillingness of television stations to provide free time for races below the presidential level. In general, television stations refused to provide free time for any candidates other than presidential contenders because of the lost revenue and concern about equal time requirements for all candidates. However, A. H. Belo Corporation, owner of seven local stations, was one of the exceptions when it offered five minutes of free broadcast time to local candidates for the Senate, House, and Governor in the seven cities where Belo owned television stations. Belo was able to get a Federal Communications Commission ruling that the plan for free air time qualified as "on the spot coverage of a bona fide news event," which exempted it from equal time provisions to all legally qualified candidates.[15]

Ad Watches

Ad watches are designated newspaper columns and television segments that are devoted to monitoring political advertising. They were created to give reporters a formal opportunity to evaluate political ads. One of the problems of media coverage of campaign ads has been its inattention to deceptive rhetoric. Because of improvements in editing and production techniques, it is easy for candidates to mislead the public through emotional visuals or the clever use of music, color, and audiotape voice-overs, as has been discussed previously.

For example, Buchanan electronically altered ads against Bush in 1992 to make the president look unappealing. Some commercials were speeded up to show a hyperactive Bush appearing to be frenetic and out of control. Others were slowed down so that Bush looked sluggish and lethargic. To the casual observer, it was not apparent that the Bush footage had been altered.

Ad watches were designed to deal with deceptive and inaccurate advertisements. As described by Jamieson, one of the originators of the concept, ad watches provide a "grammar of evaluation."[16] In their original formulation, reporters would show an ad (or provide a transcript in the case of a newspaper story) and then critique the claims presented in the commercial. Were their factual inaccuracies? Was the rhetoric overblown? Did ads mislead the public in any way?

The goal was to formalize and professionalize the evaluation process. Rather than leave ad coverage to casual observation or the vagaries of individual stories, a style of analysis was developed to help reporters and the general public be more systematic in their viewing of ads.

The 1988 presidential campaign was the first one featuring ad watches. From time to time, national newspapers printed "truth boxes" in which ad claims were assessed. The television networks ran stories containing a broadcast of an ad and a critique by a reporter.

However, focus groups conducted that year revealed that these ad watches did not achieve their purposes. Viewers often remembered the ad but not the media corrections. For example, negative ads that year, such as Bush's "Revolving Door," had such powerful visuals that replaying the ad, even with criticism and commentary, only served to boost Bush's campaign message.

Jamieson encountered the same problem in focus groups she conducted. When she showed a story by Richard Threlkeld of CBS debunking Bush's "Tank" ad, she was dismayed to learn that viewers internalized the ad message. In the Bush spot, a helmeted and obviously ill at ease Dukakis rode around in a military tank while visual text on screen claimed the Massachusetts governor opposed major weapons programs. Threlkeld ran a lengthy critique of this ad showing that Dukakis actually supported a number of weapons systems, but viewers who saw this story were more likely to believe Bush's charges against Dukakis than the news story's rebuttal.

The problem was that when Threlkeld rebroadcast the ad within his news story in order to critique it, the spot was shown full-screen. Reminiscent of Lesley Stahl's experience during the Reagan presidency, this exposed people to compelling pictures. Many of them ended up remembering the visuals, not the audio critique.

The style of coverage in the 1988 campaign was profoundly disturbing to voters, academic experts, and even reporters themselves. After the election, countless seminars, conferences, and white papers urged journalists to alter their approach to covering campaign commercials. The feeling was that by not having challenged

Bush more effectively in 1988, reporters let the candidate run deceptive ads to the detriment of the campaign dialogue.

Based on this experience, ad watches were changed in several ways. Instead of rebroadcasting ads full-screen, Brooks Jackson of CNN made an innovative effort on the show "Inside Politics" to review ads without hyping the candidate. The trick, according to Jackson, was to use what Jamieson called a "truth box" to rebroadcast the commercial in a smaller square tilted to the side so that viewers could see it was not a candidate airing of the ad.

This shrinking of the video in the ad watch is important because it undercuts the visual impact of the advertisement. Rather than forcing news analysts to compete with powerful visual images, the CNN approach allows reporters to superimpose their own graphics, such as "misleading," "false," or "unfair" over the ad. This put the news story on a fairer visual footing with the ad.

In the analysis of the spot, the dimensions of accuracy and fairness were separated from notions of strategic effectiveness so that viewers would realize there were several different standards of evaluation. It was hoped that this would overcome the tendency displayed during the 1988 presidential campaign of evaluating ads mainly on the dimension of whether they worked.

To give ad watches a distinctive identity, many newspapers created a formal box labeled "ad watch." This feature provided the complete script of the ad (along with a photo of the most important visual), an assessment of the accuracy of the ad, and a discussion of its effectiveness.

The media in 1992 devoted considerable space to ad watches. The *Boston Globe* offered some of the most comprehensive coverage in the country. It printed ad watches on forty-eight of the fifty-three commercials broadcast during the New Hampshire primary campaign alone (as well as many thereafter). Overall, the *New York Times* ran fifteen separate reviews throughout the nominating process, and the *Washington Post* ran twenty-one. The television networks also incorporated ad segments in a number of stories. The general election campaign featured twenty-nine ad watches in the *New York Times* and twenty-four in the *Washington Post*.

Ad watches had a big impact on candidates. The 1992 campaign witnessed the rise of what I call "ads with footnotes." Reporters' scrutiny forced candidates to document their claims more carefully. This led some presidential aspirants to include factual citations directly on the screen reminiscent of footnotes in a term paper. For example, Clinton ads routinely listed the source and date of publication of a quote or fact for viewers to see. Clinton would quote a statistic and cite the Bureau of the Census or a newspaper article as the source.

This was an obvious effort to boost the credibility of the Clinton ads. Because nonpartisan sources, such as newspaper articles and government reports, have greater credibility than partisan spots, ads with footnotes are a way of piggy-backing claims on the high credibility of more objective sources.

Clinton media adviser Frank Greer said his campaign's research in 1992 "consistently found that viewers believed Bush's negative ads—such as one suggesting that Clinton would raise taxes on middle-class workers—lacked documentation. . . . They [the Bush advisers] never figured out that you needed to offer people substantiation and details. Ross Perot figured that out." [17]

Because of the close attention devoted to ads by the media, it is not surprising that ad watches are noticed by the viewing public. A Boston metropolitan survey taken March 2 to 9, 1992, revealed that 57 percent of the area's residents said they had seen ad watches, 28 percent said they had not, and 15 percent did not remember. Viewers reported that they found ad watches to be helpful.

A survey in May 1992 taken in Los Angeles asked residents how helpful news stories analyzing ads had been.[18] Of those expressing an opinion, 21 percent indicated the stories had been very helpful and 47 percent said they had been somewhat helpful. Only 32 percent felt the ad watch analysis had not been very helpful.

According to reporters, ad watches were effective oversight tools. Howard Kurtz of the *Washington Post* said they were "a great step forward for democracy because they keep candidates honest." The same sentiment was expressed by Mara Liasson of National Public Radio, who said that "candidates are more careful because they know they will be scrutinized." Renee Loth of the *Boston Globe* felt that ad watches "inoculate viewers against the potion of ads." [19]

The 1996 Presidential Campaign

Recent research by Ansolabehere and Iyengar published at the beginning of the 1996 campaign concluded ad watches were almost completely ineffective.[20] Drawing on three simple experiments in which some viewers were shown a CNN ad watch while others were not, there was a surprising result. Participants developed greater support for candidates whose ads were scrutinized by reporters. This was the exact opposite of what was intended by the ad watch.

This research, though, has been challenged by Jamieson on the grounds that the particular ad watches used in the experiment were not typical of the genre. Appearing on CNN's "Inside Politics" and writing later in a January 27, 1996, *New York Times* op-ed piece, Jamieson argued that the particular commercials reviewed in the study's ad watches were judged to be accurate, not inaccurate.[21] Therefore, it was a failure of the experiment, not a failure of the ad watch, when voters responded favorably.

To see how media outlets viewed ad watches, I participated in a project that conducted a telephone survey of 261 newspapers and local television stations around the country in January and February 1996.[22] Newspaper managing editors and local television news directors were asked whether their outlet had conducted ad watches, when they started, which election campaigns were conducted, what format was used, how they evaluated their impact, and whether they planned to continue ad watches in the 1996 campaign.

Table 5-1 reveals that newspapers were much more likely (65 percent) than television stations (44 percent) to have done ad watches. Those that did them first started in 1988 with most stations having begun in 1990 and 1992. The most frequent elections covered in newspaper ad watches were those of governor (54 percent of all newspapers), followed by Senate races (51 percent), House contests (47 percent), local races (36 percent), presidential campaigns (26 percent), and referenda (1 percent). Television stations were most likely to cover Senate races (21 percent), compared to presidential races (16 percent), House contests (16 percent), gubernatorial races (12 percent), local races (8 percent), and referenda (0 percent).

Few editors felt that ad watches had reduced ad frequency, led candidates to withdraw ads, made campaigns less negative, or led candidates to be more careful in what they say. Newspaper editors expressed more support for ad watches than news directors at television stations.

Part of the problem of ad watches concerns their format. Whereas 60 percent of newspapers used ad watches to analyze

Air Wars

TABLE 5-1
Ad Watch Usage: 1996

	Newspapers	TV Stations
Done ad watches		
Yes	65%	44%
No	35	56
Year started		
1988	7%	5%
1990	18	2
1992	23	6
1994	7	6
1995	1	0
1996	2	3
DK/NA	41	77
Elections covered		
Presidential	26%	16%
Senate	51	21
House	47	16
Governor	54	12
Local	36	8
Referenda	1	0
Format used		
Ad visuals	11%	—
Ad text	52	—
Show whole ad	—	6%
Show part of ad	—	23
Candidate picture	1	0
Ad picture	33	0
Analysis of tactics	25	16
Analysis of truthfulness	60	20
Blunt language	12	10
Run analysis more than once	2	—
Use candidate response during segment	—	11
Evaluation		
Reduced ad frequency	0%	0%
Candidate withdrew ad	8	5
Campaign less negative	0	0
Candidate used ad watch in ads	6	1
Readers expressed support for ad watch	29	9
Candidates more careful what they say	—	8
Had no effect	1	0
Plan to continue in 1996		
Yes	53%	26%
No	3	0
DK/NA	44	74
Number of responses	107	154

Source: These data were collected from telephone interviews with newspaper managing editors and local television news directors around the country in January and February 1996. The information was tabulated by Darrell M. West of Brown University and collected by Sam Schreiber of the Committee for the Study of the American Electorate.

Notes: DK/NA indicates "don't know/no answer."

— indicates no data available.

truthfulness, only 20 percent of television stations did. Only one in every ten media sources used blunt language to condemn candidate ads. This shows that some of the failures of ad watches to achieve their potential are due to an unwillingness on the part of newspapers and television stations to use them to their full effect.

The 1996 nominating process saw a decrease in the number of ad watches. The *New York Times* printed eight in the spring, down from fifteen in the 1992 nominating process. The *Washington Post* ran seven ad watches, down from twenty-one in 1992. This decline represents the absence of a competitive Democratic primary and the shortened Republican process after Dole wrapped up a majority by the end of March.

In the 1996 general election, the *New York Times* ran fifteen ad watches, down from twenty-nine in 1992. The *Washington Post* conducted seven ad watches, which was fewer than the twenty-four it had done in 1992.

The ad watches that were conducted in national outlets reviewed a relatively small proportion of the ads actually broadcast by candidates. As would be expected, reporters generally picked ads that were provocative or controversial or that dealt with a central theme of the campaign. For example, *USA Today* media reporter Martha Moore developed one ad watch in the primaries and two in the summer season. Both of the summer ad watches dealt with taxes. She chose those particular ads to review because "taxes were of central importance to both campaigns and was the central issue in the campaign." [23]

Most ads were reviewed just a single time, which contrasts with the dozens of times top ads are aired before the viewing public. Of course, media outlets have more credibility with the American public than do partisan political ads. But there is an imbalance between the frequency of ads broadcast and reviews through ad watches.

Another problem that came up in 1996 was the development of different types of ad watches. Some followed the traditional model of evaluating ad accuracy. In general, based on focus groups conducted at Brown University, voters liked these segments and felt they added a valuable perspective to campaign discourse. However, other ad watches moved into the realm of strategic calculations and evaluated the goals campaigners had in running particular ads. In our focus groups, these segments were not as favorably received by voters. Ordinary citizens viewing these types felt reporters were not adding much substantive information and were focusing too much on "the game."

Our focus groups in 1996 also revealed that ads have added so much visual text on-screen and that so many different candidate, party, and independent group organizations are running spots today that voters have difficulty correctly identifying the sponsor of political ads. In one focus group on the U.S. Senate race in Rhode Island, only 50 percent correctly identified the sponsors of candidate and party ads that we showed them. In another that dealt with the presidential campaign, only 46 percent correctly identified ad sponsors despite just having seen the ad.

On average, the text identifying the sponsor of ads is on the screen for five seconds, which is not long enough for many viewers to identify the ad sponsor. In one case, that of an independent ad on retirement savings accounts broadcast by the American Council of Life Insurance, only 40 percent of our focus group participants correctly identified its sponsor immediately after having seen the ad. Twenty percent believed it was put on by the Clinton campaign, 20 percent did not know who broadcast the ad, and 20 percent erroneously believed it was sponsored by the Cato Institute because that organization had been listed in visual text on-screen at the beginning of the spot as the footnote for a claim made during the commercial.

This demonstrates that in the increasingly multifaceted world of political ads, there needs to be greater attention given to disclosing ad sponsorship. Rather than having the disclosure text be on-screen for just five seconds, the sponsorship should be shown continuously throughout the time of the ad. This would give viewers more time to determine which organization is sponsoring ads and put them in a stronger position to see where the ad message is coming from.

Ad Oversight at Other Levels

Most ad watches in national newspapers focus on presidential campaign commercials. Ads from Senate, House, and gubernatorial elections receive much less scrutiny from the television networks, *New York Times, Washington Post,* and *USA Today.* This is understandable given the viewership and readership of those outlets.

However, in 1996, a number of local television stations became more aggressive in overseeing ads from political parties and interest groups. During the U.S. Senate race in Rhode Island between Democrat Jack Reed and Republican Nancy Mayer, WJAR-TV rejected a Republican National Committee ad attacking Reed as a liberal who opposed welfare reform. The ad claimed, "Jack Reed is so liberal, he opposes making welfare recipients work for their checks. It's outrageous. Jack Reed has voted repeatedly against replacing welfare with workfare."

WJAR-TV reviewed Reed's voting record and concluded that the ad did not accurately represent his votes. Reed had voted against the Republican welfare reform bill but had voted in favor of a moderate Democratic bill. By national law, campaign ads by candidates cannot be rejected by broadcasters, even if they contain false or misleading claims. But television outlets can reject ads from political parties or interest groups on grounds of accuracy and fairness.

In 1996, this was not an isolated example. Twenty-four stations refused to air AFL-CIO ads condemning Republican House members for cutting Medicare on grounds that the votes were for slowing the rate of increased spending on Medicare rather than actual spending reductions. Boston radio station WRKO rejected an AFL-CIO spot critical of Republican representatives Peter Torkildsen and Peter Blute.[24]

A Brown University focus group in the Rhode Island U.S. Senate race found that ad watches were more positively reviewed than ads themselves. Of the ads shown to study participants, the spot having the highest believability was Reed's biography ad in which he discussed his family background and concern for education. Sixty-two percent found it very believable. This compares to 25 percent for a Mayer ad saying she was a fiscal watchdog, 12 percent for a Reed response ad questioning why Republicans have spent $1 million in ads attacking him, 12 percent for a Republican Senatorial Campaign Committee ad comparing Reed and Mayer on fiscal matters, 12 percent on a Reed spot decrying Republican cuts in student loans and Medicare, and 0 percent for a Republican National Committee ad attacking "liberal Jack Reed."

In contrast, voters felt that the ad watch broadcast by WJAR-TV was very believable (62 percent), very persuasive (50 percent), and very fair (62 percent). In general, voters found the ad watch was balanced between the two candidates and helped them understand what was happening in the U.S. Senate campaign. It shows that ad watches at the local level can be effective when done well.

The Impact of Ad Watches

Ad watches have had a substantial impact on the electoral process. First, ad critiques have made it more difficult for candidates to target specific spots on local audiences. For example, Buchanan's effort in his 1992 "Freedom Abused" spot to deliver a message about lifestyle values to conservative Republican voters in Georgia backfired when newspapers and television stations from around the country ran stories about it. Ad watches make it riskier to broadcast commercials in different parts of the country that cater to local interests.[25]

Second, candidates have more incentives to be careful in their ad claims. According to Moore of *USA Today*, "ad watches have affected the amount of time campaigns spend on documentation of the ad. Each side churns out a lot of documentation and provides criticism of ads by the opposing candidate." Media consultant Robert Shrum agreed with this, saying that ad watches "put pressure on people to be more honest. They create a more skeptical public so there is more pressure to source what you say."[26]

Finally, ad watches have affected the way ads are presented by consultants. According to Shrum,

They have restored the role of the print press in an odd way. They are used by campaigns to characterize the other side's ads. You take what the *New York Times* says about an ad and you put it in your ad saying the *New York Times* says this ad was misleading. That gives you a third-person authority.[27]

At the same time, the disparity in how news outlets covered advertisements suggests a need for further refinement of the ad watch concept. Liasson of National Public Radio notes that "the media is an organism without a head. There are no standard rules on coverage and there is no punishment if [the coverage] is not good."[28]

The visibility of ad watches falls well short of candidate advertisements. As shown in Table 5-2, only 55 percent of Americans said they saw presidential ad watches, compared to the 80 percent who said they saw Clinton's or Dole's ads. At the congressional level, only 47 percent said they saw ad watches for congressional

TABLE 5-2
View of Information Sources: 1996

	Saw	Thought Helpful If Seen
Presidential candidate ads	80%	35%
National TV news	78	—
Campaign commentators	64	60
National party ads	56	45
Presidential ad watches	55	58
Interest group ads	52	48
Free TV time	50	55
Congresional ad watches	47	59

Sources: Brown University national survey, October 28–November 3, 1996.

Notes: Entries indicate the percentage of Americans who saw and thought helpful each information source. The percentage for seeing presidential candidate advertisements was the average for Clinton and Dole. The numbers on helpfulness were the percentage saying each information source was very or somewhat helpful based on those who said they saw each source. The percentage for believing candidate advertisements were helpful was the average for Clinton and Dole.

— indicates the question was not asked.

races. Ad watch viewership also was well below the 78 percent who claimed they saw the national television news and was comparable to the 50 percent who saw candidates during free television time provided by the networks. Fifty-two percent report having seen interest groups' ads and 56 percent said they saw national party ads in the last week of the 1996 campaign.

But more people were likely to rate presidential ad watches as helpful than candidate ads themselves. Of all the information sources, campaign commentators were seen as most helpful (60 percent), followed by congressional ad watches (59 percent), presidential ad watches (58 percent), free television time (55 percent), interest group ads (48 percent), national party ads (45 percent), and presidential candidate ads (35 percent). This suggests that with proper refinement of the technique, ad watches are a helpful part of the information mix in campaigns.

Chapter 6

Learning about the Candidates

Early efforts to study the impact of ads emphasized learning about substantive matters. Do the media provide information that increases voters' knowledge of where candidates stand on the issues? To the pleasant surprise of scholars, research from the 1970s revealed that voters who watched ads—as opposed to network news—were remarkably better informed about the policy views of presidential aspirants.[1] Experimental work also supported claims about the educational virtues of commercials.[2] Ads did not help candidates create new political images based on personality. Instead, political commercials allowed viewers to learn about the issues.

The undeniable trend of these studies notwithstanding, researchers have persisted in their efforts to examine the effects of advertising. Great changes have taken place in the structure of political campaigns since earlier research was completed. New electoral arenas have arisen that do not have the stabilizing features of past settings. Furthermore, recent campaign experiences run contrary to interpretations that emphasize the educational virtues of commercials. Television is thought to have played a crucial, and not very positive, role in a number of races, a state of affairs that has renewed concern about the power of ads to alter citizens' beliefs.[3]

Indeed, recent studies have found that voters do not cast ballots based on the issues very often, and their evaluations of candidates' qualities and views about electoral prospects are often decisive. Citizens form many impressions during the course of election campaigns, from views about candidates' issue positions and personal characteristics to feelings about the electoral prospects of specific candidates. As ads have become more gripping emotionally, affective models—which describe feelings—are crucial to evaluations of candidates' fortunes.[4]

Favorability is an example of an affective dimension that is important to vote choice. There is a well-documented relationship between voters' likes and candidate preferences. Citizens often support the candidates they like and oppose those they dislike. If all are disliked, they vote for the one they dislike the least. Anything that raises a candidate's favorability also increases his or her likelihood of being selected.[5] Candidates devote great attention to presenting themselves in ways that make them appear more likable. For example, it is a common strategy in political campaigns to appeal to basic community and family values. Values that are widely shared, such as patriotism and pride in national accomplishments, help candidates increase their favorability ratings among voters. Conversely, hard-hitting ads are used to pinpoint flaws of the opposition.

The opening up of the electoral process has brought new factors such as electability and familiarity to the forefront. *Electability* refers to citizens' perceptions of a candidate's prospects for winning the November election. Because many citizens do not want to waste their vote on a hopeless choice, impressions of electability can increase voters' support of a candidate; people like to support the winner. Familiarity is important as a threshold requirement. Candidates must become known in order to do well at election time. In earlier epochs, most campaigners were nationally known. But today's candidates may not be well known, and they have to use ads to raise their name recognition. The development of a campaign structure that encourages less widely known candidates to run makes citizens' assessments of a candidate's prospects potentially a very important area of inquiry.

Advertising and Electoral Context

Past work on television advertising has focused on a particular kind of electoral setting—presidential general elections. For example, Patterson and McClure's findings were based on the campaign that ended in Nixon's 1972 landslide victory over McGovern. The apparent absence of effects of ads on voters' assessments of the personal qualities of candidates in the two-and-a-half-month span of that campaign is not surprising in light of the lopsided race and the fact that by the time of the initial sur-

vey in September, public perceptions of the two candidates had
largely been determined. In that situation, it was appropriate for
Patterson and McClure to conclude that people "know too
much" to be influenced by ads.[6]

However, as Patterson and McClure themselves have pointed
out, other electoral settings display greater opportunities for
advertising to have measurable effects. Nominating affairs and
Senate races show extensive shifts in voters' assessments of the
candidates. Presidential nominations often have unfamiliar contenders vying for the votes of citizens who hold few prior beliefs
about the candidates. In these settings, television commercials can
play a major role in providing crucial information about the candidates.

Advertising is particularly important when news media time is
scarce. Ken Bode, then a reporter for NBC, recounted a letter written to him by Senator Dole following the 1980 nominating campaign: "Dear Ken, I would appreciate knowing how much coverage my campaign received by NBC from the date of my announcement to my final withdrawal. I've been told my total coverage by
NBC amounted to fourteen seconds."[7]

Senate races also have become heavily media oriented. Candidates spend a lot of money on television advertising, and Senate
contests have taken on the roller-coaster qualities of nominating
affairs. Many Senate elections feature volatile races involving
unknown challengers. Because some observers have speculated
about the effects of advertising, it is important to study advertising
in nominating and Senate campaigns to determine whether the
impact of advertising varies with the electoral setting.

Citizens' Knowledge and Evaluations of Candidates

Elections in recent decades represent an interesting opportunity
to study the impact of political commercials. Structural changes
have allowed individuals who are not very well known nationally
(such as McGovern in 1972, Carter in 1976, Hart in 1984,
Dukakis in 1988, and Clinton and Perot in 1992) to run for president and do surprisingly well. Other changes include a growing
independence of voters, rising skepticism about the Washington
establishment, and increasing prominence of the media in campaign affairs. Again we face questions about the role of ads in
changing citizens' impressions of candidates.

TABLE 6-1
Citizen Evaluation of the Candidates: October 1996

Appeal	Clinton	Dole	Perot
Recognition	84	75	68
Likability	51	25	18
Electability	83	10	2
Leadership	57	41	—
Honesty	41	50	—
Caring	52	24	12
Protect Medicare	48	24	8
Bring fiscal discipline	30	29	22
Protect environment	52	17	5

Source: Brown University national survey, October 28–November 3, 1996.

Notes: N = 724. Entries represent the percentage of respondents recognizing the candidate, evaluating him favorably, seeing him as most electable, and feeling that he has the indicated personal qualities and policy views.

—indicates question not asked.

Opinion surveys provide one way of determining how the public felt about the candidates. Information is available on a number of different contests at various levels from 1972 through 1996: Senate contests for 1974, 1990, and 1992; presidential nominating races for 1976, 1988, 1992, and 1996; and presidential general elections for 1972, 1976, 1984, 1988, 1992, and 1996. These surveys give a sense of the public's recognition of the candidates, views about favorability, and impressions of each candidate's electability. By comparing elections over a period of years and at several levels, one can see how ad effects change in different contexts.

In looking at these surveys, there were wide variations in citizens' assessments of the candidates, depending on electoral setting. Presidential general election candidates were the best well-known, with a range of recognition levels from a low in 1992 for Clinton (73 percent) and Perot (67 percent) to a high for Ford (95 percent) in 1976. The average recognition level in presidential general elections was significantly higher than for nominating candidates or Senate contenders. In 1996, Dole started the nominating process with a relatively low recognition of 46 percent, but this rose to 73 percent by mid-March. By October 1996, 75 percent recognized Dole, 68 percent recognized Perot, and 84 percent recognized Clinton (see Table 6-1).

There have been extensive variations in citizens' perceptions of candidates' likability and electability. Of recent nominees, Reagan has been the best liked (66 percent in 1984) and Bush (23 percent in 1992), Dole (25 percent in 1996), and Perot (18 percent in 1996) the least liked. In regard to electability during the fall, McGovern in 1972 was the candidate who was seen as least electable (1 percent), whereas Bush in 1988 was seen as the most electable (85 percent). Eighty-three percent believed Clinton was the most electable in the fall of 1996, compared to 10 percent who named Dole and 2 percent who cited Perot.

Voters furthermore have a sense of the policy issues and personal traits associated with each candidate. Foreign policy considerations were prominent in 1972 for McGovern and Nixon because of the Vietnam War, whereas domestic matters dominated thereafter. In terms of personal traits, this period began with candidates' experience being the most cited and ended with leadership being the most cited.

In 1996, Clinton was seen as having stronger leadership skills (57 percent) than Dole (41 percent) and being more caring (52 percent for Clinton, 24 percent for Dole, and 12 percent for Perot). But Dole was seen as more honest (50 percent) compared to Clinton (41 percent). In terms of the issues, Clinton held a big advantage over Dole and Perot in protecting Medicare. Forty-eight percent believed he would protect Medicare, compared to 24 percent who thought Dole would and 8 percent who felt Perot would. More people (52 percent) believed Clinton would protect the environment than Dole (17 percent) or Perot (5 percent). The numbers were more evenly split on the crucial subject of who would bring fiscal discipline to the federal government. Thirty percent believed Clinton would, whereas 29 percent named Dole and 22 percent named Perot.

Of course, it remains to be seen how political commercials influenced perceptions of recognition, likability, and electability. I looked at statistical tests showing the significance of percentage differences in citizens' knowledge and evaluation of candidates between the low and high ends of ad exposure scales. These measures were used to compare those with high and low ad exposure on their impressions of the candidates. Ads cannot be proved to be the cause of the association, but at least we can identify relationships that warrant additional analysis. For example, if 70 percent of the least attentive television watchers recognized Clinton, whereas 85 percent of the most attentive did, the recognition difference would be +15 percentage points. In general, Senate races showed the strongest advertising effects, with exposure to campaign ads associated with high recognition of political contenders. The average difference in recognition between respondents who scored high on ad viewing and those who scored low was 27 percentage points.[8] Senate campaigners typically are not as well known as presidential contenders, which means that political commercials can be more influential in raising the visibility levels of those who run for senator.

Presidential elections showed a lower, albeit still significant, association for recognition based on advertising exposure. The largest general election difference in recognition came during the 1988 Bush-Dukakis race. These men were among the least known of the recent party nominees. Dukakis was not known nationally; and, despite having been vice president for eight years, Bush was not particularly visible in that office.

In the nominating process, the magnitude of the difference varied according to how well known the individuals were. Candidates who were not well known used advertising to advance their name recognition. For example, in April 1976, polls from the Pennsylvania primary revealed that Carter had a difference of 21 points and Morris Udall a difference of 48 points between the high and low ends of their ad exposure scales. Dukakis and Senator Gore (D-Tenn.) also showed substantial differences in 1988—18 and 21 percentage points, respectively. In 1992 Buchanan had the greatest rating differential for visibility, whereas in 1996, Forbes had the highest difference (15 percentage points) in recognition between those seeing and not seeing his ads.

Ads also had effects on citizens' perceptions of favorability; the strongest were for Senate and nominating races.[9] In both the 1974 and the 1990 Senate campaigns, ad viewing produced favorability gains for Democratic and Republican candidates. The effects were not as consistent in the nominating process, but there were strong differences for Gore and Bush in 1988. Both ran aggressive advertising campaigns, and their strategies appear to have paid off. Gore, for example, emphasized a populist image designed to win the support of white southerners. Bush ran a hard-hitting campaign designed to persuade voters that he was the logical heir to the Reagan legacy. It is interesting to note that Dukakis's ads were not associated with changes in favorability ratings. The Massachusetts governor had difficulties during the fall in overcoming public impressions that he was cool and aloof.

In 1992 Buchanan displayed the highest improvement in favorability (12 percentage points) between the low and high ends of his ad exposure scale. He ran the spring's most prominent ad, "Read Our Lips." This commercial painted a negative picture of Bush and questioned the president's character for breaking his promise of no new taxes. The ad featured a catchy narrative related to betrayal of the common person. Eventually, according to Bush adviser Richard Teeter, the president was able to beat back the Buchanan challenge through attack ads that told voters "[Our] guy's the goddam president and the other guy's a goddam typewriter pusher, and the toughest thing he's had to do in his whole life is change the ribbon on his goddam Olivetti." [10]

Senator Tsongas (D-Mass.) suffered the ignominy of a negative relationship in 1992, as frequent viewers of his ads were *less* favorable by 16 percentage points toward him than those people who did not see his commercials, a difference that was statistically significant. Tsongas clearly had difficulty using the paid media to his advantage after his surprise New Hampshire victory. Clinton showed a difference score of +13 percentage points in the October 1992 phase of the general election campaign, whereas Perot had a difference of +15 points.

In 1996, none of the Republican candidates showed a statistically significant difference during the nominating process in favorability based on ad exposure. Even Buchanan, who had done well in boosting his favorability through ads in 1992, was not able to duplicate this feat. People who saw his 1996 ads were 3 percentage points more likely to view him favorably, but the difference was not significant. Dole showed a 3-percentage-point loss in favorability based on ad viewing during the Republican primaries. Forbes had a 5-percentage-point gain in favorability.

In terms of electability, ads were associated with significant effects for Nixon in fall 1972, Carter in spring and fall 1976, Dukakis and Bush in spring 1988, Buchanan and Clinton in spring and fall 1992, respectively, and Clinton in 1996.[11] Seeing ads for these candidates was related to believing that the candidate was politically strong. Dukakis's ads created the impression of electoral strength. Despite the fact that his commercials did not make voters feel any more favorable toward him, they helped generate a sense of inevitability about his campaign. Of the races examined in this study, Bush in 1992 was the only one whose ad exposure actually hurt the perception of electability. Frequent ad viewers were 11 percentage points less likely to see him as electable than infrequent viewers were. The difference was statistically significant. None of the Republican candidates in 1996 had significant gains in electability based on ad exposure.

One of the most persistent criticisms of campaign advertising has been that advertising can manipulate citizens' views about candidates. If one looks at the most prominent issues and personal traits, 1972 stands out. For 1972 the results of the presidential race conform to the findings of Patterson and McClure that the effects of advertising on citizens' perceptions of issues were substantially larger than the influence on assessments of personal traits.[12] Recall that 1972 was the election they studied. However, other races show different patterns. For example, in 1976 Carter ran an image-based campaign that produced stronger advertising effects for evaluations of personal traits than of issue positions.[13] In the 1988 nominating process, Dukakis, Gore, and Bush had ads with strong effects on both assessments of issues and traits.[14]

Clinton was able to use his 1992 and 1996 campaign commercials to help viewers see him as caring and capable of handling the economy. He used ads in 1992 to tell the story of a family having problems in affording quality health care. Visuals in these commercials allowed him to convey his positive, caring side. His fall ads helped project an image of hopefulness and being able to improve the economy, which was important to voters discouraged by the dismal economy. His campaign slogan in 1992 emphasized that the contest was a "race of hope against fear," and ads were run noting Clinton's origins in a town called Hope, Arkansas.[15] In 1996, Clinton talked incessantly about "A Bridge to the Twenty-First Century," and ran ads contrasting his youthful vigor with Dole's aging presence.

It is interesting to note that Bush was the only major candidate in 1992 who was unable to boost impressions of himself either on his positions on issues or on his character.[16] This was true for both the nominating and the general election campaigns. Part of the problem obviously was structural in nature. When domestic problems prove intractable, it is nearly impossible for incumbents to improve their political image through advertising. But Bush also had serious problems developing ads that could resonate with voters and attract favorable media coverage. For these reasons, he was unable to repeat his successful 1988 experience in 1992.

The Importance of Prior Beliefs

The analysis to this point has suggested a tie between advertising and voters' assessments of candidates. It is likely, of course, that other factors influence this relationship in meaningful ways. Advertisements are merely one part of the cacophony of information heard by voters during election campaigns. Various sources of citizens' impressions must be examined to determine whether ads have any independent effect. For example, partisanship and ideology are often important to how people respond to ads. Citizens bring different values and beliefs to the political arena, and they are likely to see the same event in very different ways. Selective exposure may influence the results based on the differential impact of educational attainment, race, age, and gender. Finally, interest in politics and exposure to the media in general may make a difference, because impressions can be altered in ways that are independent of campaign ads.

Regression models are widely used in the social sciences to determine the impact of particular factors on citizens' impressions, controlling for other influences. Using models that produce estimates of the magnitude and direction of relationships, one can evaluate the independent effect of commercials on voters' assessments. These models have the virtue of incorporating a significance test, which ensures that the particular results obtained do not arise purely by chance.[17]

Even after the controls were incorporated, ad viewing still had a major impact on citizens' impressions. Those who saw Nixon ads in 1972 were more likely to see him as wishing to uphold commitments made to other nations. The same phenomenon emerged in the 1988 nominating process. During that year, exposure to ads influenced people's perceptions of the issue positions of Dukakis (on the military), Gore (on unfair competition from Japan), and Bush (on deficit reduction). The 1992 race helped viewers understand Buchanan on the economy, Clinton on the economy, and Tsongas on competition from Japan. Each candidate ran ads that made these subjects a central part of his campaign. Buchanan's ads from New Hampshire criticized Bush for insensitivity on the economy, Clinton emphasized the need for a middle-class tax cut, and Tsongas called for reinvigorated efforts against Japan's trade practices.

Clinton's 1992 nominating strategy was marked by a tendency to run ads filled with lists of matters of concern to him. His sixty-second ad "The Plan" illustrates this approach. According to Elizabeth Kolbert of the *New York Times,* as soon as this ad started airing in New Hampshire, Clinton strategists found their candidate jumped 13 percentage points in tracking polls. The commercial was "designed to counter the Tsongas plan. It provided a sense of specificity for Clinton," said Kolbert.[18] It furthermore had the long-term effect of staking out claims to particular issues, in order to prevent Republicans from trespassing on traditionally Democratic issues, as Bush had done in 1988 when he campaigned on promises to become the environmental and education president. But his strategy also created problems for Clinton. One of the criticisms directed against him in spring focus groups was that he was difficult to pin down: "If you asked his favorite color he'd say 'Plaid,'" stated one focus group participant.[19]

However, the effects of ads were not simply that citizens learned about policy matters. If that were the case, critics would have much less ammunition against political commercials. Instead, ads also had an impact on assessments of candidates' images, likability, and electability that was at least as strong as the effect on assessments of issue positions. In terms of perceptions of likability, seeing commercials had a significant impact in many elections. For Gore and Bush, ad exposure was related to favorability ratings during the 1988 nominating process, and the same was true for Buchanan and Perot in 1992 and for Senate candidates in 1974 and 1990.

Political commercials furthermore had an impact on perceptions of electability. The strongest impact came with Dukakis in the 1988 nominating process, but effects were present for Nixon in 1972, Carter in 1976, Buchanan and Clinton in 1992, and Clinton in 1996. Conversely, people who saw Bush's ads in 1992 had a negative sense of the president's electability.

In addition, campaigners were able to mold public perceptions of personal traits. Those who watched Carter ads saw him as an able leader, and those who saw Gore ads felt he was likely to care about people. Those who watched Clinton ads in spring 1992 believed that he was a caring individual. The ads helped create a positive view of his character, which counterbalanced the negative coverage received after Gennifer Flowers came forward to claim he had an affair with her.

Tsongas was hurt in spring 1992 because his advertisements did not help him create a more positive image. Several members of a focus group study conducted on the nominating contest mentioned Tsongas's low-key personality and unkempt appearance. One described him as having "the charisma of a bull dog." Another said, "He looks like an unmade bed. He looks like he got out of bed in the morning, threw on the first thing that he picked up off the floor, like my son does sometimes, and combed his hair with a piece of toast." [20]

In the 1996 presidential general election, I developed a model looking at the tie between believing Clinton was electable and seeing the national television news and ads for Clinton, Dole, and Perot. Those who said they saw Clinton's ads were much more likely to cite him as electable, whereas those who saw Dole's ads were significantly more likely to say he was not electable (see Table 6-2). There was no impact on electability from seeing Perot's ads or the TV news.

These results are interesting because they demonstrate how successful Clinton was in producing a sense of inevitability about his campaign. Through presidential-looking visuals and graphics proclaiming Dole was "Wrong in the Past, Wrong for the Future," the president's ads carefully cultivated an image of electability.

The weak results for Perot's ads contrast clearly with the situation in 1992. In that year, Perot's ads were the most memorable and provided a dramatic boost for the Texan in the closing weeks of the campaign. In contrast, people in 1996 who said they saw Perot's ads were not more likely to recognize him, like him, or feel that he was electable.[21]

Part of the problem related to Perot's ad-buy strategy. Unlike 1992, when he dumped $60 million in ads during the last month of the election and dramatically outspent both Clinton and Bush, he was not able to do this in 1996. Because he received the Reform Party nomination in late August and needed to spend early in an unsuccessful attempt to achieve high enough poll standing to be included in the presidential debates, he spread his $29 million in overall campaign spending out over an eight-week period. He saved money for major ad buys in the last two weeks, but it did not produce the same improvements in favorability that had been seen in 1992.

TABLE 6-2
TV News and Ad Coefficients with Citizens' Perceptions of Candidates: 1996

	TV News	Clinton Ads	Dole Ads	Perot Ads	N
Clinton recognition	.28 (.14)[1]	−.20 (.20)	.30 (.21)	.01 (.16)	520
Dole recognition	.19 (.12)	.24 (.16)	−.19 (.18)	.09 (.14)	517
Perot recognition	−.03 (.11)	.37 (.14)[2]	−.12 (.16)	−.05 (.12)	518
Clinton likability	.02 (.04)	−.04 (.05)	.10 (.05)[1]	−.05 (.04)	480
Dole likability	.02 (.04)	.05 (.05)	−.07 (.05)	.02 (.04)	471
Perot likability	.08 (.04)[1]	−.07 (.05)	.01 (.06)	−.03 (.04)	460
Clinton electability	−.05 (.16)	.35 (.20)[1]	−.48 (.23)[1]	.13 (.16)	509
Dole electability	.01 (.17)	−.51 (.21)	.54 (.24)[2]	.08 (.18)	509
Perot electability	.23 (.66)	1.76 (.90)[1]	−.26 (.81)	−1.65 (.76)[1]	509

Source: Brown University national survey, October 28–November 3, 1996.

Note: Entries are logistic regression coefficients for TV news and ad exposure to each candidate, with standard errors in parentheses. A positive coefficient means that seeing the TV news and each candidate's ads was associated with recognizing, liking, and thinking the specified candidate was electable. Coefficients marked with superscripts were statistically significant. Effects of control variables (party identification, education, age, gender, race, ideology, and political interest) are not shown. The coefficients for likability are based on ordinary least squares regression.

[1] $p < .05$ [2] $p < .01$

In addition, Perot's 1996 ads simply were not as memorable as in 1992. Perot's ads in his first race were vivid because of their scrolling text up the screen, his novel infomercials, and their targeting on an important issue—the legacy of national debt being left to our children—that other politicians were ignoring. His 1996 ads were not visually appealing, were no longer novel, and in them he had difficulty pinpointing a substantive rationale for his candidacy. Most of his September ads, for example, whined about his exclusion from the presidential debates (see "Where's Ross?" ad text in the Appendix).

There also were interesting relationships between seeing TV news and candidate ads and how candidates' personal qualities and political views were seen. As Table 6-3 shows, those who saw Clinton's commercials were more likely to be negative on Dole's leadership and less likely to believe that Dole was honest. Individuals seeing Dole's ads thought he was honest and that Dole would bring fiscal discipline to the federal government and that Perot

TABLE 6-3
TV News and Ad Coefficients with Citizens' Perceptions of Candidates' Personal Qualities and Political Views: 1996

	TV News	Clinton Ads	Dole Ads	Perot Ads	N
Clinton leadership	-.04 (.03)	-.04 (.04)	.02 (.05)	-.02 (.04)	488
Dole leadership	.06 (.03)[1]	-.12 (.05)[2]	.07 (.05)	.01 (.04)	448
Clinton honesty	-.01 (.04)	-.01 (.05)	.03 (.05)	-.07 (.04)[1]	455
Dole honesty	.06 (.04)	-.11 (.05)[1]	.09 (.05)[1]	.02 (.04)	425
Clinton caring	-.06 (.14)	-.13 (.19)	.17 (.20)	-.06 (.15)	480
Dole caring	-.09 (.15)	-.05 (.20)	.04 (.21)	-.12 (.17)	480
Perot caring	.26 (.17)[1]	.19 (.21)	-.24 (.21)	.16 (.16)	480
Clinton to protect Medicare	.31 (.14)[2]	-.25 (.17)	.16 (.19)	-.14 (.14)	431
Dole to protect Medicare	-.09 (.16)	.17 (.19)	.02 (.20)	.01 (.15)	431
Perot to protect Medicare	-.33 (.18)[1]	.24 (.24)	-.41 (.25)[1]	.26 (.19)	431
Clinton has fiscal discipline	.13 (.14)	-.23 (.18)	.16 (.20)	-.35 (.14)[2]	441
Dole has fiscal discipline	-.06 (.14)	-.18 (.18)	.31 (.19)[1]	-.03 (.14)	441
Perot has fiscal discipline	-.04 (.13)	.44 (.19)[2]	-.46 (.20)[2]	.33 (.14)[2]	441
Clinton will protect environment	.10 (.15)	.11 (.19)	-.11 (.20)	-.28 (.15)[1]	410
Dole will protect environment	-.02 (.17)	-.29 (.20)	.29 (.22)	.29 (.17)[1]	410
Perot will protect environment	-.14 (.23)	.37 (.31)	-.36 (.30)	.09 (.25)	410

Source: Brown University national survey, October 28–November 3, 1996.

Note: Entries are logistic regression coefficients for TV news and ad exposure to each candidate, with standard errors in parentheses. A positive coefficient means that seeing each candidate's ads was associated with believing the specified candidate had the particular personal quality or political view. Coefficients marked with superscripts were statistically significant. Effects of control variables (party identification, education, age, gender, race, ideology, and political interest) are not shown. The coefficients for leadership and honesty are based on ordinary least squares regression.

[1] $p < .05$ [2] $p < .01$

would not. Those who saw Perot's ads were more likely to think Clinton was not honest, would not bring fiscal discipline to the federal government, and would not protect the environment. They also were more likely to believe Perot would bring discipline to the federal government.[22]

Electability and the Vote

Advertising is important for voters' assessments of electability, but it has not yet been shown to have electoral consequences.[23] Recent nominating campaigns offer interesting opportunities to investigate the vote as well as strategic interactions among the candidates. The 1988 Democratic nominating process was a wide-open, seven-candidate affair with no well-known front-runner until Dukakis began to forge ahead at the time of the March Super Tuesday primaries. The 1992 Republican process, in contrast, featured a two-person race between President Bush and challenger Buchanan. (The third candidate, David Duke, was not a serious factor.) The 1996 Republican nominating process was a multicandidate field with Dole being the clear front-runner in terms of money, endorsements, and organization.

At the time of the 1988 Super Tuesday contests, a number of candidates were running hard-hitting ads challenging the substantive positions and personal qualifications of their opponents. For example, Gephardt's ads in Iowa and South Dakota criticized Dukakis for claiming naively that farmers could reverse their financial problems by planting Belgian endive. Dukakis's ads later accused Gephardt of flip-flops on policy matters.[24] Gore and Jesse Jackson also ran strong campaigns in key southern states.

The victories by Dukakis on Super Tuesday were vital to the inevitability that began to surround his candidacy. Prior to this time, Dukakis had put together a strong organization and had been very successful in terms of fund raising. But it was the support expressed at the time of Super Tuesday that began to propel him toward the nomination. As summarized by Jack Germond and Jules Witcover right after Super Tuesday, "Dukakis was now clearly the front-runner, in terms of both the number of delegates he had captured and the strength demonstrated in winning not only in the Northeast but also in the Far West and South."[25]

But how did this sense of momentum develop? A two-stage path analysis of the Dukakis vote during the critical period of the 1988

Super Tuesday primaries deals with the possibility of reciprocal relations between voters' preferences in candidates and views regarding electability.[26] Electability clearly was quite decisive for the Dukakis vote. The more he was seen as being electable, the more likely voters were to support him.

Other factors—race, gender, and party identification—were also directly linked to support for Dukakis. Race was important, owing to the presence of an African American candidate (Jackson) in the contest. There was a clear polarization of voters, with Jackson receiving the vast majority of the black vote and Dukakis and Gore dividing the white vote. Gender and party identifications had a strong effect on support for Dukakis, with women and strong Democrats being most likely to vote for him.[27]

Dukakis's advertising had indirect consequences for the vote through views regarding electability. The strongest predictor of electability in this model was exposure to spot commercials. Ads shown prior to Super Tuesday, more than race, gender, or partisanship, influenced voters to see the Massachusetts governor as the most electable Democrat.[28]

These results hold up when strategic considerations are incorporated into the model. Voters do not make decisions about candidates in isolation. They see ads for all the major contestants and form impressions based on the campaigns' strategic interactions. The major competition for Dukakis among white voters on Super Tuesday was Gore. As a senator from Tennessee, Gore had a home-region advantage in southern states. Other than Jackson, whose base was black voters, Gore was the major obstacle to Dukakis's nomination drive at the time of Super Tuesday.

When the ads of competing candidates are included in the model, the results correspond to those just reported. Seeing ads for the Massachusetts governor was positively correlated with feeling Dukakis was the most electable Democrat. Electability also had a clear impact on the vote.[29] Spot commercials thus were important even when strategic interactions were factored into the model.

In the 1992 Republican primaries, advertising played a different role. At the start of the race, President Bush was on the defensive over his handling of the economy and his inattention to domestic politics in general. Buchanan ran a series of ads castigating Bush for breaking his famous "no new taxes" pledge. In part because of saturation coverage of the New Hampshire and Massachusetts markets, these commercials achieved a remarkably high level of visibility. Tom Rosenstiel, a news reporter for the *Los Angeles Times* who covered the media, noted that "little kids all over New Hampshire were running around schoolyards chanting, 'Read our lips, No new taxes.'"[30]

A March survey of the Boston metropolitan area asked viewers which ad run by a Republican presidential candidate had made the biggest impression. Of the 590 people interviewed, ninety-two (about 16 percent of the entire sample) were able to name a specific ad. The most frequently named commercial by far was Buchanan's "Read Our Lips" spot, which was cited by sixty-four people, followed by Buchanan's "Freedom Abused" spot against the NEA, which was named by eleven people. Overall, eighty-five viewers cited specific ads for Buchanan, compared with six for Bush and one for Duke.

The situation for Democrats was different: Eighty-six people (14 percent) named specific ads, but the ads mentioned were spread among the candidates: Bob Kerrey ($N = 29$), Tsongas ($N = 25$), Tom Harkin ($N = 23$), Clinton ($N = 6$), and Jerry Brown ($N = 2$). The most frequently cited ads were Kerrey's hockey rink ad about foreign imports ($N = 20$), Tsongas's bio spot showing him swimming ($N = 17$), and Harkin's empty mill ad complaining about high unemployment ($N = 10$).

Not only were Bush's commercials unmemorable, they also had a negative impact on views about the president. Rosenstiel said the president's ads about the need for change "weren't connected to reality. People smelled that. They knew he wasn't the candidate of drastic change." In contrast, Buchanan's advertisements "weren't bull. They were real. Bush had broken campaign promises." When people were exposed to ads from both candidates in a path model, they were less likely to see the president as electable and also less likely to vote for Bush.[31] These results are surprising not only because they are negative but because they contrast so clearly with Bush's 1988 ad performance. In that election, Bush's commercials dominated those of Dukakis.

Part of the problem was that Bush's 1992 spots simply were not as catchy as Buchanan's. The challenger's ads, according to Rosenstiel, had a "crude simplicity that suggested someone who was not slick, someone who was an outsider type of candidate." Rosenstiel felt that Bush's commercials started out effectively but lost their punch close to the New Hampshire primary, just when people started paying attention to the race.

Bush's advertising did not successfully use visual symbols and narrative to develop his connection with salient issues. In one ad, for example, he referred to the Persian Gulf War and also attacked Congress to show how strong he was. According to Robin Roberts, Bush's ad tracker, this spot was the most frequently run in the nominating process.[32] But the main issue of concern to voters—getting the economy going again and helping the unemployed with new jobs—did not relate to this appeal.

The president suffered because media coverage of his 1992 nominating campaign was quite negative. Reporters in New Hampshire questioned Bush's campaigning ability, concern about human suffering, and disjointed speaking style (which also was mimicked by comedian Dana Carvey). This pattern of coverage undermined the president's message and made it difficult for him to impress people who saw his ads. Although he ultimately was able to win his party's nomination, Bush's spring commercials did not lay a strong foundation for the fall campaign.

In the 1996 Republican primaries, Dole's early lead produced a political situation in which other candidates, such as Forbes, went on the attack in an effort to undermine the front-runner's support. A late January and early February 1996 national survey conducted at Brown University before the Iowa caucuses found that Forbes's ads achieved a high level of visibility. Whereas 51 percent indicated they had seen ads for Dole, 40 percent said they had seen Forbes's ads, 24 percent indicated they had seen ads for Buchanan, 20 percent had viewed Gramm's ads, and 10 percent had seen ads for Alexander.

Of the 927 individuals interviewed in this survey, 24 percent were able to cite a commercial that had made a big impression on them (higher than the 16 percent in 1992). Among the top individual ads mentioned were Forbes's flat tax ad (eighteen mentions), Democratic National Committee ads for Clinton against Republican cuts in Congress (ten mentions), Forbes's ad on Dole raising taxes (six mentions), Dole on Forbes's untested leadership (two mentions), Alexander on working for the people (two mentions), Dole on balancing the budget (one mention), Dole's biography ad on his war injuries (one mention), and Buchanan's anti-NAFTA ad (one mention). Overall, seventy-seven individuals cited Forbes's ads, sixty-three cited Dole's, forty cited Democratic National Committee ads for Clinton, eighteen cited Gramm's, nine cited Alexander's, and eight cited Buchanan's. Spots for Buchanan clearly were less memorable than in 1992, where his ads were the most frequently cited for having made a big impression.

But as the primary process wore on, Buchanan's spots rose in memorability. Buchanan's ads targeted clear and emotionally provocative topics such as his views on the evils of NAFTA and the danger of immigration. Much like he had done in 1992, Buchanan was able to develop vivid ads on graphic issues. Viewers began to cite his ads more frequently and those of Forbes less frequently. For example, a survey with 311 Rhode Island voters after the Iowa caucuses, New Hampshire primary, and the New England Yankee primaries found that thirty-two people mentioned ads for Dole, twenty mentioned ads for Buchanan, fifteen mentioned ads for Forbes, eight mentioned ads for Alexander, and four mentioned ads by the Democratic National Committee for Clinton.

Dole's ads achieved a high degree of visibility but were not especially memorable to viewers. People remembered seeing the ads but could recall few of their specific details. When asked which specific ad had made the biggest impression on them, the top ads named were Forbes's ad on flat tax (seven mentions), Buchanan's ad on protecting jobs for American workers (two mentions), Alexander's ad showing him in one of his flannel shirts (two mentions), and Alexander's ad proclaiming him having fresh ideas (two mentions). No Dole ad got more than a single mention.

But Dole's advertising situation improved in the fall. When voters were asked which ad had made the greatest impression on them, more people named ads for Dole (sixty-four mentions) than Clinton (fifty-six mentions) or Perot (forty-eight mentions). The most frequently cited specific ad in the general election was Dole's MTV ad (twenty-one mentions), which replayed videotape of Clinton saying he would inhale when smoking marijuana if he were doing it over again. The second most commonly named ad was Perot's "It's Your Country" spot (sixteen mentions), which told viewers they should make up their own minds and not be told how to vote. Clinton's ads on Medicare cuts were the third most frequently cited ads, with ten mentions.

Chapter 7

Setting the Agenda

Few subjects are more central to the political system than agenda formation. It is well established that issues come and go and that at any given time only a few matters receive serious consideration by government officials.[1] *Agenda setting* refers to the process by which issues evolve from specific grievances into prominent causes worthy of government consideration. In a political system in which citizens pay only limited attention to civic affairs, it is a mechanism through which the public can influence official deliberations by conveying its sense of which problems are important. Agenda setting is also a means of maintaining popular control in democratic societies because the process provides a link between citizens' concerns and the actions of leadership.

One avenue of agenda setting that has attracted considerable attention is the mass media.[2] There has been extensive discussion of how television shapes priorities and influences public perceptions about the nation's most serious problems. Television is thought to play a crucial role in presidential strategies of going public. Iyengar and Kinder's experimental work strongly supports a model of media agenda setting. The respondents to their study of network news regarded any problem covered by the media as "more important for the country, cared more about it, believed that government should do more about it, reported stronger feelings about it, and were more likely to identify it as one of the country's most important problems."[3]

However, there has been little extension of this work to political advertising. No one has used an agenda-setting model to determine whether ads influence citizens' policy priorities. In a campaign, agenda setting is potentially very important. Candidates often use election contests to dramatize issues that previously were

124

not high on the public agenda or to show their awareness of issues that are. They also try to deemphasize matters that may be problematic for themselves. Bush's strategy in 1988 clearly involved a redefinition of the agenda away from certain aspects of Reagan's record and toward furloughs and flag factories (Dukakis's vulnerable areas) in an effort to move the campaign debate onto terms more advantageous for Republicans. Candidates' advertising therefore should be assessed to gauge its ability to change citizens' perceptions of what is important and how the campaigns are run.

The Media's Role in Agenda Setting

At its most general level, agenda setting entails studying the wide range of actors who turn personal concerns into matters deserving political action. There are a large number of societal problems that warrant government attention. Some are domestic in nature, involving fundamental questions of poverty, justice, and social welfare. Others include the broad contours of macroeconomic performance. War and peace are recurring concerns, as are more general issues of foreign affairs.

But not all matters of social concern get defined as political problems that deserve government attention. In the United States, many problems are considered to be outside the sphere of government. According to Stanley Feldman, it is common in the individualistic political culture of the United States for subjects to be defined as private matters related to the personal characteristics of individuals. Whereas other societies attribute responsibility for difficulties more generally, a belief in economic individualism weakens attributions of collective responsibility in the United States.[4]

Some areas are seen as problematic but not a priority for institutional deliberations. Only a few questions occupy the attention of government decision makers at any point. Paul Light demonstrates convincingly in his study of presidential agenda setting how important it is for leaders to conserve their political capital and focus their attention on a limited number of issues.[5] The chief executives who are the most successful develop specific priorities and are able to communicate their preferences clearly to voters.

From the standpoint of researchers, the most interesting question is how topics move from private concerns to top priorities and what role the media play in this process. Roger Cobb and Charles Elder argue that agenda setting is a way for citizens to convey preferences to leaders in a system characterized by limited participation. They demonstrate how the characteristics of particular policy areas (such as concreteness, social significance, long-term relevance, complexity, and novelty) influence the scope and intensity of political conflicts. These authors suggest that the media—because of their crucial role in defining the nature of conflict—can "play a very important role in elevating issues to the systemic agenda and increasing their chances of receiving formal agenda consideration."[6] Their conclusions are in line with a number of public opinion studies that have found that media exposure is a major factor in how people rank policy concerns.[7] Issues that receive a lot of attention from the press generally are seen as important problems facing the country. Saturation coverage by the media, as occurred during the Watergate scandal, can have a decisive effect on the public agenda.[8] Likewise, it also is true that journalists pay a lot of attention to issues of general public concern.

Other scholars have been more sanguine about media influence. John Kingdon studies agenda formation using lengthy interviews with leaders as well as detailed studies of congressional hearings, presidential speeches, polling data, and media coverage. It is interesting to note that his interviews reveal that few leaders attributed much of an agenda-setting effect to the mass media. Instead, policy entrepreneurs who advocate new policy proposals were seen as very significant, and there also was emphasis placed on interest groups (named as important by 84 percent) and researchers (named by 66 percent). In contrast, only 26 percent of the leaders Kingdon interviewed said the media were important.[9]

Kingdon does suggest ways in which the media can elevate particular issues. Reporters often influence agenda formation by acting as a conduit of information for policy makers. Kingdon cites the case of federal officials who were unable to gain access to the White House. One day a report about their concern was published in the *Washington Post,* and the president immediately called up the secretary of the relevant department to resolve the problem.[10] Because policy makers are swamped with the daily demands of governing, it is not uncommon for them to use media coverage to determine which problems deserve immediate attention.

The press also can act as a triggering mechanism for agenda setting by using particular styles of coverage. Through crisis reports or investigative journalism, the media can magnify particular events and turn them into catalysts for official action. Even when there is widespread agreement regarding the importance of a particular policy problem, it still takes a specific incident to galvanize public attention and move the concern onto the formal agenda of government.

The exact magnitude of the media's impact appears to depend considerably on institutional setting. For example, Light's analysis of agenda setting in the presidency attributes more influence to the media than much of the work conducted on Congress. Light finds, like Kingdon, that the media often act as an indirect channel to the White House. Although they rarely serve as an incubator of new ideas, they are a "source of pressure." One of Carter's aides is quoted as saying, "We all read the papers and we notice if an event is causing a reaction. We watch the evening broadcasts and recognize the lead stories. If an item makes a stir and we haven't noticed it, we are in trouble." [11]

Preliminary investigations have documented the impact of television ads on the public agenda during campaigns. For example, Atkin and Heald studied advertising in a 1974 open seat election to the House of Representatives.[12] Through a survey of 323 voters in the closing weeks of the campaign, they found that ad exposure altered voters' impressions of the most important policy issues in the race. Bowers, meanwhile, examined a number of Senate and governor's races in 1970 and demonstrated that exposure to newspaper ads corresponded with survey results about most important issues.[13]

Policy and Campaign Components of the Public Agenda

Agenda-setting studies commonly have investigated people's perceptions of the policy agenda, the substantive problems deemed worthy of government attention. In the campaign world, though, the agenda also includes a number of other matters. In recent years, the campaign agenda has been dominated by matters such as who is doing well and who has made major progress or blunders. The media devote most of their attention to nonpolicy matters. Such topics often have consequences for candidates' fortunes. For example, the so-called character issue effectively derailed the fortunes of candidates Hart and Joseph Biden in the 1988 presidential campaign and threatened to do the same thing to Clinton in spring 1992.[14]

The policy agenda and the campaign agenda have different characteristics. The policy agenda is generally rooted in the real conditions of people's everyday lives. If unemployment rises, there will be a parallel increase in concern about jobs. When oil tankers spill their cargo, worry arises regarding the environment. In contrast, campaign issues are more ephemeral and less rooted in objective realities. Questions related to momentum and mistakes often arise quickly, based on electoral developments and media coverage.[15] The mass media are quick to jump on unexpected events. They provide saturation coverage of things that are politically surprising, and this can influence the dynamics of the electoral contest.

Opinion polls from 1972 through 1996 have included a series of open-ended questions examining citizens' views about the most pressing policy concerns for the country and about the most important campaign events.[16] From the 1970s through the 1990s there was a fundamental shift in priorities. In 1972, foreign affairs and economic matters dominated the fall general election campaign between Nixon and McGovern. By the 1974 Senate races, inflation was starting to rise nationally; at the same time, the Watergate scandal that forced the resignation of President Nixon in August of that year was renewing public concern about honesty in government. Economic issues returned to the forefront in 1976, when both unemployment and inflation were cited as the most important problems. In the 1980s, foreign affairs returned as the most important problem after a period off the list of most pressing needs. Tax and spending issues also emerged for the first time during this period as the most important problem. Both Reagan and Bush devoted great attention in their advertising and political speeches to keeping down the size of government. Bush's most famous line in the 1988 campaign occurred during his convention speech, when he said, "Just read my lips—no new taxes." [17] But in 1992, prosperity disappeared and the economy and concern over unemployment again emerged as the top issues. The 1996 agenda emphasized fundamental questions about the proper role of government, including taxes, the economy, crime and drugs, and Medicare and Medicaid (see Table 7-1).

Surveys also asked about the most notable campaign events from 1976 through 1996. In 1976, that Carter and Reagan did well and won key primaries were the top developments in the spring, whereas the presidential debates were the most notable

TABLE 7-1
Most Important Problems and
Campaign Events: 1996

Most important problem	
Government spending and deficit	19%
Economy and jobs	17
Crime and drugs	14
Medicare and Medicaid	10
Most important campaign event	
Debates	18%
Clinton scandals	3
Perot candidacy	2
Dole fall	2
N	(724)

Source: Brown University national survey, October 28–November 3, 1996.

Note: Entries represent the percentage of respondents citing the particular problem or event as most important in 1996 in open-ended questions.

events in the fall. The 1984 CBS News/*New York Times* survey broke down the most important campaign events for individual candidates, and 60 percent cited Reagan's mistakes in the debates. In 1988, 54 percent named Bush's attacks on Dukakis as the most important development of the fall campaign. The 1992 primary race saw voters naming Buchanan's unexpected showing in New Hampshire and Clinton's scandals as the most important developments of the nominating campaign, and Perot's candidacy and the debates as the most important aspects of the general election campaign. The 1996 campaign showed the debates, Clinton's scandals (such as Whitewater, Travelgate, and contributions from foreign sources), Perot's running on the Reform Party banner, and Dole's fall from a campaign platform as the most important campaign developments.

Ads and Agenda Setting

Candidates seek to influence citizens' priorities and to base their strategies on issues that are already on the public's mind, but it is not obvious how ad exposure corresponds to the agenda. An analysis shows that in 1972, 1976, and 1984, ads were not associated with particular policy views. Many of the differences were either not very large or not in the expected direction. For example, the top issue cited in 1972 was foreign affairs, and there were no significant differences based on ad exposure. Concern over the economy actually was stronger among those who were not ad viewers than among those who were. There also were weak effects in 1976 on unemployment and inflation and in 1984 on peace and arms control as well as on tax and spending matters.

However, there were exceptions in the 1974 and 1990 Senate races, Bush's 1988 general election campaign, and Clinton's fall 1992 campaign. Honesty in government was significantly linked to advertising in the 1974 Senate races.[18] Thirty-four percent of people who reported not seeing ads cited honesty in government as the most important problem, compared with 42 percent of those who had paid close attention to ads, a statistically significant difference of 8 percentage points. In 1990, those who saw ads were more likely than others to cite the economy and budget matters as the most important problem. Bush's 1988 ads on tax and spending matters paid off in a big way, as did Clinton's 1992 ads. Among those who did not watch ads, 21 percent cited tax and spending matters as most important in 1988, whereas 46 percent of those who had paid attention to Bush's ads cited tax and spending issues, a whopping difference of 25 percentage points.

Differences also occurred on citizens' assessments of campaign events. In 1976, 27 percent of those who did not watch ads cited Carter's doing well as the most important development in the campaign, compared with 36 percent of those who had paid attention to ads, a difference of 9 percentage points. In June of that year, Reagan also achieved a 9-point difference among ad viewers, with attentive viewers more likely to report that his doing well was the most notable aspect of the campaign. The Californian experienced a substantial effect of 26 percentage points based on ad viewing for those who cited his debate performance as the most important thing he did in the campaign.

There were also advertising effects in 1988 regarding which campaign events were most important. Eight percent of those who had not seen ads cited Bush's campaign as his top accomplishment, compared with 14 percent of those who had paid attention to Bush's ads. There were significant differences based on ad exposure in criticism of Dukakis for not responding to Bush. Among those with low attentiveness, 6 percent named this problem, whereas among those with high attentiveness, 17 percent mentioned it.[19]

A series of regression analyses was conducted for mentions of most important problems and most notable campaign events. Several policy problems (honesty in government in 1974, tax and spending matters in 1988, the economy and budget in 1990, and unemployment in 1992) showed significant advertising effects. Even after controls were introduced, exposure to advertising was associated with naming the most important problem facing the country. In 1974, seeing and paying attention to ads were linked to citing honesty in government as the most important problem. In a similar way, in 1992, ad exposure was related to naming unemployment as the country's most important problem. In 1996, seeing Clinton's ads was associated with thinking crime and drugs were the most important problems and that Medicare and Medicaid were not as important (see Table 7-2 for a list of ad coefficients with mentions of the most important problems and most notable campaign events).

There were significant advertising effects related to a number of notable campaign events. Ad watching was linked to mentions that Carter was doing well, that Reagan had performed poorly in television debates, that Reagan had restored pride in the United States, that Dukakis had erred in not responding to Bush during the 1988 campaign, and that the debates were the most important campaign event in 1992. In 1996, those who saw ads for Perot were more likely to believe that Clinton's scandals were the most important campaign event. Characteristics of the phenomenon under scrutiny appear to affect the ability of the media to influence people. As shown in the previous chapter in regard to electability, ephemeral qualities are amenable to ad effects. Just as it is possible to shape people's impressions of how well candidates are doing, television ads can influence views about the campaign agenda.

The Influence of Individual Ads

General exposure to campaign ads are associated with citizens' assessments of the public agenda. But what about individual ads? Most past work has examined ad exposure in aggregated form with no distinction being made between ads. To explore the impact

TABLE 7-2
Ad Coefficients with Mentions of Most Important Problems and Most Notable Campaign Events: 1996

	TV News	Clinton Ads	Dole Ads	Perot Ads	N
Most important problem					
Government spending/deficit	.27 (.15)[1]	-.19 (.19)	.26 (.20)	.03 (.14)	525
Economy and jobs	-.17 (.16)	.31 (.24)	.01 (.25)	.01 (.17)	525
Crime and drugs	-.49 (.16)[2]	.47 (.25)[1]	-.29 (.26)	.20 (.18)	525
Medicare and Medicaid	.02 (.18)	-.50 (.22)[2]	.39 (.27)	-.15 (.19)	525
Most important campaign event					
Debates	-.01 (.13)	-.24 (.16)	.27 (.18)	-.14 (.13)	525
Clinton scandals	-.12 (.50)	.91 (1.01)	-.55 (.77)	.90 (.47)[1]	525
Perot candidacy	.33 (.34)	-.20 (.36)	.00 (.38)	.26 (.31)	525
Dole fall	-.27 (.40)	.27 (.56)	-.02 (.58)	.35 (.44)	525

Source: Brown University national survey, October 28–November 3, 1996.

Note: Entries are logistic regression estimates for TV news and ad exposure to each candidate, with standard errors in parentheses. A positive coefficient means that seeing the TV news and each candidate's ads was associated with believing that problem or event was the most important one. Coefficients marked with superscripts are statistically significant. Effects of control variables (party identification, education, age, gender, race, ideology, and political interest) are not shown.

[1] p < .05   [2] p < .01

of individual ads, I analyzed the most frequently named ads in the 1984, 1988, and 1992 presidential general elections. In 1984 the CBS News/*New York Times* survey asked, "Both presidential candidates had a lot of television commercials during this campaign. Was there any one commercial that made a strong impression on you? (If so) Which commercial?" The top Mondale ad named in the postelection survey was the "Future" commercial, whereas Reagan's top ad was the "Bear in the Woods" ad (see Appendix). In 1988, the CBS News/*New York Times* poll again asked which ads made the biggest impression: "Tell me about the commercial for [Bush/Dukakis] that made the biggest impression on you." Viewers picked the "Revolving Door" as Bush's top ad and the "Family/Education" ad for Dukakis.

In 1992 an October 26 to 31 survey asked, "Which television ad run by a presidential candidate this fall has made the biggest impression on you?" Of the people questioned, 145 people (24 percent of the sample) were able to name a specific ad. Perot received by far the most mentions: 109 people cited his ads, twenty-seven cited Clinton's, and nine cited Bush's. Perot's most memorable ads were his infomercials, mentioned by thirty-eight people, followed by his spot discussing job creation ($N = 19$), his sixty-second spot discussing the legacy of national debt being left to our nation's children ($N = 18$), and the commercial in which he discusses having received a purple heart in the mail from a supporter ($N = 10$). Clinton's top commercials were "How're You Doing?" ($N = 7$) and "Read My Lips" ($N = 5$). Bush's top ad accused Clinton of wanting to raise taxes ($N = 3$). (See Appendix for descriptions.)

In 1996, the top ad was Dole's MTV ad in which Clinton indicated he would inhale marijuana if he were doing it over again. The second most frequently cited ad was Perot's "It's Your Country" spot, in which a series of young people talk about how important it is to make up your own mind and vote the way you would like to.

The conventional wisdom is that commercials for Reagan, Bush in 1988, and Clinton were effective, whereas those for Mondale, Dukakis, and Bush in 1992 were not. But these judgments are based on the views of political professionals, not the assessments of the American public. To see what effects these ads had on citizens' views about the policy agenda, I conducted an analysis of ad exposure on those matters seen as the country's most pressing policy problems, controlling for party identification, education, age, race, gender, ideology, political interest, and media exposure.[20]

In the case of Bush, Dukakis, Clinton, and Perot, the findings conform to conventional wisdom. However, with regard to Reagan and Mondale, the common view is not supported. Mondale's "Future" ad on defense matters was very effective, at least from the standpoint of having the strongest tie to people's priorities. Among those who had not seen the ad, 20 percent cited peace and arms control as the most important problem, whereas 38 percent of those who had seen it did, a difference of 18 percentage points. Mondale's ads also influenced beliefs that restoring pride in the United States had been the most important aspect of the 1984 campaign.

It is interesting to note that for all the attention devoted to Reagan's "Bear in the Woods" ad, in which the bear was seen as a symbol of the Soviet Union, this commercial had no significant effect on either of the concerns noted: peace and arms control or restoring pride in the United States. Part of the problem may have been the abstractness of the ad. Although the Reagan campaign was apparently confident of the public's ability to understand this ad, the spot contained abstract allusions both to dovishness—the bear may not be dangerous—and hawkishness—we need to be strong. The complexity of this ad may have limited its effect on the agenda.

In 1988, Bush's "Revolving Door" ad was linked to mentions of crime and law and order as the most important problems facing the United States.[21] Among those who had not seen the ad only 5 percent cited these problems, whereas 12 percent of those who had seen the ad named this area. This fits with longitudinal evidence cited by Marjorie Hershey, who found that "the proportion of respondents saying that George Bush was 'tough enough' on crime and criminals rose from 23 percent in July to a full 61 percent in late October, while the proportion saying Dukakis was not tough enough rose from 36 to 49 percent."[22] It is interesting to note that the Dukakis ad did not produce significant effects on any domestic policy dimension.[23]

In 1992, Perot's infomercials were quite effective at focusing attention on the economy, as was Clinton's "How're You Doing?" ad on unemployment. Perot's ads had a simplicity and directness that in an antipolitician year appealed to viewers. Clinton's spot was able to raise public awareness of jobs as an important problem. Focus group tests within the Clinton campaign showed that his commercial "zoomed off the charts" when played for voters.[24]

The Special Case of Women and the Revolving Door Ad

No commercial since the "Daisy" ad has generated more discussion than Bush's "Revolving Door." This spot was aired frequently during the evening news and extensively discussed by news commentators. In looking at the effects of this ad on agenda setting, fascinating differences arise based on the personal circumstances of viewers.

I broke down group reactions to ads for Mondale, Reagan, Bush, and Dukakis in regard to agenda setting. Among the people most likely to cite crime as the top problem after seeing Bush's "Revolving Door" commercial were midwesterners and young people. Reagan's "Bear in the Woods" ad, meanwhile, had its greatest effect on peace concerns among men and those aged thirty to forty-four. Mondale's ad about the future was quite influential among women, young people, and those who lived in the Northeast and West. Dukakis's "Family/Education" ad had its strongest agenda-setting effect on women.

But most significant were the differences between men and women in regard to Bush's 1988 ads. One of Bush's strongest agenda-setting effects from his "Revolving Door" ad, for example, was among women on the crime issue.[25] After seeing this commercial, as well as the widely publicized Horton ad produced by an independent political action committee, women became much more likely than men to cite crime as the most important issue.

The fact that the ads mentioned rape clearly accentuated their impact on women. According to Dukakis's campaign manager Susan Estrich, "The symbolism was very powerful ... you can't find a stronger metaphor, intended or not, for racial hatred in this country than a black man raping a white woman.... I talked to people afterward.... Women said they couldn't help it, but it scared the living daylights out of them."[26]

The "Revolving Door" case demonstrates how the strategies of campaign elites and the overall cultural context are important factors in mediating the significance of advertisements. The way in which this commercial was put together—in terms of both subject area and timing—was a major contributor to its impact on view-

ers. If Horton had assaulted a fifty-year-old black man while on
furlough from a state prison, it is not likely that the "Revolving
Door" ad would have affected voters' policy priorities as it did.[27]

The Strategic Dimensions of Agenda Control

Agenda setting is an interactive process in political campaigns.
It was not just Bush's use of attack ads in 1988 that was important
to the outcome of the election. Instead, it was the combination of
Bush's attack strategy with the high road taken by Dukakis. One
must go beyond ads aired by particular candidates to examine the
strategic interactions of electoral competition.[28]

Strategic interactions revolve around two key campaign decisions—what subjects to cover in advertisements and whether to
attack the opposition. Topics often are chosen with an eye toward
public saliency. Matters that have attracted citizens' concern, such
as rising unemployment, oil spills, or ethics in government, are the
natural subjects of television advertising.

The decision to "go negative" is another important part of
strategic decision making. In the past decade, it has become widely accepted that negative ads work. Most recent contests have produced a high proportion of commercials devoted to attacking the
opposition. Yet how negative ads influence viewers is not well
understood. Attack commercials may help candidates control the
agenda, thereby enabling them to set the tone of the campaign. An
axiom in politics is that the person "who sets the agenda, wins the
election." The rationale is simple. Setting the agenda allows candidates to define the terms of debate and to dictate the dynamics
of the campaign.

No case provides a better illustration of campaign strategy than
the Bush-Dukakis race in 1988. Bush seized the initiative at the
very beginning of the fall campaign. Recognizing that Dukakis was
one of the least known nominees in recent years, Bush advisers
developed a plan designed to define the terms of the campaign.
When it became obvious that Dukakis was the likely Democratic
nominee, Lee Atwater gave his staff instructions for what
euphemistically is called opposition research—that is, digging for
dirt on the opponent's background. Speaking to Jim Pinkerton, the
research head of Bush's campaign, Atwater said, " 'I want you to
get the nerd patrol. . . . We need five or six issues, and we need
them by the middle of May.' . . . I gave him a three-by-five card

and I said, 'You come back with this three-by-five card, but you can use both sides, and bring me the issues that we need in this campaign.' " [29]

The Bush campaign also picked up attack clues from Dukakis's Democratic opponents in the nominating process, for example, Senator Gore. This included the case of Horton and Dukakis's veto of legislation that would have mandated the recitation of the Pledge of Allegiance in schools.[30] After testing these themes in a series of focus groups, the Bush campaign consciously pursued agenda control through an attack strategy. As stated by Bush's media adviser Roger Ailes, "We felt as long as the argument was on issues that were good for us—crime, national defense, and what have you—that if we controlled the agenda and stayed on our issues, by the end we would do all right." [31]

Dukakis, however, chose a very different route. He had earned the nomination by generating a sense of inevitability about his campaign. Through early fund raising, the development of a strong organization, and cultivation of the view that he was the most electable Democrat, Dukakis was able to play the role of the long-distance runner in the race. Because his advertising generally was positive (with the exception of his timely attack on Gephardt's flip-flops), he did not offend his opponents' voters. Dukakis thereby was able to gain opposition support when voters' preferred candidates bowed out. The lesson he learned from the nominating contest, then, was that if he was patient and took the high road, victory would come eventually.

According to his campaign manager Estrich, Dukakis decided that his fall race would, among other things, center on character and integrity. She said, "An important element of our fall strategy . . . would emphasize competence . . . [and] the value of integrity. You saw this at the convention and throughout the campaign— that Mike Dukakis stood for high standards. That's the kind of campaign he would run, the kind of governor he had been, the kind of President he would be." [32] Along with the nomination experience, which had rewarded a positive campaign, this decision inevitably led to the choice of a high-road strategy, one that would not respond to Bush's fierce attacks.

However appropriate this approach may have been in the nominating context, with its sequential primaries and Democratic supporters of other candidates to be wooed as their top choices dropped out, it was disastrous in the two-candidate context of the general election. Dukakis's decision allowed Bush to set the tone of the campaign and to define the terms of debate. It was Bush's issues—flags, patriotism, "tax-and-spend" liberalism, and crime—that became the agenda of the campaign. Little was heard about homelessness, rising poverty, and the unmet social needs of the Reagan years.

The consequences of these campaign choices are reflected in an analysis of a paired-ads design. This technique was developed specifically to look at strategic interactions. People were questioned regarding whether they had seen each candidate's top ads: Bush's "Revolving Door" and Dukakis's family education ad. The answers were jointly evaluated through techniques designed to determine whether responses had any agenda-setting and voting implications.

The results illustrate how strategic behavior helped set the tone of the campaign when ads of both candidates were seen. Bush was able through his "Revolving Door" commercial to widen the perception of crime as the most important problem facing the country. In contrast, exposure to Dukakis's ad decreased the saliency of crime. Viewers who thought crime was the most pressing policy problem also were more likely to say they would cast ballots for Bush over Dukakis.[33]

Bush's attacks took a toll on the Massachusetts governor. Not only did they allow the vice president to dictate the terms of debate in the campaign, they created the perception that Dukakis was not a fighter. As stated by Estrich, "The governor was hurt by the attacks on him—the mental health rumors, the attacks on patriotism, the harbor and furlough issues—and perhaps most of all by the perception that he had failed to fight back, which went to his character. . . . We did fight back on occasion. The problem is we didn't fight back effectively, and we didn't sustain it. We created a perception that we weren't fighting back, and I think that hurt us much more."[34]

Dukakis's decision was even more harmful in light of the very favorable media coverage reaped by Bush. Kiku Adatto undertook an intensive analysis of network news coverage in 1988. She found that newscasts ran segments from the "Revolving Door" ad ten times in October and November, making it the most frequently aired commercial of the campaign. Overall, twenty-two segments about Bush's crime ads were rebroadcast during the news, compared with four for Dukakis's ads. Only once was the deceptive information from Bush's crime ads challenged by reporters.[35]

These news reports reinforced Bush's basic message. A number of stories appeared during the general election campaign citing political professionals who believed that Bush's tactics were working and that Dukakis's strategy was a complete failure. Because these assessments appeared in the context of news programs, with their high credibility, they were more believable than if they had come from paid ads.

Redefinition of the Agenda in 1992

The agenda in 1992 differed significantly from that of 1988. The 1988 race took place in a setting characterized by a fluid agenda. Because the economy was still growing, no single concern dominated the agenda. Instead, a variety of concerns, such as taxes, government spending, social welfare, and crime, were on people's minds. In 1992, everyone in the Clinton campaign's favorite line about the agenda was that the top three issues were jobs, jobs, and jobs. Clinton campaign adviser James Carville kept a sign posted in the Little Rock headquarters reminding workers, "THE ECONOMY, STUPID." About two-thirds of Americans identified the economy and unemployment as the crucial problems facing the country. These numbers did not drop during the campaign.

The presence of a fixed agenda altered the strategic terrain of the presidential campaign. Rather than attempting to redirect people's priorities, as had been the case in 1988 when peripheral concerns such as crime were made central to voters, candidates geared their appeals to jobs and economic development. In the case of Clinton and Perot, the message was simple. Economic performance was dismal under Bush, and a new plan was needed to reinvigorate the economy. President Bush also discussed the economy, although he wavered between claiming that things were not as bad as his opponents charged and admitting that the economic picture was terrible but blaming congressional Democrats. Because Clinton led in the preelection polls throughout the summer and fall, he had the strategic luxury of targeting his economic message to eighteen states. Bush, by contrast, ran many of his ads on the national networks in order to raise support across the country.

The one effort at agenda redefinition attempted by Bush—raising questions about Clinton's character in order to deflect attention from Bush's own record—was not very successful. After being urged privately by Ailes to "go for the red meat [and] get on the bleeping offensive," the president challenged Clinton on numerous personal dimensions in speeches, interviews, the debates, and spot commercials.[36] In one of his most hard-hitting ads, Bush used a series of ordinary men and women to criticize Clinton's integrity: "If you're going to be President you have to be honest." "Bill Clinton hasn't been telling anything honestly to the American people." "The man just tells people what they want to hear." "About dodging the draft." "I think he's full of hot air." "I wouldn't trust him at all to be Commander in Chief." "I think that there's a pattern, and I just don't trust Bill Clinton." "I don't think he's honorable. I don't think he's trustworthy." "You can't have a President who says one thing and does another." "Scares me. He worries me. You know, and he'll just go one way or another." [37] It is interesting to note that the campaign edited out a criticism about Clinton's trip to Russia because a backlash of hitting below the belt developed against Bush on this charge. In a play on Carville's sign, the Bush people also posted a message in their headquarters: "TRUST AND TAXES, STUPID."

But national opinion surveys demonstrated little increase in concern about Clinton's character during the fall campaign. For example, in a CBS News/*New York Times* survey taken September 9 to 13, 42 percent of the respondents thought Clinton responded truthfully to the charge that he had avoided the draft and 25 percent did not. Seventy-nine percent felt the allegation would have no effect on their vote.[38] In an October 12 to 13 poll by CBS News/*New York Times,* 79 percent claimed that their votes were unaffected by Bush's attacks on Clinton's antiwar activities at Oxford University.[39] Clinton's focus groups revealed little damage: "Many people indicated that they thought he [Clinton] had been evasive or had even lied, but they said that wouldn't affect their vote." [40]

Bush's efforts to redefine the agenda were unsuccessful because of unfavorable media coverage and the strategic response by Clinton and Gore. Although the media devoted considerable time and space to Bush's allegations, the spin on the story generally was negative to Bush and his chief adviser, Jim Baker. Headlines repeatedly emphasized Bush's "assaults" on Clinton and "smears" on Clinton's character. Spokespeople for the Arkansas governor meanwhile labeled the tactics McCarthyite. News of State Department searches of the passport records of Clinton, as well as of his mother, brought this stinging rebuke from Gore: "The American people can say we don't accept this kind of abuse of power. We've had the Joe McCarthy technique and the smear campaign; now we have the police state tactics of rummaging through personal files to try to come up with damaging information."[41] Combined with sympathetic news coverage, this response undermined the legitimacy of Bush's attack strategy.

In addition, Bush's advertising attacks suffered because they were unfocused. After the election, Bush's advisors said their efforts were hampered because "we never knew if we were focusing on Arkansas or Clinton's character or big spending. I don't think it ever clicked. I don't think the character assault was framed very well."[42] Bush's focus groups furthermore revealed a boomerang effect from voters on the trust issue: "They didn't trust Clinton's word or Bush's performance." For a while, Bush's advisers had the candidate substitute truth for trust. But new wording did not change the final outcome.[43]

The 1996 Agenda

The biggest change in the agenda between 1992 and 1996 was the move from a fixed agenda dominated by the economy to a fluid one that was broader and more diffuse. Whereas 60 percent of voters in 1992 cited the economy as the most important problem facing the country, the types of issues named in 1996 were quite varied: government spending, high taxes, crime rates, the drug problem, and the possible budget reduction of Medicare and Medicaid.

In addition, voters were far more positive about the economy. In 1996, according to network exit polls on election night, 59 percent of Americans rated the economy as excellent or good. In 1992, 19 percent gave the economy excellent or good ratings. This upturn in consumer confidence raised people's spirits and made a majority of voters feel the country was headed in the right direction.

The fluidity of the agenda in 1996 made that year look more like 1988 than 1992. Rather than having to frame every part of their message around the 800-pound gorilla of the economy, Clinton, Dole, and Perot enjoyed greater strategic flexibility. The result was that the campaign centered on competing conceptions about the country's direction. Clinton successfully framed the election's choice as a referendum on the Republican Revolution. Did voters want to "CUT MEDICARE," "SLASH EDUCATION," and "GUT THE ENVIRONMENT"? Through ads, speeches, and news events, Clinton pounded the message that Republicans were uncaring and insensitive and not to be trusted with America's future.

Dole, in contrast, attempted to redefine the agenda along several different dimensions. His first frame developed at the Republican convention and continued through mid-September was on his economic plan of a 15-percent across-the-board tax cut. Unfortunately for him, according to a national public opinion poll, only one-quarter of Americans believed he would actually deliver a tax cut for them. When his economic program failed to arouse much voter interest, Dole shifted to crime and drugs in September. He aired the MTV ad, accused the president of failed liberal policies, and made some short-term gains in the polls. But the movement in his direction did not persist. It was not until the closing weeks of the campaign, when a series of Democratic fund-raising misdeeds came to light and Dole began to push the character attack, that polls tightened, and by election day Dole did better than expected. Rather than losing by the expected 15 points, Dole lost by 8. Polls in congressional races around the country also showed a movement in a Republican direction in the last two weeks, which helped the GOP retain control of Congress. The character issue resonated with people in a way the tax cut issue and attacks on Clinton's crime and drug policies did not. The allegations of the Democratic National Committee's fund-raising illegalities were designed to portray Clinton as a politician who was not to be trusted. This turned out to be Dole's most successful effort at agenda redefinition during the fall campaign.

Chapter 8

Changing the Standards

Citizens rarely incorporate all available information into their political decisions.[1] Politics is but one of many activities for American voters. Most people are involved in several social, religious, and educational communities, and therefore face multiple demands on their time. Some pay extensive attention to election campaigns, whereas others devote only sporadic attention to them. The traditional notion that individuals review every option before making choices has been supplanted by models that incorporate information grazing, or sporadic searches for material.

Priming is a new theoretical model that builds on this way of thinking about political information. Developed in regard to the evening news, the priming model proposes that people use readily available material to evaluate candidates and that in the media age one of the most accessible sources is television. By its patterns of coverage, television can influence voters' choices between candidates by elevating particular standards of evaluation. For example, television shows that devote extensive coverage to defense matters can increase the importance of defense policy in citizens' assessments. Likewise, news accounts that dwell on environmental concerns can raise the salience of those matters in voting choices.[2]

Priming has attracted growing attention in relation to television news, but there has been little attention paid to its conceptual counterpart, *defusing*. This term refers to efforts on the part of candidates to decrease the importance of particular standards of evaluation. Candidates often have problematic features, such as being seen as weak on defense or lacking a clear vision for the future. It obviously is in their interest to defuse their shortcomings. They can do this either by lowering the overall salience of the topic to the public or by shortening the distance between the candidates to the point at which the subject no longer affects the vote.

The concepts of priming and defusing are particularly applicable to the study of campaign advertising. Impressionistic evidence is available regarding the ability of television commercials to prime (or defuse) the electorate by shifting the standards of evaluation. This chapter examines priming and defusing through campaign ads and demonstrates that commercials can alter the importance of various factors in voters' decision making. Bush in 1988 was a masterful candidate whose political ads helped him defuse some standards that could have been problematic.[3]

Informational Shortcuts

To understand priming we need to understand the notion of information costs. This idea has been popularized by game theorists and incorporated into theories of social psychology. The assumption is that acquiring information costs people time and effort. Particularly during election campaigns, it is not easy for ordinary citizens to compile a full record of candidates' backgrounds, policy views, and personal attributes. Citizens lack the inclination to search for all relevant material.

Given the time it takes to acquire information, it is not surprising that people look for informational shortcuts, or what Kahneman, Slovic, and Tversky call *heuristics*.[4] Rather than conducting a complete search that incorporates every nugget of material about candidates, voters use readily available information. In the media era, television provides some of the most accessible material. By its patterns of coverage and emphasis on particular information, the electronic medium plays a significant role in influencing the standards of evaluation used in voters' selection of candidates.

For most elections, voters can call on many standards to evaluate candidates: views about their prospects for election, assessments of their positions on issues, and feelings about their personal attributes. Candidates attempt to prime the electorate by promoting standards that benefit themselves. If their strength lies in foreign policy as opposed to domestic policy, as was true for Bush in 1992, they seek to elevate foreign policy considerations in voters' decision making. If their strength is being seen as the most caring or trustworthy candidate, they will try to persuade voters to make personal qualities the basis of their choice.

Candidates conversely attempt to defuse matters that may be problematic for them. They try to lower the salience of problem areas. Bush, for example, was seen as wimpish and uncaring at the start of the 1988 presidential campaign. He obviously was not able to remake his personality, but Bush did alter the terms of the campaign in a way that defused those perceptions, emphasized his toughness, and focused voters' attention on other matters that were not as problematic for him.[5]

Considerable evidence has surfaced about the ability of television to prime viewers, although little attention has been devoted to defusing. Iyengar and Kinder as well as Krosnick and Kinder have undertaken pathbreaking work on priming; they have shown that television can shape standards of evaluation in regard to presidents and political candidates.[6] Iyengar and Kinder have analyzed a range of filtering mechanisms that allow voters to deal with complex political phenomena without being paralyzed or overloaded with information. Briefly, their research documents the power of priming through the evening news: "By calling attention to some matters while ignoring others, television news influences the standards by which governments, presidents, policies, and candidates for public office are judged." [7]

Krosnick and Kinder demonstrate the importance of priming with regard to a real-world issue, the Iran-contra affair, which was demonstrably salient to voters in late 1986. Using data from surveys taken before and after the revelation of the scandal, this study showed that intervention in Central America "loomed larger" in popular evaluations of President Reagan after saturation coverage by the media than before the event was publicized. Priming was also more likely to occur among political novices than experts.[8]

Neither project, though, has addressed the role of television commercials in altering voters' standards. Candidates have obvious incentives to attempt to change the importance of matters in ways that benefit themselves.[9] In fact, based on recent campaigns, political commercials appear to be particularly influential as a means of altering voters' assessments of candidates. Ads are designed to be persuasive, and campaigners frequently seek to shift voters' standards of evaluation. The power to mold the judgments of voters through commercials, if demonstrated, would represent a major strategic resource for the contesting of elections.

Standards of Evaluation

The study of priming during election campaigns is complicated by uncertainties concerning the nature of voters' evaluations and the kind of standards actually used to evaluate candidates.[10] Past work has devoted little attention to the mechanism by which a voter's heightened interest in a subject leads to the incorporation of that factor into the voter's assessments of candidates. For example, Krosnick and Kinder assume in their study of the Iran-contra affair that the increased coverage of the scandal led to the decline in support for Reagan. However, Brody and Shapiro argue that the criticism of Reagan by elites of both parties was the crucial factor in the decline, not simply the news of the arms-for-hostages deal.[11]

Both studies, though, ignore a third possibility: the strategic behavior of the participants. In the campaign arena, voters' assessments depend on media coverage, the views of political elites, and the strategic actions of the candidates. In fact, the candidates' activities may be the crucial mechanism because they generate coverage by news organizations and reaction by political elites.

Electoral strategies generally involve efforts to alter voters' concerns about domestic and foreign policy, views about the personal traits of candidates (such as leadership, trustworthiness, and appearance of caring), and impressions of the electability of particular candidates. The large number of determinants distinguishes electoral from nonelectoral priming. Government scandals, such as the Iran-contra affair, typically provoke a change in policy standards. But in the electoral arena, other types of standards are also important to voters' assessments.[12]

Experimental studies have solved the problem of how to determine which standards are most salient to voters by assumption. Iyengar and Kinder conducted a series of experiments in which viewers were shown newscasts emphasizing defense. They found that if the evening news emphasized defense matters, that subject became important in evaluations of the president. Factors that did not appear on the nightly news showed no effect on voters' decision making.[13] But outside of the experimental setting, there is no way of knowing whether citizens actually would incorporate defense as a factor in their vote choices. This research technique simply cannot guarantee that voters in the field will act the way they did in the lab.

Other studies, such as that of Krosnick and Kinder, ensure salience by using an issue—in this case the Iran-contra scandal—which had obvious relevance for citizens.[14] Iran-contra received saturation coverage from the mass media over a period of several months. There were banner headlines and numerous stories on the latest disclosure. That kind of reporting all but guaranteed salience for voters.

However, neither making assumptions nor choosing obviously salient issues solves the relevancy problem. Voters use many standards to evaluate candidates, and these dimensions are neither obvious nor stable over time. Studies of priming and defusing in electoral settings must recognize the diversity of possibilities and develop a research approach that deals with the complexity.

One way to address the saliency matter is to ask citizens which factors were most crucial in their voting choices. After determining overall relevance based on self-reports, one can measure whether exposure to television ads altered the importance of the factors cited. There are clear limitations to relying on self-reports, especially given evidence that voters are not aware of the standards they employ. But this technique can be a starting point in the analysis of voters' standards of evaluation.

In 1984 and 1988, CBS News/*New York Times* surveys inquired about which general factors were most important to voters. In 1984 the survey asked in its pre- and post-election waves: "When you vote/voted for president on Tuesday, what will be/was more important in deciding how you vote/voted—the economy of this country, or the U.S. military and foreign policy, or mainly the way you feel/felt about Reagan and Mondale?" In 1988 the item was, "Some people choose among Presidential candidates by picking the one closest to them on important issues. Some other people choose the one who has the personal characteristics—like integrity or leadership—they most want in a President. Which is most important when you choose—issues or personal characteristics?"

One of these questions emphasizes the agenda and the other focuses on vote choice. But the results show that voters differ in what is considered important to them. The top factor cited by voters in 1984 was the economy (49 percent), followed by the candidates (37 percent), and foreign policy (14 percent). Issues were

named in 1988 as the most important factor by 76 percent of the
sample, and 24 percent cited personal characteristics as more
important.

The crucial question for this research is, "What impact does
television advertising have on these assessments?" As people saw
and paid more attention to ads, did their standards of evaluation
change? A voting model that reflects how the importance of particular standards changed with different levels of ad exposure can
be used to investigate the interpretations of priming, defusing,
and no effect. A priming effect is present when the impact of the
factor on the vote rises with level of ad exposure. In contrast,
defusing is evidenced by a reduction in the importance of the factor, and no effect is demonstrated by a flat line for importance of
the factor based on ad exposure or a zig-zag line revealing random fluctuations.

I undertook a regression analysis of the effect of each of the factors on the 1984 and 1988 vote, respectively. Four levels of ad
exposure, from low to high, were incorporated, as were controls
for intervening factors (party identification, education, age, gender,
race, ideology, political interest, and [for 1988] media exposure).
Vote choice was a dichotomous measure of candidate preference
for Reagan or Mondale in 1984 and Bush or Dukakis in 1988.
Because coefficients are used to indicate the statistical significance
of each relationship, I use them to show the importance of each
factor for the vote.

In 1988, there was little evidence of priming or defusing for people who felt that issues or personal characteristics were important.
The lines zig-zagged, indicating that among those with low or high
ad exposure, there was no systematic difference in the weighting of
issues or personal characteristics as factors in vote choice.

However, in 1984, there was significant evidence of priming.
Foreign policy moved from unimportant to important as a determinant of the vote as level of exposure to television ads increased.
Those who watched ads were much more likely than those who
did not to cite foreign policy matters as influencing their vote for
Reagan. There was also a significant priming effect for economic
matters. The more ads people saw, the more likely they were to cite
economic matters as an influence on their vote. The sharp change
in the slope of these lines indicates that campaign ads raised the
importance of foreign and economic policy matters as factors in
vote choice.

It is interesting to note that although a number of media stories proclaimed the power of Reagan's personal traits, there was no evidence of ad priming in regard to personal candidate qualities in 1984. Politicians were unable to shift standards in this area despite journalists' reporting on Reagan's "Great Communicator" status. According to voters, ads actually had more influence on substantive than on personal dimensions of evaluation.

Nixon and the Politics of Inevitability

Ads can influence general standards of evaluation, but it remains to be seen whether political commercials can prime or defuse specific factors in vote choice. Self-reporting methods are limited by their dependence on the subjective impressions of voters. Citizens may feel that particular factors are important to their vote choice when in reality other things matter more.

Elections since 1972 present an interesting opportunity to examine ad priming and defusing in greater detail. Individual elections need to be investigated to determine exactly how ad exposure influences the factors generally considered to have been important standards of evaluation. The years 1972 through 1996 cover a range of general election and nomination settings. They encompass election campaigns that exhibited a variety of political features: both victories and losses of incumbents, differing levels of political visibility, and so on. Each of these races has received extensive analysis, which aids our reconstruction of the factors that were important in the contest.

The 1972 presidential general election is an interesting setting for an examination of priming. Nixon's general strategy in this race was to characterize himself as a trusted, capable, and responsible leader, in sharp contrast to what he portrayed as an irresponsible and not very trustworthy McGovern. Nixon also sought to portray the McGovern candidacy as hopeless, in a clear effort to elevate electability as a standard of evaluation.[15]

The question in this case is whether the president's ads shifted the standards of evaluation to magnify the significance of personal traits and electability. Respondents were asked to rate the salience of various personal qualities: "Now would you tell us how you personally feel about the unimportance or importance of some of the personal qualities needed by a President?" (rating on a 1 to 7 scale). Trustworthiness was the most commonly cited important trait (61 percent). This item indicates directly what quality was significant to respondents, thereby resolving the salience problem. In addition, the survey asked about the most important policy problems facing the country. Foreign affairs (36 percent) and the economy (33 percent) were ranked as the most important problems. Assessments of Nixon's electability also were used to determine how likely respondents thought he was to win the November election.

I investigated how important each of these qualities was for the general election vote (a dichotomous measure of support for Nixon versus McGovern) by level of ad exposure, controlling for demographic, political, and media-exposure factors. There were weak priming effects in regard to the policy problems of foreign affairs and the economy. Neither played a strong role in voters' decision making, and there appears to have been little significant variation based on exposure to campaign ads.

However, there were stronger priming effects for personal traits and electability. The more ads viewers saw, the more likely they became to elevate trustworthiness in their voting decisions. Trustworthiness went from being an unimportant consideration in the vote among those who were not exposed to ads to a statistically significant factor among those who watched many ads.

Electability also displayed strong evidence of priming. Its role in voters' decision making became much more important as viewers were exposed to ads. Among those who had not seen ads, electability was a statistically insignificant contributor to vote choice. But among attentive viewers, electability had a substantial impact on the vote.

These effects were consistent with the general strategy employed by Nixon against McGovern. Based on his media advertising, the president appears to have shifted the standards of evaluation in a way that elevated personal traits and electability.[16] Voters who saw his ads were more likely to incorporate these factors in their decisions and to use standards favorable to the president.

There also were interesting shifts in the importance of these qualities during the course of the campaign. Between September and November, 28 percent of the sample shifted from not seeing to seeing trustworthiness as the most important trait. Seven percent shifted in the opposite direction, 33 percent cited trustworthiness as most important in both waves, and 32 percent mentioned it at neither point.

Campaign advertising appears to have had some influence. Among those who consistently rated trustworthiness as important, 31 percent of those who did not see ads and 37 percent of those who saw many ads thought trustworthiness was important, a statistically significant difference of 6 percentage points. Political ads therefore demonstrated a priming effect over time.

Defusing Potential Problems: Bush in 1988

Bush started his fall presidential campaign in a difficult position. Dukakis held a substantial lead in the early summer polls. Bush was reeling from bad publicity surrounding the Reagan administration's negotiations with Panamanian dictator Manuel Noriega and disclosures that Nancy Reagan had consulted an astrologer during her husband's presidency. Bush himself was seen as weak and ineffective.[17]

However, according to the theory of priming and defusing, careful advertising can help a candidate by shifting the standards of evaluation. This is exactly what Bush set out to do in 1988. Through priming, Bush sought to elevate factors advantageous to himself. Meanwhile, matters that hurt him would be defused through television ads and favorable coverage from the news media. If he could not remove his own negatives, he could at least shift the standards to his advantage.

I undertook an analysis of the influence of various factors on the Bush vote.[18] On certain issues, there was little evidence of priming or defusing. For example, there was little shift in the importance of the death penalty. The impact this matter had on the vote did not vary with ad exposure. There was also little evidence of priming on defense issues.

The most significant effect was defusing on the salience of the environment and the view that Bush cared about people. These matters actually became less relevant to the vote as people saw more ads. Either the overall salience of the factors decreased or the distance between the candidates was reduced to the point that voters saw no practical difference between them. Both the environment and caring were potentially harmful areas to Bush. As an oil-state representative, Bush had never had strong environmental credentials. Because the environment as a political issue had become very important to voters by 1988, this issue was potentially very negative for him. But the vice president was able to defuse the issue by noting his concern about the environment in ads. In one of his most famous ads, Bush also cast doubt on Dukakis's environmental credentials by arguing that the Massachusetts governor had not cleaned up Boston Harbor.

Bush defused the personality issue of caring about people by reducing its centrality to American voters. Among those who watched few ads, the matter of whether Bush cared about people was significantly linked to the vote. However, voters who saw and paid more attention to ads considered Bush's personality less relevant.

These effects were consistent with the strategic goals of Bush's campaign. They demonstrate how well-organized advertising pitches can improve a candidate's fortunes. Bush achieved defusing effects, and he was therefore able to change the standards of evaluation in ways that benefited himself.

The Gantt-Helms Senate Race in 1990

The 1990 North Carolina Senate campaign turned into one of the fiercest battles in the country. Pitting controversial Republican Jesse Helms against Harvy Gantt, a black Democratic former mayor of Charlotte, Helms started the race as a clear front-runner. Having beaten the popular Gov. James Hunt Jr. in 1984, the conservative Republican seemingly held a firm grip on his seat.[19] Helms appeared to be in even stronger shape after Democrats nominated Gantt, a black liberal with limited statewide name recognition.

Helms opened the contest with the same type of liberal-bashing that had proved successful against Hunt. Seeking to characterize Gantt as an ideological extremist, Helms portrayed him as a man outside the political mainstream of North Carolina. However, Gantt responded with an aggressive campaign accusing Helms of neglecting "pressing social needs." [20] These appeals helped Gantt surge in preelection polls to the point where he actually led in some polls during the closing weeks of the campaign. Press accounts cited issues such as the environment, abortion rights, and education as the crucial ones that had revived Gantt's fortunes and helped him develop key support among young people.[21]

Helms, though, came back with television commercials accusing Gantt of supporting unrestricted abortion and gay rights, opposing the death penalty, and backing racial quotas. One ad in the waning days of the campaign, Helms's infamous "White Hands" commercial, generated a national uproar by blatantly claiming that the quotas supported by Gantt would lead to the loss of jobs for whites. The spot ad showed a white man's hands crumpling what clearly was a job rejection letter. "You needed that job and you were the best qualified," the announcer says. "But they had to give it to a minority because of a racial quota. Is that really fair? Harvey Gantt says it is. Gantt supports Ted Kennedy's racial quota law that makes the color of your skin more important than your qualifications." [22]

A survey undertaken at the University of North Carolina at Chapel Hill was designed to explore the impact of ads on voters' assessments. Although the fieldwork was completed in late October, before the "White Hands" ad had aired, the polling information still can be used to see how convictions about issues ranging from off-coast oil drilling, abortion, the role of the United States in the world, and the death penalty were affected by viewing campaign spots. [23]

Analysis reported in earlier chapters demonstrates how effectively Helms used advertising on social issues, such as the death penalty, to boost support for his position. But priming and defusing also played a role in this election. Helms and Gantt altered the standards of evaluation used by North Carolina voters. Abortion clearly was one of the major battlegrounds throughout this contest. Both candidates sought to define the controversy to their advantage. The analysis undertaken reveals that Gantt was able through advertising to increase the salience of abortion to his vote. Even with controls included, abortion became a stronger factor in citizens' assessments as exposure to Gantt's ads increased.

Meanwhile, Helms's commercials had more of a defusing effect in regard to offshore drilling for oil and gas. In a manner reminiscent of Bush's defusing of the environment as a problematic issue, there was a strong association between seeing Helms's ads and making the offshore drilling less of a factor in vote choice.

Both priming and defusing were particularly important given the closeness of the race. The free media devoted considerable attention to the commercials of each candidate because the vote margin was thought to be so narrow. Charles Black, a leading Republican consultant to Helms, described the advertising battle this way: "You spend a million and move an inch and the other guy spends a million and a half and moves an inch back." [24] In the end, Helms was able to defeat Gantt on a 52 percent to 48 percent vote.

Clinton and the Economy in 1992

Clinton advisers James Carville, Stanley Greenberg, and Mandy Grunwald report that in April 1992 they were worried. Their candidate had sewed up the nomination early, but they felt uneasy about the upcoming fall campaign. In a memo that month, Carville and Greenberg noted that Clinton's negatives had risen to a damaging 41 percent and that he trailed Bush by 24 percentage points on the crucial dimensions of trustworthiness and honesty. Focus group participants regularly complained that "no one knows why Bill Clinton wants to be president" and called him "Slick Willie."[25]

The Clinton advisers moved into action. In a top-secret memo prepared for what Grunwald euphemistically called the Manhattan Project in honor of the 1940s crash program to build a nuclear bomb, Greenberg wrote, "The campaign must move on an urgent basis before the Perot candidacy further defines us (by contrast) and the Bush-Quayle campaign defines us by malice." According to the *Newsweek* account of this plan, Clinton's problem was not so much Gennifer Flowers's accusations about adultery, avoiding the draft, or having once tried to smoke marijuana, but "the belief that Bill Clinton is a typical politician." The report noted many of the inaccurate impressions people had of Clinton: that he was rich and privileged, that he and Hillary Rodham Clinton were childless, that he could not stand up to the special interests, and that "Clinton cannot be the candidate of change." The campaign, the report said, must "take radical steps" to "depoliticize" its candidate.

Early in the summer the Clinton camp began to pretest its fall themes of a New Covenant, fighting for the forgotten middle class, and putting people first. At a series of focus groups in New Jersey, the reactions of voters were stunningly negative. One participant said the New Covenant was "just words . . . glib . . . insulting . . . like blaming the victims." The notion of fighting for the middle class drew these comments: "baloney . . . propaganda." After hearing these comments, Greenberg remarked, "They think he's so political the message stuff gets completely discounted. In fact, it makes it worse."

With the help of a coordinated research program of public opinion surveys and focus groups, the Clinton campaign embarked on an effort to redefine its candidate. At a meeting late in May, Carville suggested, "We need to mention work every 15 seconds." Grunwald agreed and said, "By the end of the convention, what do we want people to know about Clinton: that he worked his way up; that he values work; that he had moved people from welfare to work; that he has a national economic strategy to put America back to work."

The next day, they met with Bill and Hillary Clinton to lay out their plan. The proposal, as described by Greenberg, was based on the idea that "in the 1980s the few—leaders in the corporations, the Congress and the White House—neglected the many. The consequences were that work was not honored, good jobs were lost, everyone but the few felt insecure. . . . The answer for the 1990s had to be a plan to do right by the American people. A plan means a contract. It's not 'Read my lips.'" The campaign then sketched out a plan to coordinate paid ads on the economy in a small group of targeted states and hope for the future with a variety of media appearances on the network morning shows, "Larry King Live," and the "Arsenio Hall Show." The talk show appearances would put Clinton in more intimate settings and allow viewers to get to know him better. They also would bypass traditional reporters, who liked to ask hard-hitting questions.

This plan was remarkably successful. Because some interpretations of the 1992 elections have labeled pocketbook voting the sole reason for Clinton's victory and have asserted the absence of media effects, it is important to recognize the ways in which Clinton's media campaign encouraged economic voting. For example, Clinton was able through his advertising to focus public attention on the economy and his own ability to improve economic performance. Even controlling for a variety of political and demographic factors, people who had high ad exposure were more likely than those of low exposure to make the economy a factor in their votes. They were also more likely to support the view that Clinton had the ability to improve the economy.[26] At the same time, Clinton was able through advertising to strengthen his own image on the trustworthiness and honesty dimension.

These results demonstrate that people's views about the economy do not merely reflect their daily experiences but instead can be shaped by the candidates' strategies. The 1992 experience suggests that citizens' predictions for the economy can be more pessimistic than warranted on the basis of objective economic statistics. One of the reasons forecasting models based purely on economic factors failed to predict Clinton's victory was their failure to take into account the ability of candidates and the media to prime voters.[27] Clinton's advertising and the media coverage of the campaign were part of the reason why Bush got blamed for the country's poor economic performance.

Clinton in 1996

The 1996 election featured a different dynamic than 1992. The country was at peace and people generally were feeling prosperous. The recession that had aborted the reelection effort of President Bush was over and a majority of Americans believed the country was headed in the right direction.

But Clinton faced a new problem during his reelection campaign. The country was experiencing peace and prosperity, but Republicans wanted to revise the role government played in American society. The Gingrich Revolution proposed to downsize government and reduce the rate of growth in spending on a wide variety of social programs.

In order to combat this new Republican challenge, Clinton moved to the center, reclaimed his old credentials as a New Democrat, and adopted Republican language on the importance of balancing the budget and protecting American values. His first ad, aired in June 1995, touted his crime bill and showed Clinton surrounded by a bevy of police officers. In the winter of 1995 and spring of 1996, the Democratic National Committee broadcast commercials attacking Republicans Gingrich and Dole for their efforts to cut popular social programs.

This two-track message of compassion for the downtrodden and a sense of fiscal responsibility was a powerful component in Clinton's reelection. As shown in Figure 8-1, the impact of each factor on the vote rose in importance as people viewed more ads. The idea that Clinton "cared about people like you" had been important in 1992 as Americans struggled with the economy and President Bush appeared oblivious to the suffering of ordinary people. It remained important in 1996 following Republican efforts to cap the social safety net. As people moved from low to

Figure 8-1 Priming the Clinton Vote: 1996

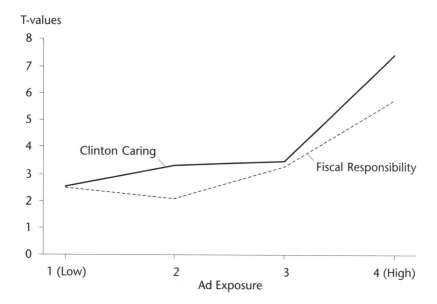

Source: Brown University national survey, October 28–November 3, 1996.

Note: T-values are the impact of each factor on the vote.

high Clinton ad exposure, the sense that Clinton was caring and compassionate rose in importance to the vote.

The same was true on the crucial dimension that Clinton would bring fiscal discipline to the federal government. As people saw more ads, the president's image as fiscally responsible exerted a stronger tie to the vote. It was a strategy that helped Clinton fight off Dole and defuse the potential problem of being called a tax-and-spend liberal. As a result, he become the first Democratic president to win reelection since Franklin Delano Roosevelt.

Chapter 9

Playing the Blame Game

It has become conventional wisdom based on recent campaigns that attack ads work. The widespread acceptance of this view explains in part the frequency of negative campaigns. This perspective, though, ignores contrary evidence. Negative commercials are advantageous when they help candidates define the debate and pinpoint liabilities of the opponent. In 1988, Bush was able to dominate the agenda and prime voters. Yet it also is clear from other elections that Bush in 1992 and Forbes, Dole, and Gingrich in 1996 were the objects of a backlash in reaction to the negative ads that enabled their opponents to attract voters.

From the standpoint of candidates, negative ads are risky as a strategic device because it is hard to get the benefits of attack without suffering the blame for an unpleasant campaign. Attack strategies must be used with great prudence. Simply going on the offensive is not necessarily going to be effective. If attributions of blame outweigh the benefits of controlling the agenda, attacks are likely to backfire. As the following case studies reveal, for negative ads to work, they must help candidates define the terms of debate without also making them come across as mean-spirited.

Blame Dukakis

In the 1988 presidential campaign, Bush played the blame game masterfully. A survey by the CBS News/*New York Times* that year asked voters two questions in an effort to measure attributions of responsibility for the negativity of the campaign: "Did most of Bush's [Dukakis's] TV commercials that you saw explain what George Bush [Michael Dukakis] stands for, or did most of the commercials attack George Bush [Michael Dukakis]?" and "Who

158

is more responsible for the negative campaigning there has been this year, George Bush or Michael Dukakis?"

Although Bush is generally acknowledged as having been the more aggressive campaigner that year, he did not reap a disproportionate share of the blame for negativity. More people in October saw his ads as attacking the opponent (37 percent) than explaining his views (21 percent), but the same was true for Dukakis (34 percent thought his ads attacked and 25 percent believed they explained his views). (See Table 9-1.) Not until the end of the campaign did Bush receive the majority of the blame.

If one compiles the ratio of attack/explain responses each for Bush and Dukakis at different points in the campaign, viewers were evenly split in their ratios between Bush (1.8) and Dukakis (1.3) in October. By November, though, Bush's attack/explain ratio was 3.1, whereas Dukakis's was only 1.3.[1] These figures were in line with reality. A study of CBS news stories involving ads during the 1988 general election reveals that 75 percent of Bush's commercials aired during the news were negative about Dukakis, whereas only 33 percent of Dukakis's ads were negative about Bush.

Blame Bush

The picture in 1992 could not have been more different. In September, almost twice as many people said Bush's commercials attacked Clinton (46 percent) than said the ads explained his own views (24 percent). In contrast, more people thought Clinton's ads explained his views (37 percent) than attacked the opponent (31 percent). People also were more likely to name Bush (39 percent) than Clinton (21 percent) as being responsible for the negative campaigning. By late October, Bush was being blamed by the even larger margin of 60 percent to 13 percent. In early November 1988, 25 percent had blamed Bush and 16 percent Dukakis for campaign negativity.

To some extent Democrats anticipated Bush's 1992 attack ads and focused attention on the blame game.[2] In an effort to inoculate himself against Republican attacks, Clinton and his fellow Democrats talked about GOP tendencies to engage in attack politics as early as the Democratic convention. In his acceptance speech, Clinton warned: "To all those in this campaign season who would criticize Arkansas, come on down . . . you'll see us struggling against some of the problems we haven't solved yet. But

TABLE 9-1
Tone of Ads and Responsibility
for Negative Campaigning: 1988–1996

1988 Campaign	October	Early November	Mid-November
Bush ads			
Explain his views	21%	14%	14%
Attack opponent	37	36	43
Both	9	11	10
Don't know/No answer	33	39	33
Dukakis ads			
Explain his views	25	24	24
Attack opponent	34	26	31
Both	9	11	8
Don't know/No answer	32	39	37
Responsibility for negativity			
Bush	—	25	30
Dukakis	—	16	19
Both	—	24	24
Neither	—	3	3
Don't know/No answer	—	32	24

1992 Campaign	September	October
Bush ads		
Explain his views	24%	16%
Attack opponent	46	56
Both	16	10
Don't know/No answer	14	18
Clinton ads		
Explain his views	37	46
Attack opponent	31	24
Both	17	12
Don't know/No answer	15	18
Responsibility for negativity		
Bush	39	60
Clinton	21	13
Both	22	18
Neither	4	3
Don't know/No answer	14	6

1996 Campaign	June	Oct. 10–13	Oct. 17–20	Oct. 28–Nov. 3
Dole ads				
Explain his views	32%	40%	24%	14%
Attack opponent	48	50	63	55
Don't know/No answer	20	10	13	31

TABLE 9-1
(Continued)

1996 Campaign *(Cont.)*	June	Oct. 10–13	Oct. 17–20	Oct. 28–Nov. 3
Clinton ads				
Explain his views	53	68	73	49
Attack opponent	28	19	14	21
Don't know/No answer	19	13	13	30
Perot ads				
Explain his views	—	—	—	31
Attack opponent	—	—	—	21
Don't know/No answer	—	—	—	48
Responsibility for negativity				
Dole	—	—	—	52
Clinton	—	—	—	13
Perot	—	—	—	6
Don't know/No answer	—	—	—	29

Sources: October 21–24, 1988, CBS News/*New York Times* survey; November 2–4, 1988, CBS News/*New York Times* survey; November 10–15, 1988, CBS News/*New York Times* survey; September 28–29, 1992, Winston-Salem survey; October 26–31, 1992, Los Angeles County survey, CBS News/*New York Times* survey; May 31–June 3, 1996, CBS News/*New York Times* survey; October 10–13, 1996, CBS News/*New York Times* survey; October 17–20, 1996, Brown University survey; October 28–November 3, 1996.

Note: Entries indicate percentages of individuals believing candidate explained or attacked and that the candidate was responsible for the negativity of the campaign.

— indicates no data available.

you'll also see a lot of great people doing amazing things." A delegate from Chicago, Jonathan Quinn, was more direct about likely attacks on Clinton: "I am fearful about the attacks on Clinton's character. I don't think we've seen anything yet. I think the Republicans are going to ravage him, and I'm nervous about it. . . . I think things will get brutally ugly."[3] Clinton himself emphasized the importance of not being "Dukakisized," and repeated Bush's widely publicized comment to David Frost early in the year about Bush's willingness to "do anything" to win the election.

In a clear contrast to the high-road strategy of Dukakis, the Clinton team also responded immediately to Republican onslaughts. When Bush ran attack ads in early October accusing the Arkansas governor of raising taxes, Clinton broadcast an instant rebuttal. The spot started with a bold red headline: "GEORGE BUSH ATTACK AD." The commercial went on to say, "George Bush is running attack ads. He says all these people would have their taxes raised by Bill Clinton. Scary, huh? 'Misleading,' says the *Washington Post*. And the *Wall Street Journal* says 'Clinton has proposed to cut taxes for the sort of people featured in [Bush's] ad.'"

Bush's broadcast of an ad on the draft-evasion issue using *Time* magazine's cover story asking whether Clinton could be trusted also led Clinton's media advisers to test a commercial featuring editorial responses from around the country. Though the ad was never broadcast, because people in focus groups felt it was too harsh, the spot illustrates the quick-response mentality of the Clinton team: "All across America people are hurting, and what is George Bush doing? The press calls his campaign gutter politics [*St. Petersburg Times*]. Malicious and dangerous mudslinging [the *Tennessean*]. Wrong, deceitful [*Des Moines Register*]. It's sad to see a president stoop this low [*Atlanta Constitution*]. Nasty and shrill [*New York Times*]. Deplorably sordid [*Los Angeles Times*]. Lies and attempted distraction [Hutchinson, Kan., *News*]. Bush's smear . . . new low [*USA Today*]. Cheap shot, Mr. President [*Miami Herald*]. Stop sleazy tactics and talk straight [Wilmington, Del., *News Journal*]. We can't afford four more years." [4]

The same tactic was in evidence on October 7, 1992, when Bush raised the character issue in response to a question on the "Larry King Live" show. Under prodding from the host, Bush attacked Clinton for leading antiwar demonstrations while he was a student at Oxford University: "I cannot for the life of me understand mobilizing demonstrations and demonstrating against your own country, no matter how strongly you feel, when you are in a foreign land. Maybe I'm old fashioned, but to go to a foreign country and demonstrate against your own country when your sons and daughters are dying halfway around the world, I am sorry but I think that is wrong." When asked in the same interview about a student trip Clinton made to Moscow in 1969, Bush said: "I don't want to tell you what I really think. To go to Moscow, one year after Russia crushed Czechoslovakia, not remember who you saw there. . . ." [5]

In 1988, Bush's attacks were reported favorably by the press and Dukakis's weak rebuttals were seen as evidence of passivity. Bush's 1992 attack met a different fate. Clinton took the lead in responding. In the first presidential debate, Clinton turned to Bush and accused the president of engaging in a McCarthy-style smear on his patriotism. He also reminded Bush that in the 1950s, Bush's father, Sen. Prescott Bush, had displayed courage in standing up to McCarthy.

The press response was sympathetic to Clinton. Bush was met with unfavorable headlines across the country. For example, the *Washington Post* headlined their stories, "Clinton Denounces Attacks by Bush" and "President Drops Moscow Trip Issue: Bush Denies Attacking Foe's Patriotism." The *New York Times* ran stories entitled "Clinton Says Desperation Is Fueling Bush Criticism," "Bush Camp Pursues an Offensive By Having Others Make the Attack," and "Campaign Renews Disputes of the Vietnam War Years."

The backlash against Republican attacks took their toll on President Bush. An analysis shows how attack strategies by Bush and Clinton as well as attributions of responsibility for negative campaigning influenced the vote. Using a design similar to the paired-ads design reported in previous chapters, this analysis investigates how voters responded when faced with the combination of Bush and Clinton ads. The results indicate that attacks produced a strong voter backlash. The more each candidate was seen as attacking, the more likely voters were to blame that person for negative campaigning.[6]

These attributions are important because there was an inverse correlation between blame and the vote. Voters who saw Bush as responsible for negativity were more likely to vote for Clinton. Because more people were blaming Bush than Clinton for the tone of the race, this trend clearly was a liability for Bush. Shortly after the election, Bush aide Jim Pinkerton was forced to admit in a campaign postmortem, "We've got to ask ourselves what would make a voter vote for a draft-dodging, womanizing, fill-in-the-blank sleazeball? What would drive them to it? This says a lot about us, doesn't it?"[7]

It is ironic to note that in light of its moralistic protests against Bush's attacks, the Clinton camp had prepared ads for the last week of the campaign challenging Perot's suitability for the presidency. One featured people-on-the-street interviews with former Perot volunteers saying Perot lacked character. Another said, "Ross Perot's plan? It could make things worse. He wants a 50-cent gas tax, which hits middle-class families hardest. He wants to raise taxes on the middle-class. And he wants to cut Medicare benefits." Each statement was footnoted with a page number from Perot's book, *United We Stand*.[8] The commercials were not broadcast when it was apparent right before the election that Perot represented no threat to Clinton.

Blame Forbes

The 1996 Republican primaries featured a barrage of attack ads that was unprecedented for a nomination campaign. Starting in September 1995, six months before the Iowa caucuses and New Hampshire primary, multimillionaire Forbes broadcast wave after wave of television assaults on the front-runner Dole.

One ad proclaimed, "The official *Congressional Record* documents Bob Dole's vote that increased his million-dollar, tax-paid pension. But now, he denied it." [Dole in TV interview]. "I never voted to increase pensions." [Announcer] "Bob Dole must have forgotten. The *Orlando Sentinel* reported the Senate pay raise that Bob Dole voted for increased senators' pensions by $26 million." [Dole on TV] "I never voted to increase pensions." [Announcer] "Bob Dole. A Washington politician."

Another Forbes spot condemned Dole for raising taxes: "Since 1982 Bob Dole has voted for 17 tax increases. . . . Bob Dole voted to increase income taxes. Taxes on phones, gas, even Social Security." Still another criticized Dole for supporting appropriations bills that funded ski slopes. In all, more than two-thirds of Forbes's ads run before Iowa were negative in tone, far above the level of negativity common in the nominating process.

Tim Forbes, senior advisor to his brother's campaign, explained the strategy this way: Because Steve had zero name recognition nationally just a few months before the election and was running against a well-known opponent who had a huge lead in the polls, the Forbes campaign needed something to "puncture the air of inevitability" surrounding Dole.[9] Both Dole and Gramm received much more free news coverage and had much stronger ground organizations than Forbes, so he had to rely on big ad buys to get his message out.

The decision to go negative, according to Tim Forbes, was predicated on the view that "people say they hate attack ads, but they actually respond to them. People see them as having greater credibility and are more likely to be swayed by them."

As the attack ads rained down on television viewers, political observers began to notice similarities between Forbes's strategy and that used for years by Senator Helms of North Carolina. As noted in the previous chapter, Helms's ads often featured harsh, inflammatory, and graphic appeals to gut-level issues: race, taxes, and government spending. The split-screen pictures at the end of many Forbes ads, "[picture of Dole] Washington values. [picture of Forbes] Conservative values," paralleled the on-screen convention of Helms's commercials.

This similarity was no accident. Although Forbes tried to downplay the association, his early ads were designed by two conservative veterans of Helms's North Carolina campaigns: Tom Ellis and Carter Wrenn. These consultants were the very individuals who had devised Helms's infamous "White Hands" commercials.[10]

At one level, these television attacks were remarkably successful. In the short run, they drove down voter support for Dole. From early 1995 to early 1996, Dole's support in Iowa and New Hampshire dropped by more than 30 percentage points. The ads attached negative code words to Dole, such as "Washington politician" and "raising taxes." The commercials also temporarily increased support for Forbes. By destabilizing voter judgments about the candidates, Forbes's attack ads upset the predictability of the Republican nominating process and forced voters to take another look at their choices.

But in the midst of all his ad buys, Forbes missed two basic rules of attack politics. First, voters do not like negative ads and there always is an inevitable backlash against the person seen as responsible for those types of appeals. Second, when attacked, opponents always position themselves as the victim and focus blame on the person who started the attack.

By the end of January, Dole had redeployed his ad broadcasts against Forbes. One ad said, "Steve Forbes tells us he has the experience to cut government waste. But in his one government job, he allowed $276,000 in tax dollars to be wasted redecorating the residences of a friend who was his top aide. Forbes's top bureaucrats received government pay averaging $240,000. The press called it a 'gravy train.' Two federal audits sharply criticized this lavish waste of our tax dollars as 'improper.' Steve Forbes. Untested. Just not ready for the job."

Forbes clearly did not anticipate either the voter backlash or opponent efforts to blame him for the negativity of the campaign. In that situation, Forbes could have made a strategic adjustment. He could have scaled back the attacks and mixed more positive ads with the negative spots. For example, during the 1992 general election, Clinton always tried to have one positive ad airing for every two attack commercials he was running. When questioned by opponents or journalists about why he was on the attack, Clinton always could point to a specific positive spot on the air at that moment.

In addition, Forbes could have played the blame game with opponents by inoculating himself from their complaints. Similar to Clinton, he could have warned reporters that opponents were going to go after him. After all, he was rising in the polls and Washington politicians were feeling threatened. What else would one expect them to do but to attack him in return?

Forbes did neither of these things until it was too late. After he finished in fourth place in Iowa, he canceled his negative attacks in New Hampshire for the week prior to that primary. But the backlash had already developed and engulfed Forbes in the blame game. An exit poll in New Hampshire the night of the state primary revealed that 65 percent of voters thought the ads in that primary had mainly attacked opponents rather than addressed the issues. A large number of voters blamed Forbes for this turn of events.

Ultimately, Forbes's attacks succeeded in weakening support for Dole, but Forbes was not the beneficiary of this change. Buchanan ended up winning New Hampshire and Alexander came in a strong third after Dole. Forbes's candidacy was doomed in part by his slowness in anticipating the voter backlash to his attacks.

Blame Dole

The fall campaign began unusually early. With Clinton having no opposition and Dole wrapping up the Republican nomination by the middle of March, both candidates aired commercials throughout March, April, May, and June. Many of these spots attacked the opposition. Clinton tied Dole to Gingrich and accused them both of gutting Medicare, Medicaid, education, and the environment. Dole, for his part, questioned the president's trustworthiness in light of the Whitewater allegations concerning Clinton's real estate and financial transactions in Arkansas.

Clinton won the spring phase of this campaign. By June, he had a lead of 54 percent to 35 percent among registered voters and was viewed more favorably than Dole. Whereas 48 percent viewed the president favorably and 33 percent saw him unfavorably, Dole had a favorability rating of 29 percent and an unfavorability rating of 35 percent. By early October, Dole's unfavorability rating had risen to 41 percent with a favorability rating of 29 percent. Clinton was viewed favorably by 47 percent and unfavorably by 36 percent. His lead was 53 percent to 36 percent.

But more surprising was how well Clinton did on the blame game. When asked in May 1996 whether the candidates were spending more time explaining views or attacking the opponent, more blamed Dole than Clinton. Thirty-two percent of voters thought Dole was explaining his views and 48 percent believed he was attacking the opponent. In Clinton's case, 53 percent thought he was explaining his views and only 28 percent felt he was attacking the opponent.

By early October 1996, even more blamed Dole than Clinton. In a national survey from October 10 to 13, 50 percent believed Dole was attacking the opponent and 40 percent thought he was explaining his views. This contrasts with the 19 percent who believed Clinton was attacking the opponent and 68 percent who felt he was explaining his views.[11]

The blame for Dole got even worse later in October. After the final debate and a week in which Dole attacked Clinton's character on everything from the president's unsuccessful Whitewater real estate investment to his ethics in the White House, 63 percent felt Dole was attacking his opponent and only 14 percent believed Clinton was doing so.[12]

By the last week of the campaign, 55 percent felt Dole was attacking his opponent, 21 percent believed Clinton was doing so, and 21 percent thought Perot's ads were attacking the opponent. When asked who was most responsible for the negative campaigning for that year, 52 percent cited Dole, 13 percent Clinton, and 6 percent Perot.

As they had done successfully in 1992, the Clintons used an inoculation strategy as early as April 1996 to warn people that Republicans would launch "a relentless attack" of negative advertising and misinformation. Speaking before 1,000 Democratic women at Emily's List, an organization devoted to raising early money for female candidates, First Lady Hillary Clinton predicted: "Get prepared for it and don't be surprised by it. When you've got no vision of how to make the world a better place for yourself or your children, then you go negative." After Dole went negative in the fall, Clinton White House advisor George

Stephanopoulos characterized Dole's public persona this way: "All you ever see him doing on TV is carping, attacking, whining."[13]

The Clinton people shielded themselves from the backlash against negative campaigning by developing a new genre in the advertising area—the positive attack ad. Recognizing that voters do not like negative advertising, the Clinton campaign broadcast attack ads that combined negative and positive appeals. An example is an ad Clinton ran as a response to Dole's attack on Clinton's drug record. The ad criticized Dole for opposing the creation of a drug czar and Congress for cutting monies for school drug prevention programs but then went on to explain that Clinton had sought to strengthen school programs and that he had expanded the death penalty to drug kingpins. By using attack ads as a surgical tool, not as a sledge hammer, the Clinton campaign sought to attach negatives to the opponent while also sheltering themselves from blame by voters upset about negative ads.

Blame Gingrich

The 1996 campaign was unusual in being one of the few national elections to be framed around the Speaker of the House. In 1982, Republicans had made an ad making fun of what they called Speaker Tip O'Neill's tired old liberalism that concluded with the tagline, "The Democrats are out of gas." But this targeting of a sitting Speaker was atypical. Elections are more likely to be framed around general public perceptions about the two parties, such as Republicans being uncaring and insensitive and Democrats being tax-and-spend liberals. However, owing to Gingrich's high unpopularity in national public opinion polls, numerous Democrats around the country in 1996 made use of ads that directly attacked Gingrich by name. About 75,000 ads, 10 percent of all the political spots that aired in 1996, were broadcast against Gingrich, according to the Speaker's own estimate. Local Republican candidates were shown standing next to Gingrich with the suggestion that they were Gingrich robots who mindlessly sought to gut education, Medicare, and the environment.

Other Democratic spots relied on new video technology to show the local Republican being "morphed" into a picture of the Speaker. The general text of these ads was to claim that a vote for the Republican was a vote for the unpopular House Speaker.

One Republican in Madison, Wisconsin, though, made creative use of morphing to protect himself from the Gingrich backlash. When moderate Republican Scott Klug ran for reelection against Paul Soglin, the mayor of Madison, he broadcast an ad that started with an image of Gingrich's face and Klug's lips saying, "You've heard a lot of talk lately about how Scott Klug and Newt Gingrich are the same person." After boasting that he was the "ninth most independent" Republican in the House, newspaper headlines appear trumpeting Klug's votes against the Gingrich Revolution. Gingrich's face then is morphed into Klug's with an announcer proclaiming, "The next time someone tells you Scott Klug is Newt Gingrich, tell them they've got the wrong picture."

But the ad produced the following response from Klug's Democratic opponent: "Do you think Newt Gingrich is right 84 percent of the time? Scott Klug does. That's how often Scott Klug votes with Newt Gingrich." [14]

As congressional Democrats ran against Gingrich, Republicans responded with a series of ads produced by the Republican National Committee that accused Democratic candidates of being liberal, ultra-liberal, and super-liberal. Many of these ads took the guise of "issue advocacy" spots designed to educate the public, not influence the election. This exempted the commercials from federal campaign laws and meant the party organization was not limited in how much it could spend on local races and was not forced to disclose the contributors who financed the spots.

A series of such spots aired in the Rhode Island U.S. Senate campaign between Democrat Jack Reed and Republican Nancy Mayer at the cost of more than $1 million, as was discussed in Chapter 5. Starting in early May 1996, one ad began with a picture of Reed with text on screen proclaiming "Opposes the Balanced Budget Amendment." An announcer intoned,

You already know liberal Jack Reed opposes the Balanced Budget Amendment. But, it gets worse. [on-screen text: Opposes making welfare recipients work for their checks.] Jack Reed is so liberal that he opposes making welfare recipients work for their checks. It's outrageous. [on-screen text: Voted repeatedly against workfare.] Jack Reed has voted repeatedly against replacing welfare with workfare. [on-screen text: That's liberal.] That's liberal. [on-screen text: That's Jack Reed.] That's Jack Reed. [on-screen text: That's wrong.] That's wrong. Call liberal Jack Reed. Tell him his record on welfare is just too liberal for you. Tell him to vote for the Governor's plan to replace welfare with workfare.

In response to this, the Reed campaign aired an ad that began,

Newt Gingrich, Bob Dole, and the national Republicans have brought their negative politics into Rhode Island to smear Jack Reed. The truth is Jack Reed has voted for a balanced budget amendment—one that protects Social Security. But he opposed the Gingrich budget that slashes Medicare and education in order to pay for a massive tax cut for the wealthy. Reed has voted to require welfare recipients to work. But he opposed the Gingrich cuts in child nutrition. Jack Reed. Fighting for the working families of Rhode Island.

As the RNC ads continued throughout the rest of the Senate campaign, the press coverage of the advertising barrage was negative. One story by *Providence Journal* reporter Scott MacKay was headlined, "Reed Counterattacks GOP's Negative TV Ad." A column by the state's leading political columnist, M. Charles Bakst of the *Providence Journal,* was titled, "Saying It Straight: Political Attack Ads Fill Air with Garbage." [15] After Reed challenged the accuracy of some of the RNC ads, a local television station refused to air one of the spots on the grounds that the ad substantially distorted Reed's voting record in the House.

As part of their polling, the Reed campaign tracked the percentage of voters who felt Reed was "too liberal." The number reached a high point of 29 percent midway through the campaign and dropped after that. Even after the RNC accelerated their expenditures on "liberal Jack Reed" ads, the number did not rise higher. Reed's polls also found that more voters blamed Mayer for the negativity of the campaign compared to Reed.[16]

A focus group conducted October 2, 1996, at Brown University found that viewers did not like the ads or find them very believable. Voters were asked to rate the U.S. Senate candidates on a series of dimensions such as favorability, leadership, honesty, caring, fiscal discipline, and responsibility for negative campaigning. They then were shown a series of six television commercials being broadcast in the U.S. Senate campaign as well as an ad watch broadcast September 19, 1996, on a local television station that evaluated U.S. Senate campaign ads. After seeing each ad and ad watch, voters were asked to rate and discuss the presentations on persuasiveness, believability, the degree to which the candidates conformed to the participant's values, and sense of fairness in the campaign. They also were asked to identify the sponsor of the ad. After seeing the six ads, they were asked to rerate candidates Reed and Mayer and then to rate them again after seeing the ad watch.

In general, voters did not find the "liberal Jack Reed" attack ad sponsored by the RNC as part of its national advertising strategy against Democratic candidates around the country very persuasive (0 percent), very believable (0 percent), conformed to their values (0 percent), or was very fair (12 percent). Few found that an ad sponsored by the Republican Senatorial Campaign Committee comparing the records of Reed and Mayer was very persuasive (0 percent), very believable (12 percent), conformed to their values (12 percent), or was very fair (12 percent).

Voters had considerable difficulty correctly identifying the sponsor of the ads and distinguishing between ads run by candidates and party organizations. Only 50 percent were able to correctly identify the sponsors of the ads. Just 12 percent correctly identified the sponsor of the Republican Senatorial Campaign Committee ad. Indeed, some thought it was sponsored by the RNC, and others believed it was sponsored by the Mayer campaign and the Republican party.

When discussing the RNC ads, voters volunteered a number of criticisms. One person described the ad as "offensive." Another said, "It gives me a good reason to dislike the Republican National Committee." Another said, "If they looked up in the dictionary the true meaning of the word liberal, . . . liberal is having an open mind."

Of the ads shown to study participants, the ad having the highest believability was Reed's biography ad in which he discussed his family background and concern for education. Sixty-two percent found it very believable. This compares to 25 percent for a Mayer ad saying she was a fiscal watchdog, 12 percent for a Reed response ad questioning why Republicans have spent $1 million in ads attacking him, 12 percent for a Republican Senatorial Campaign Committee ad comparing Reed and Mayer on fiscal matters, 12 percent on a Reed spot decrying Republican cuts in student loans and Medicare, and 0 percent for a Republican National Committee ad attacking "liberal Jack Reed."

Most of these ads did not alter the impressions of voters about the candidates. Reed gained the most in terms of a 0 (cold) to 100 (warm) feeling-thermometer rating, moving from 54 at the beginning of the discussion to 61 at the end. Mayer moved from 54 to 55 on her feeling-thermometer score. Fifty percent gave Reed favorable ratings after seeing the ads, compared to 38 percent who had at the beginning of the discussion. Mayer went from a

50 percent to 38 percent favorability rating after seeing the six ads.

In terms of responsibility for the negativity of the campaign, many more at the beginning of the discussion were likely to blame Mayer for the negativity of the campaign (62 percent) compared to Reed (12 percent). After seeing the ads, 75 percent blamed Mayer and 12 percent blamed Reed.

Both candidates were seen as more honest and caring after the series of six ads. Each was less likely to be seen as bringing fiscal discipline to the federal government after ad viewing, although more (25 percent) were likely to see Mayer as bringing fiscal discipline than Reed (12 percent). Reed ended up winning the seat by a margin of 63 percent to 35 percent.

Chapter 10

Advertising and Democratic Elections

In this book, I have investigated television advertising from a number of different perspectives. The questions I have tried to answer include, What is the strategic use of political commercials? How do the media cover ads? What impact do campaign spots have on viewers? In brief, I found that commercials influence how voters learn about the candidates (Chapter 6), what they identify as priorities (Chapter 7), their standards of assessment (Chapter 8), and attributions of blame (Chapter 9). Ads have their strongest impact with little known candidates and electoral settings of low visibility and in situations in which journalistic coverage reinforces the ad message. Strategic elements within each election are also crucial. Both the timing and content of ads and decisions on when and where to attack shape viewer responses to advertisements.

This chapter examines the implications of these results for democratic elections. Elections are crucial to democratic systems. They are a means by which citizens choose who occupies positions of formal responsibility. There is little doubt that ads have altered the way citizens make electoral decisions. Yet the research reported here has shown that not all electoral arenas face the same problems. Because the impact of an advertisement depends considerably on the campaign context, the same type of commercial can pose very different challenges in various settings. It therefore is important to determine under what conditions ads are most worrisome.

Democratic Expectations

Few aspects of democracy have been discussed over the course of American history as much as the quality of information provided during the election process. Candidates are expected to address the subjects at stake in a given election and provide some indication of where they stand in regard to those matters. In fact, this information allows voters to hold leaders accountable. Failure to provide suitable material undermines the representative basis of American democracy.[1]

As an intermediary institution, the media are expected to devote enough attention to candidates' character attributes and to the issues to help voters bridge the gaps left by candidates' communications. Not many people directly experience election campaigns. Voters are dependent on the media to help them interpret political realities. When reporters provide the type of information that educates citizens regarding the choices facing them, the election process is significantly enhanced.

However, there is disagreement over exactly how detailed information from candidates and the media should be. The classical model of democracy calls for specific, issue-oriented material.[2] Candidates are expected to have detailed positions on the major issues facing the country and to communicate these views clearly to voters. Issue-based voting models as well as textbook descriptions of American elections emphasize the policy aspects of campaigns.

Other scholars, though, have argued that popular control can be achieved through other approaches. For example, the party-responsibility model uses partisanship as the means of accountability. Parties foster representation because they encapsulate general lines of thinking about major policy positions. Therefore, according to this model, voters can make substantive judgments about candidates based purely on party labels.[3] In a similar way, retrospective evaluations have become widely accepted as a means of popular control. Advocates of this system argue that the candidates' approach to issues alone is not an appropriate test because voters can be sophisticated and rational without engaging in issue-based voting. As long as leaders can be held accountable for the broad direction of government performance, democratic tenets are satisfied.[4]

Still others have argued that knowledge about the character of potential leaders is vital to democratic elections.[5] Elections are seen as a means of evaluating the judgment of leaders who will do the deliberating in a representative democracy. According to this perspective, assessments about leadership qualities and character are quite relevant to voters' decision making.

The emergence of thirty-second ads and nine-second sound bites as the primary means of political communication represents a potential challenge to each of these models.[6] Because classical democratic theory places a premium on detailed policy information, the chief danger under this model is deception and distortion by the candidates in regard to their positions on issues. Ads that mislead viewers or distort an opponent's record are particularly dangerous. Numerous campaigners have used ads to create impressions of themselves that turned out to be inaccurate (including Johnson as the peace candidate in 1964 and Bush as the "no new taxes" man of 1988). The same logic applies to models centered on leaders' judgment. The primary danger of ads in this view is their potential to manipulate views about personal traits—leadership, trustworthiness, and independence. In 1984, for example, Hart was remarkably successful at getting people to see Mondale, who had formidable Washington experience and interest group support, as just another old-style politician currying favor with special interests.

But these are not the only risks from advertisements. The party-responsibility model assumes that long-term party identification will protect ad viewers against excesses by candidates. Yet even this model recognizes that party attachments have loosened in recent years and that new arenas based on intraparty nominating contests have arisen. These settings are precisely where ads achieve their greatest impact. The combination of unknown candidates, volatile preferences, and shared party labels gives ads enormous influence. The emergence of independent candidates, such as Perot, has put the party-responsibility model in even greater danger in regard to general elections, because party ties are less decisive in a three-way race. In these settings, advertising takes on great strategic significance. The ability to win with a plurality of the vote encourages candidates to use commercials to appeal to narrow pockets of voters.

The pocketbook-voting model also raises important normative questions. This approach appears on the surface to be the least vulnerable to ads. Because vote choice is presumed to be based on citizens' views about the economy, which are in turn rooted in people's personal experiences, ads would not seem too influential on electoral decisions. But a closer inspection reveals that even this model requires voters to assign blame for unsatisfactory performance and to assess candidates' capabilities to deal with economic matters.[7] In 1992, for example, Clinton—primarily through advertising—was able to boost public perceptions about his ability to improve the economy and to show people that he was a caring individual. At the same time, he and Perot were able to blame Bush and the Republicans for the nation's poor economic performance.

Attributions of responsibility are particularly open to media influence. Through techniques based on priming and defusing, ads can elevate or lower particular standards of evaluation. In fact, during eras of scarce resources, elections often rest on how well candidates play the blame game.[8] Therefore, although traditional voting models diagnose the problem of advertisements quite differently, each one identifies particular dangers regarding the quality of information presented to voters and the ability of citizens to engage in informed decision making.

The Risk of Manipulation

The concerns expressed about American elections did not originate with television. Writers have long complained about the dangers of outside influences on voters. Nineteenth-century reformers, for example, fought outright bribery in an era when cash payoffs to citizens in exchange for votes were quite common. The extension of voting rights in this century precipitated wild debates regarding the impact of external agents: opponents of expanded suffrage claimed that newly enfranchised women would be unduly influenced by their husbands and that Catholic immigrants would become pawns of the pope!

Several features of democratic systems have been thought to reduce the danger of external manipulation. Widespread acceptance of the democratic culture by political elites is seen in pluralist models as providing a sufficient guarantee of fair and open competition. Self-regulation, it is said, weakens the threat from candidates and helps to ensure that election appeals are made fairly. At the same time, a variety of intermediary institutions supposedly protects citizens from overly ambitious campaigners. People can express opinions and hold leaders accountable through organizations representing their political perspectives. Parties and interest groups have been seen as the most important links in modern theories of democracy. Because these organizations facilitate the joint activity of citizens having common points of view, they are a means of bridging the gap between citizens and leaders.

The problem with this view of democracy is that its proponents have been strangely quiet about key aspects of leadership behavior. In the rush to reconcile less than optimistic views of citizens' behavior with hopes for democracy, sight has been lost of the crucial responsibilities of candidates in the election process. Pluralist perspectives, for example, ignore the fact that elite competition can go beyond the bounds of fair play when there is no referee to penalize players for making deceptive appeals. With the powerful advertising tools at candidates' disposal, citizens are exposed to potent campaign appeals.[9]

The decline of self-regulation by candidates' organizations would not be quite so problematic if there were a universally acknowledged body to protect citizens against subtle manipulation of their standards of evaluation. Unfortunately, there is no external referee with the authority to police electoral competition. Political parties and interest groups have lost much of their grip on elections. Government agencies (such as the Federal Election Commission and the Federal Communications Commission) meanwhile cannot regulate campaign appeals, because political speech is constitutionally protected.

The weakness of external regulators at a time when candidates control influential communication technologies has given candidates great incentives to attempt manipulation of voters through the airwaves. The classic problem of electoral deception involves substantive manipulation, whereby leaders deceive citizens about policy matters. According to Page and Shapiro, "To the extent that the public is given false or incorrect or biased information, or is deprived of important relevant information, people may make mistaken evaluations of policy alternatives and may express support for policies harmful to their own or society's interests, or in conflict with values they cherish."[10]

If elections were primarily about public policy, substantive manipulation would remain the most dangerous threat to the political system. However, contests involve perceptions about electability and personal images as well. Many races in recent years have turned on questions of momentum, likability, and mistakes. How the game is played often has become more important than the actual task of setting the future course of government action.

The fact that elections generally involve short-term campaign phenomena creates another type of deception, which I call *strategic manipulation*. In this situation, efforts are made to shift impressions of the campaign in a direction favorable to particular candidates. For example, candidates often seek to influence short-term evaluations. Specifically, spot commercials can be employed to alter views about an opponent's likability; they can lead to exaggerated claims regarding a contender's electoral prospects; they can be used to change campaign dynamics and distract voters from pressing matters of the day.

Television commercials are particularly problematic because they combine audio and visual technologies. Sounds, colors, and visual presentations can be used in deceptive ways, as was discussed earlier. For example, Buchanan's ad consultants in 1992 occasionally speeded up or slowed down Bush's physical movements to create unfavorable impressions of the president. Independent ad producer Floyd Brown also admitted that he had doctored a 1992 ad showing Clinton's hand raised high with Senator Kennedy's. The joint picture was faked by combining separate pictures of the men alone.[11]

In the 1996 U.S. Senate race in Virginia, Sen. John Warner was forced to fire consultant Greg Stevens after Stevens admitted doctoring a photo used in a spot linking Mark Warner with President Clinton by replacing the head of Sen. Charles Robb with that of his Democratic opponent, Mark Warner.[12] This type of editing, which tried to link Mark Warner with other candidates said to be liberal, poses obvious problems for viewers. People may remember the visual image but not be in a position to recognize electronic chicanery.

Strategic manipulation has not attracted as much study as substantive or symbolic manipulation, but in a media era it is a serious threat. A campaign structure that is open, volatile, and heavily dependent on media coverage gives candidates clear incentives to seek advantage strategically. The rise of new technologies and the employment of professional campaign managers in the United States have broadened the range of tactics considered acceptable and given campaigners extraordinary tools for influencing voters.

Different Arenas, Different Threats

The susceptibility of voters to advertising appeals has long generated despair from political observers. McGinniss's book, *The Selling of the President,* and Spero's volume, *The Duping of the*

American Voter, express common fears about the dangers of advertisements.[13] But these authors failed to recognize that not all electoral arenas are subject to the same threat. The visibility of the setting makes a big difference.

The major threat in highly visible arenas, such as presidential general election campaigns, is substantive manipulation. The 1988 general election gave a textbook illustration of this danger, as the relatively unknown Dukakis saw his entire campaign shattered by Bush's successful efforts to move the campaign from past performance to flags, furloughs, and patriotism. Bush used advertising on tax and spending matters as well as crime that year to fill in the public profile of the relatively unknown Dukakis. The vice president was able to dominate the campaign because few voters knew much about the Massachusetts governor, 1988 was a year with a fluid policy agenda, and Dukakis did not successfully defend himself. Bush painted a portrait of the Massachusetts governor that many observers considered grossly exaggerated; Bush pictured an unrepentant liberal who was soft on crime and out of touch with the American people. Combined with uncritical coverage from the media, Bush's ads in this election had consequences that were both substantial and quite disturbing because he gained an electoral advantage through deceptive means.

Less visible electoral arenas, such as presidential nomination campaigns, are more vulnerable to strategic manipulation. Because they are less visible contests that are heavily influenced by campaign dynamics, they contain fewer of the countervailing forces than are present in presidential general elections. Democrats compete against Democrats and Republicans against Republicans in a sequential nominating process.[14] In this situation, party identification is not central to vote choice. The setting limits the power of long-term forces and makes it possible for short-term factors, such as advertising and media coverage, to dominate.

Senate races share some features with nominating races. These contests are susceptible to ad appeals because relatively unknown candidates compete in races that resemble roller-coaster rides. There often are wild swings in electoral fortunes during the course of the campaign. The absence of prior beliefs about the candidates makes advertising especially influential.[15] It is easier to create a new political profile (for one's self or one's opponent) than to alter a well-defined image. Candidates who are the least known are the most able to use advertisements to influence the public. But they also are the most susceptible to having an opponent create an unfair image of themselves through television.

Slicing and Dicing the Electorate

Campaign advertisements also pose problems for democratic elections on the systemic level. Even if ads influence voting behavior only in certain circumstances, they have consequences for the way in which the campaign is viewed. Advertisements are one of the primary means of communication, and much of how people feel about the electoral system is a product of how campaign battles are contested.

In contemporary elections it is common for political consultants to divide voters into advertising segments based on public opinion polls and focus groups: the committed (those who are for you), the hopeless (those who are against you and about whom little can be done), and the undecided (those who could vote either way). The last group, of course, is the central target of campaign tactics.

Ads are developed to stir the hopes and fears of the 20 percent to 30 percent of the electorate that is undecided, not the 70 percent to 80 percent that is committed or hopeless. Narrow pockets of support are identified and targeted appeals are made. Many Americans complain that campaign discussions do not reflect their concerns. Their complaints are legitimate. With advertising appeals designed for the small group of voters who are undecided, it is little wonder many voters feel left out.

In this system of segmentation and targeted appeals, candidates have clear incentives to identify pockets of potential support and find issues that will move these voters. Whether it is the backlash against affirmative action among white rural dwellers in North Carolina (one of the winning issues for Helms in 1990) or Bush's attacks on Clinton for his 1969 antiwar demonstrations (which did not save the election for Bush), the current electoral system encourages candidates to find divisive issues that pit social group against social group.

It is not surprising in this situation that Americans feel bad at the end of election campaigns. Candidates engage in an electronic form of civil war not unlike what happens in polarized societies. The battleground issues often touch on race, lifestyle, and gender, which are among the most contentious topics in America. Ads and sound bites are the weapons of choice in these confrontations.

The long-run dangers from the electronic air wars are ill feelings and loss of the sense of community. Clinton addressed these fears in his 1992 nomination acceptance speech. Long before his patriotism had been challenged, Clinton warned about the danger of divisiveness and the importance of community: "The New Covenant is about more than opportunities and responsibilities for you and your families. It's also about our common community. Tonight every one of you knows deep in your heart that we are too divided. It is time to heal America. . . . Look beyond the stereotypes that blind us. We need each other . . . this is America. There is no them. There is only us." [16]

What Can Be Done

The controversies that have arisen concerning television commercials have produced cries for serious reform. These calls undoubtedly reflect deep frustration over the uses of advertisements in the United States. [17] But it is far too simple to blame ads for electoral deficiencies. The problem of political commercials is as much a function of campaign structure and voters' reactions as of candidates' behavior. Structural and attitudinal changes have loosened the forces that used to restrain elite strategies. The rise of a mass-based campaign system at a time when candidates have powerful means of influencing viewers rewards media-centered campaigns.

At the same time, voters are vulnerable to candidates' messages because the forces that used to provide social integration have lost their influence. Intermediary organizations no longer organize political reality. Consensus has broken down on key domestic and foreign policy questions. Voters are bombarded with spot ads precisely because of their proven short-term effectiveness, as has been evident in recent races.

Recent court rulings make an outright ban on campaign commercials unlikely. Most court decisions have treated candidates' expenditures on advertisements as tantamount to free speech. [18] Because ads are a form of expression, they are subject to constitutional protection and are thereby quite difficult to restrict. Most attempts at direct regulation have been resisted as unconstitutional encroachments on free speech. [19] Self-monitoring efforts, such as those proposed by the National Association of Political Consultants, are of limited value.

However, there is an informal mechanism in the advertising area that, when combined with regulatory reform, promises more success: the media. In the case of candidates' advertising, government regulation clearly would be inadequate without direct and effective media oversight. Reporters have the power to make or break the regulation of advertising by how they cover spot commercials.

For example, follow-up reporting by the news media would enable viewers to link ad sponsorship to responsibility. Journalists who aggressively focused on negative commercials would help the public hold candidates accountable for ads that crossed the threshold of acceptability. This attention would alter the strategic environment of campaigns and create clear disincentives for the excessive or unfair use of attack ads.

Currently, advertising coverage falls far short of what would be needed to uphold democratic elections. Reporters devote plenty of attention to candidates' ads, but not necessarily in a way that furthers citizens' knowledge. They are more likely, for example, to use ads to discuss the horse race than the policy views of the candidates.

But with a different approach to ad coverage, television could become an enlightening force in American elections. Journalists in the United States have an unusually high credibility with the public. American reporters are seen as being more fair and trustworthy than in other countries. A recent comparative study of five countries illustrates this point. Whereas 69 percent of the Americans surveyed had great confidence in the media, only 41 percent of Germans and 38 percent of the British gave high ratings to journalists.[20]

What is needed in the United States is a "truth in political advertising" code that would feature a prominent oversight role for the media. Both Jamieson and Broder have suggested that journalists should exercise their historic function of safeguarding the integrity of the election process.[21] The media could use their high public credibility to improve the functioning of the political system.

There are several tenets to this code that would improve the quality of electoral discourse. Reporters must use ad watches to evaluate the accuracy of candidates' claims, especially in races below the presidential level. Candidates periodically make exaggerated claims in their efforts to win votes. Journalists need to look into their claims and report to voters on their accuracy. The 1992 race was notable because journalists made detailed assessments of candidates' claims. Newspapers routinely printed the text of commercials in ad watches, with sentence-by-sentence evaluations of their honesty. In addition, television reporters reviewed videos of commercials with an eye toward false claims, exaggerated promises, or unrealistic commitments.[22]

These efforts are valuable, but journalists must go beyond fact checking to true oversight. Commercials have become the major strategic tool for the contesting of American elections. Candidates devote the largest portion of their overall campaign budgets to advertising. Their ads feature their own appeals as well as comments about their opposition. Arbitrators are needed to ensure that ads are not misused and that the electronic battle is fought fairly. Almost every election now features claims and counterclaims regarding the fairness of television ads. Voters are not usually in a position to assess these claims, and the Federal Election Commission has chosen not to adjudicate them.

The media are left with the responsibility to expose manipulation, distortion, and deception, not just inaccurate use of facts. Candidates who exceed the boundaries of fair play should be brought to task by reporters. Unfair tactics or misleading editing needs to be publicized. Commercials that engage in obvious appeals to racism, for example, should be condemned. Media pressure could protect the airwaves, as happened when the "Daisy" ad was condemned in 1964.

Television has a special obligation because it is the medium through which most Americans receive their political news. CNN pioneered the ad watch technique of broadcasting the spot in a smaller square on the side of the screen so that the ad would not overpower the analysis. This valuable innovation should become a model for the rest of the electronic media.

Aggressive ad watches are especially important in spots involving race, lifestyle issues, gender, or other topics with emotional overtones.[23] The danger in focusing on such commercials is that viewers will remember the candidate's message, not the critique. Because ads on hot-button issues using well-recognized code words are becoming quite common, reporters need to check candidates' messages to limit manipulatory appeals.

These actions will help protect the integrity of the electoral process. Reporters are the only major group with the credibility vis-à-vis the American public to arbitrate electoral advertising. In fact, a 1985 Gallup Poll revealed that citizens would like the media to undertake an aggressive watchdog role.[24] Government regulators at the Federal Communications Commission or the Federal

Election Commission would not be as effective in such a role. Nor would political elites be seen as credible because they are associated with partisan politics.

There is some danger for the media in openly assuming this role. Many Americans already are concerned about what they believe is excessive influence and bias on the part of the news media.[25] If journalists aggressively challenge candidates' statements, they may be viewed as part of the problem rather than the solution. There are increasing signs of a backlash against the media, and reporters could become subject to more stringent criticism regarding their overall influence and objectivity.

In 1991, for example, Louisiana gubernatorial candidate David Duke tried to foster antipathy to the media through a last-minute ad directly criticizing coverage of his campaign: "Have you ever heard such weeping and gnashing of teeth? The news media have given up any pretense of fair play. The liberals have gone ballistic. The special interests have gone mad. The politicians who play up to them are lining up on cue. Principles lie abandoned and hypocrisy rules the day. I raise issues that must be discussed, and get back venom instead. Try a little experiment. Next time you hear them accuse me of intolerance and hatred, notice who is doing the shouting." Bush attempted to build support for his 1992 reelection in his slogan: "Annoy the media: Reelect Bush." In 1996, Dole attacked the "liberal press," saying "They don't put any anti-Clinton stories in the *New York Times.* Only anti-Dole stories in the *New York Times.*"[26]

A national survey conducted during the last week of the 1996 presidential campaign found that 49 percent believed the news media had done an excellent or good job, 48 percent thought it had been only fair or poor, and 4 percent had no opinion. These numbers were down from comparable figures from the fall of 1992. In that year, 54 percent rated the media as having done an excellent or good job of covering the presidential campaign whereas 44 percent thought the media had done only a fair or poor job. In the 1992 campaign, 43 percent felt reporters had been biased against particular candidates and 49 percent said they had not been. When asked to identify which campaigner had received the most biased coverage, 43 percent named Bush, 32 percent named Clinton, 21 percent named Perot, and 4 percent cited other candidates. Content analysis from the Center for Media and Public Affairs reveals that Bush earned the highest percentage of negative comments (71 percent) from network evening newscasts, compared with Clinton (48 percent) and Perot (55 percent). The content analysis also fit with evidence that reporters were more likely to report Democratic leanings in 1992 than in earlier years.[27] In 1996, 47 percent of news stories about Clinton were positive, and 40 percent of those about Dole were positive.

Despite the drawbacks, oversight by the media is vital enough to the political system to warrant the risk of backlash. The quality of information presented during elections is important enough to outweigh the practical difficulties facing the fourth estate. Nothing is more central to democratic elections than electoral discourse. Without informative material, voters have little means of holding leaders accountable or engaging in popular consent.[28] By encouraging candidates to address the substantive concerns of the electorate, media watchdogs will raise the caliber of the political process and help voters make meaningful choices.

Legal Remedies

There are limits in the ability of voluntary approaches to restrain some of the more deleterious consequences of political advertising. It is no surprise that observers unhappy with political commercials have turned to legal remedies to ameliorate the problems of advertising. A review of state laws around the country finds that most states have vague rules on political advertising with violations of the law categorized as a misdemeanor with fines from $1,000 to $2,000. Some states have penalties of imprisonment for up to one year.

The most common legal requirement is the disclosure of ad sponsorship. This generally involves showing the name and address of the candidate or the independent sponsoring organization at the end of the ad. Some states gear their rules to those promulgated by the Federal Election Commission in national statutes.

In a few states (such as Connecticut), voluntary truth in campaign advertising codes has been considered by legislatures. In subscribing to the code, candidates would agree not to distribute fraudulent, forged, or falsely identified writing, personally approve all literature or advertising for his or her campaign, and immediately retract or correct any claim discovered to be inaccurate.

But almost nowhere have these codes actually been enacted into law. For example, the Connecticut bill was passed in the House with two amendments, but it died in the Senate. Kentucky has a bill pending that would ban ads using "false, deceptive, or misleading" statements. New Jersey considered but rejected a truth in campaign act that would have created a commission to investigate complaints that an ad contained "any false statement of material fact." The penalty would have been $5,000 for the first offense and $10,000 for each subsequent offense. In an effort to deal with independent expenditures, South Dakota considered but did not pass a similar bill requiring individuals who run ads mentioning a candidate at least ten days before an election to provide a copy of that ad to the mentioned candidate.

A few states have considered rules aimed at media consultants as opposed to candidates. Michigan, for example, had a bill that passed the Senate but died in the House that would have fined media consultants up to $1,000 for producing ads in violation of disclosure laws.

Some states do have rules regulating ad content on the books. Montana has a statute making it unlawful for a person to make a "false statement" about a candidate's public voting record or to make a "false statement" that reflects unfavorably on a candidate's character or morality. North Dakota has a law banning statements that are "untrue, deceptive or misleading." Oregon has a statute banning ads with "false statements." Unlike other states, this law also has a significant penalty: "If the finder of fact finds by clear and convincing evidence that the false statement of fact reversed the outcome of the election, the defendant shall be deprived of the nomination or election." Washington has a statute requiring that pictures of candidates used in ads must have been taken within the past five years. Political ads also must not contain "a false statement of material fact."

In general, state courts have not been very sympathetic to legal restrictions. A Pennsylvania statute required candidates in the last eight days prior to an election who run ads referring to an opposing candidate to provide copies of the ad to that candidate and the county board of elections at least twelve hours before the ad appears. But the Pennsylvania Supreme Court in the case *Pennsylvania v. Frank J. Wadzinski* struck down this provision on grounds that it was an unconstitutional infringement on freedom of expression.

Because of the weakness of current laws, there have been calls for changing the structure and regulation of campaign advertisements. One idea involves shortening campaigns. The idea behind this proposal is that if citizens have less exposure to ads, they would be less likely to be influenced by them.

The clear limitation of this proposal is that shorter campaigns do not address the problem of late-deciding voters. It is not the people who make up their minds early who are most at risk from advertising. These individuals are well informed, have firm beliefs about public affairs, and are least in danger of being manipulated by ads. Late-deciders are much more vulnerable to campaign commercials because they are less informed about politics and have fewer strong beliefs. Because short campaigns come at the expense of the beginning not the end of the electoral cycle, this initiative leaves unprotected the most vulnerable category of voter.

Others at the national level have suggested it is time to reconsider the hands-off approach to regulating ad content that has been common in the campaign arena. This approach would extend to political commercials the types of content restrictions that are appearing in other areas.

For example, Congress has passed legislation limiting the number of commercials that can be aired during children's programming. It directed the Federal Communications Commission to use the extent that local stations serve children's education needs as a condition of license renewal.

This move parallels recent efforts imposing content restrictions on sex, violence, and drug and tobacco use on television. Similar to the children's programming limits, legislation has been enacted requiring broadcasters to curb violent or sexually offensive programming. Parents can equip their television with a so-called V-chip to block out materials they believe are undesirable.

The Federal Trade Commission has become much more aggressive in regulating the truthfulness of advertising claims regarding health and the environment. It has become quite common for food manufacturers to attribute either health benefits or the absence of health risks to their products. In many cases, the commission has found these claims to be excessive. For example, the federal agency found that Kraft General Foods exaggerated the calcium content of its Kraft Singles cheese slices. This followed regulatory penalties to Fibre Trim for deceptive spots regarding diet products and Sara Lee for claiming its light cheesecake was low in calories.

Because of concerns expressed about political commercials, a number of national bills have been introduced to regulate the content and sponsorship disclosures of campaign ads, especially in regard to attack ads. This concern became quite prominent after the 1988 presidential campaign brought forth a host of criticisms. Democratic nominee Dukakis said after the election, "I said in my acceptance speech at Atlanta that the 1988 election was not about ideology but about competence. I was wrong. It was about phraseology . . . and going negative. . . . I made a lot of mistakes in the '88 campaign. But none was as damaging as my failure to . . . respond immediately and effectively to distortions of one's record." [29]

These and other criticisms have led many to propose "clean air" regulations for campaign commercials. One proposal introduced in 1989 by Sens. John Danforth and Ernest Hollings would require that candidates personally appear in television ads referring to their opponent. Another measure proposed by Sens. Bob Graham and Richard Bryan would stiffen disclosure rules on sponsorship of television and radio ads. Still another suggested by Sen. Wendell Ford would require candidates to appear at least 50 percent of the time in their spot ads to qualify for public funds.

The rationale behind these proposals is that negative appeals would become less likely if candidates felt they had to make the pitch personally and therefore risk being held accountable for their statements. These ideas also aim to hold outside groups accountable by imposing stronger disclosure rules so that viewers would actually know who paid for the ad in question.

These reforms offer some hope of making improvements in campaign advertisements. They increase the level of personal accountability, thereby furthering an important requirement of democratic elections. It would be interesting to see, for example, if the Bush "Revolving Door" ad would have had the same impact if the candidate had been forced to make the pitch personally.

These legal changes also would open up the disclosure process in a way that would increase citizen awareness. If the public had full information regarding ad sponsorship and candidate rhetoric, it would improve attributions of responsibility for negative campaigns. The public would be in a stronger position to assess blame if viewers were confident which candidate had sponsored the ad.

Issue Advocacy Ads

When in 1976 the Supreme Court decided its landmark case, *Buckley v. Valeo*,[30] it ruled that groups independent of the campaign could spend whatever amount of money they wanted as long as there was no coordination with the candidate's staff. Over the two decades since that decision, there has been an outpouring of independent expenditures on behalf of certain candidates. In 1992, for example, Bush and Clinton each were the beneficiary of nearly $20 million in spending by groups outside the official campaign.

As long as the group expressly advocates the defeat of particular candidates, it is required by the Federal Election Commission to register as a political action committee (PAC). This subjects the groups to detailed disclosure laws and requires them to adhere to limitations on the amount of contributions they can accept. That way, the public can see who is funding the expenditure and how the money is being spent.

Increasingly though, there is emerging a new category of spending called issue-advocacy ads. These are public education appeals run by interest groups or political parties that do not expressly advocate the election of particular candidates. Under current rules, unless groups run ads or produce material including words like "vote for or against Representative Smith," they are not required by the Federal Election Commission to register as political action committees, disclose their contributions, or reveal how they are spending their money.[31]

The most famous of these public education groups was GOPAC, the organization headed by Representative Gingrich. Though it implied by its name that it was a political action committee, GOPAC did not register with the Federal Election Commission on the grounds that it devoted less than 10 percent of its time to express electoral advocacy at the federal level. This allowed it to refuse at least initially to disclose its contributors to the public or abide by contributor limits. The Federal Election Commission sued GOPAC on the grounds that it was the fundraising arm of Gingrich's election machine and that its activities on behalf of building the Republican party base around the country was illegal unless it registered as a PAC. After several years of litigation, a federal appeals court ruled against the Federal Election Commission and said GOPAC did not meet the threshold of express advocacy.

Another lawsuit came following the 1992 election when the Christian Action Network (CAN) ran a television ad across the country right before the general election titled "Clinton's Vision for a Better America." This ad urged voters to defeat Clinton and

Gore because they favored radical homosexual rights that the group argued were bad for America. The ad featured visuals that were unflattering to Clinton, showed leather-bound men marching in a gay pride parade, and exhorted viewers to oppose Clinton's agenda of homosexual rights. The ad concluded by asking "Is this your vision for a better America?"

None of the group's $2 million in expenditures that year was publicly disclosed, because the group did not register as a political action committee. That information came to light only after the Federal Election Commission sued CAN for failure to register as a political action committee.

The key legal issue in the CAN case was whether a television ad visually and through other means could convey the message "don't elect Clinton," even if the words "don't vote for Clinton" were absent from the ad. I was hired as an expert witness by the Federal Election Commission to evaluate this ad. My judgment was that through techniques of audiotape voice-overs, music, visual text, visual images, color, code words, and editing, this ad expressly advocated the defeat of Democratic candidates Clinton and Gore in the 1992 presidential general election. However, after seeing briefs and hearing oral arguments by opposing counsels, a federal judge in Virginia ruled against the Federal Election Commission and said the public education campaign run by CAN did not constitute express advocacy. This meant that the group was not required to register as a political action committee and disclose its contributors.

Recognizing that the current system of campaign rules had big loopholes, the AFL-CIO announced in the spring of 1996 that it would spend $35 million running ads in the districts of Republican members of Congress who opposed labor objectives. Its top targets were Jim Bunn of Oregon (where it spent $1,050,000), J. D. Hayworth of Arizona ($750,000), Randy Tate of Washington ($630,000), Rick White of Washington ($630,000), John Ensign of Nevada ($575,000), Martin Hoke of Ohio ($475,000), and Fred Heineman of North Carolina ($460,000).[32] Even though these ads were broadcast right before the election and mentioned the names of the Republican representatives along with unfavorable commentary on their voting records, the AFL-CIO declared these expenditures as issue advocacy and therefore not subject to federal disclosure rules.

Shortly after this labor initiative, a consortium of thirty-five business groups including the U.S. Chamber of Commerce, National

Restaurant Association, and National Association of Manufacturers said it would spend $17 million on a probusiness advocacy campaign defending the targeted Republican incumbents (but this consortium ultimately raised just $3 million). Because these efforts were under the guise of public education as opposed to electoral advocacy, they were not subject to federal campaign laws.

The Sierra Club spent $7.5 million and the League of Conservation Voters $1 million on political activities related to the 1996 elections. The Sierra Club focused on ten Senate races and fifty House races and included spending on advertising as well as national distribution of 1.3 million voter guides on environmental issues.[33]

One of the biggest practitioners of issue advocacy has been the Christian Coalition. For several years, the Christian Coalition has engaged in a wide variety of activities, such as issuing voter guides outlining the legislative records of elected officials, mailing letters to its coalition members, and running telephone banks to urge the election of Republican candidates. In 1996, it distributed 46 million voter guides to worshipers at 125,000 churches. Although the Coalition has argued that its efforts are public education, it has been sued by the Federal Election Commission for not disclosing its expenditures as required by law. This is likely to be a landmark case in the history of issue advocacy.

Political parties also have entered the world of issue advocacy as part of election campaigns. In 1996, the Republican National Committee aired cookie-cutter commercials in several states complaining that Democratic U.S. Senate candidates were "liberals" who oppose welfare reform and a balanced budget. Because the Republican National Committee said this and other ads fell under the category of public education as opposed to appeals expressly designed to hurt the prospects of a particular candidate, they did not count against the campaign contribution limits that the committee could give to Republican senatorial candidates.

Both the Republican and Democratic National Committees spent millions on public education in the 1996 campaign. The Democratic National Committee spent more than $20 million in educational advertising featuring President Clinton and attacking "extremist" Republicans such as Senator Dole and Speaker Gingrich. The Republican National Committee launched a $20-million campaign before the August convention promoting Dole and attacking Clinton. To make sure these expenditures did not count against the $12 million limit that each party can spend during the general election promoting its presidential nominee, both parties labeled these issue advocacy that was independent of the actual campaign.

But according to a Common Cause study of campaign receipts, abuses were so prevalent in the 1996 presidential campaign that it required the appointment of a special prosecutor to investigate both parties. Clinton and Dole were accused of illegally funneling some of their parties' "soft money," funds dedicated to party-building, to their own campaigns. Supposedly "independent" ads run by the Democratic National Committee and the Republican National Committee used identical footage to that of Clinton and Dole advertisements, respectively. In some cases, the national committees hired the very same media consultants who worked for the presidential candidates.

What started as a trickle of issue-advocacy ads has become a torrent on every conceivable topic. In the past few years, groups interested in health care, tort reform, term limits, and a balanced budget have blanketed the airwaves with commercials promoting their point of view. Once the exception more than the rule, television ads have become the latest form of political volleyball on controversial issues.

This has created several problems for our political system. Issue advocacy is taking place outside of any required public disclosure of spending or contributors. Direct gifts and campaign contributions to legislators must be disclosed, but there are no rules requiring disclosure of issue-advocacy campaigns. This threatens the public's right to know who is funding campaigns, how much is being spent, and in the case of presidential campaigns limits on how much each candidate can spend.

According to a Brown University national survey in fall 1996, 76 percent of Americans believe interest groups running public education campaigns about the issues should disclose who is paying for the ad. Seventy-four percent believe these groups should be subject to the same campaign finance rules as candidates.

Issue advocacy ads criticizing candidates for office right before an election illustrate the inadequacy of current legal distinctions between issue and electoral advocacy. Even when these ads seek to influence the election by criticizing a candidate right before a national election, courts have been loath to define the spot as a campaign communication.

At one level, this concern for First Amendment rights of free expression is perfectly understandable. The Bill of Rights is the bedrock of American democracy. Freedom of expression is crucial to our system of democratic government.

But our current campaign finance system needs to balance freedom of expression with fairness in political competition. If monied interests on either side of the political spectrum can secretly finance public education ads right before an election, it eviscerates federal disclosure rules. It takes us back to the secrecy and deception of the pre-Watergate system for contesting American elections.

Appendix

Survey Data

The research used in this book relies on survey data in combination with content and media measures to explore viewers' reactions to campaign advertisements on television since 1972. A number of surveys taken from 1972 through 1996 were used to analyze advertising effects. The only presidential election during this period for which independent survey data (not connected with candidates' organizations) was unavailable was 1980.

Most of the opinion data come from sources other than the biennial National Election Study conducted at the University of Michigan. The reason is simple. Only a few times in the 1952–1996 period has the National Election Study included any questions on political advertising: The exceptions were 1974 in regard to Senate campaigns, 1988 during the nominating stage of the presidential campaign, and 1992 and 1996 in the general election study. The 1988 data are quite limited because the question asked, "In the past week, did you see any television commercials for a presidential candidate?" (yes or no), aggregates ad exposure for all candidates who competed in the nominating process. It is therefore impossible to compare results for individual candidates or to evaluate the strategic aspects of advertising. The question also does not separate the Republican and Democratic nominating processes.

The survey data used in this study come from several different sources. In 1972, Patterson and McClure conducted a general election panel survey in Syracuse, New York. Three sets of personal interviews were conducted prior to election day with the same participants. Preelection interviews took place in September ($N = 731$), October (reinterviews with 650 people), and early November $(N = 650)$. In addition to data on exposure to advertising, a wealth of information about views of the candidates was collected. For example, questions were asked concerning recognition, favorability, and electability for Nixon and McGovern, respectively. Impressions of candidate personality traits and positions on issues were compiled, as were views about the most important problems facing the country.

A 1974 National Election Study explored advertising in Senate campaigns. This survey was a postelection, nationwide questionnaire of 1,575 respondents. Individuals were interviewed between November 5 and January 31 following the election. Questions were asked about ad exposure and impact in Senate races.

In 1976, Patterson conducted a larger panel study in Los Angeles, California, and Erie, Pennsylvania. These surveys were designed to investigate the nominating and general election phases of the campaign. Respondents were asked about their exposure to ads, views about the candidates, assessments of personal qualities and issue positions, views about candidates' electability, and opinions on the most important problems facing the country. Overall, 1,236 people were interviewed in this series. Major interviews were conducted in February (N = 1,002), April (N = 897, of whom 772 had been interviewed in the earlier wave), and June (N = 907, with 720 coming from the original panel). A general election panel took place in October. Advertising items were asked during the April, June, and October panels.

The CBS News/*New York Times* poll conducted a national pre- and postelection survey in 1984 that included relevant questions. All together 1,994 respondents were interviewed between October 31 and November 2. Of these, 1,794 were reinterviewed on November 8 to 14, after the election. Questions were asked concerning views about the campaign, candidates' issue positions, and the most important problems facing the country. Additional CBS News/*New York Times* polls conducted in 1988 included advertising items: a regional survey of Super Tuesday primary states from February 28–March 2 (N = 2,251), an October 21–24 questionnaire (N = 1,827), a preelection survey from November 2–4 (N = 1,977), and a postelection interview from November 10–15 with 1,627 of the preelection respondents.

The 1990 Rhode Island survey was sponsored by the A. Alfred Taubman Center for Public Policy and American Institutions at Brown University. It was designed to explore the Senate race between Claiborne Pell and Claudine Schneider. The preelection poll was a statewide probability sample of 414 likely voters aged eighteen or older. It was undertaken September 16–19, 1990. Responses were weighted by gender and age in proportion to actual census numbers. Interviews were conducted by telephone. Overall, the survey had a margin of error around 5 percentage points.

The 1990 North Carolina Senate election study was conducted by the School of Journalism and the Institute for Research in Social Science at the University of North Carolina at Chapel Hill. From October 28–31, 1990, 833 randomly selected adult residents of North Carolina households were interviewed by telephone. The data were weighted for household size to correct for the under-sampling of members of large households. The expected margin of error is 4 percentage points.

The 1992 presidential surveys were sponsored by the National Science Foundation and the MacArthur Foundation and developed at the A. Alfred Taubman Center for Public Policy and American Institutions at Brown University. Part of a larger project on the 1992 campaign, they were designed to explore both the nominating and general election stages. Nominating polls were taken in the Boston metropolitan area March 2–9, 1992 (N = 590), and another in Los Angeles County May 18–31, 1992 (N = 484). General election surveys were conducted in Winston-Salem (N = 616) from September 28 to 29 and Los Angeles County (N = 601) from October 26 to 31. Interviews were conducted by telephone with a random sample of adults aged eighteen years or older. Overall, these surveys had a margin of error around 4 percentage points.

The 1996 national nominating study was sponsored by the *Providence Journal-Bulletin* and the A. Alfred Taubman Center for Public Policy and American Institutions at Brown University. This poll was a national probability sample of 927 adults nationwide aged eighteen or older. It was undertaken January 29–February 4, 1996. Interviews were conducted by telephone. Overall, it had a margin of error around 3 percentage points.

The 1996 Rhode Island nominating survey was sponsored by the A. Alfred Taubman Center for Public Policy and American Institutions at Brown University. It was designed to explore the aftermath of the Republican presidential nomination following the Yankee primary. This poll was a statewide probability sample in Rhode Island of 311 registered voters aged eighteen or older. The telephone interviews were conducted March 10–14, 1996. Overall, the survey had a margin of error around 5 percentage points.

The 1996 national general election study was sponsored by the A. Alfred Taubman Center for Public Policy and American Institutions at Brown University. This poll was a national probability sample of 724 adults nationwide aged eighteen or older. It was undertaken October 28–November 3, 1996. Interviews were conducted by telephone. Overall, it had a margin of error around 4 percentage points.

Memorable Ads: 1984–1996

Mondale, "Future," 1984

Crosby, Stills, Nash, and Young sing portions of the lyrics from their song "Teach Your Children," while images of missiles shooting out of underground silos are juxtaposed with closeups of children's faces. The ad concludes with a picture of a forest of trees shaking from an explosion and a young girl's face appearing on screen. Then a globe fills the screen and the words "Mondale/Ferraro" rotate into view.[1]

Reagan, "Bear in the Woods," 1984

(A bear lumbers through the woods.) "There's a bear in the woods. For some people the bear is easy to see; others don't see it at all. Some people say the bear is tame; others say it's vicious and dangerous. Since no one can be sure who is right, isn't it smart to be as strong as the bear—if there is a bear!"[2]

Bush, "Revolving Door," 1988

(Dissonant sounds are heard: a drum ... music ... metal stairs.) "As governor, Michael Dukakis vetoed mandatory sentences for drug dealers." (A guard with a rifle climbs the circular stairs of a prison watchtower. The words "The Dukakis Furlough Program" are superimposed on the bottom of the prison visual.) "He vetoed the death penalty." (A guard with a gun walks along a barbed wire fence.) "His revolving door prison policy gave weekend furloughs to first-degree murderers not eligible for parole." (A revolving door formed by bars rotates as men in prison clothing walk in and back out the door in a long line. The words "268 Escaped" are superimposed.) "While out, many committed other crimes like kidnapping and rape." (The camera comes in for a closer shot of the prisoners in slow motion revolving through the door.) "And many are still at large." (The words "And Many Are Still At Large" are superimposed.) "Now Michael Dukakis says he wants to do for America what he's done for Massachusetts." (The picture changes to a guard on a roof with a watchtower in the background.) "America can't afford that risk!" (A small color picture of Bush appears, and the words "Paid for by Bush/Quayle '88" appear in small print.)[3]

Dukakis, "Family/Education," 1988

(At night a young man flips dough in a pizza parlor.) "Jimmy got accepted to college, but his family couldn't afford tuition." (Dukakis appears on the screen.) A voice-over says: "Mike Dukakis wants to help. . . . If a kid like Jimmy has the grades for college, America should find a way to send him." [4]

Clinton, "The Plan," 1992

"The people of New Hampshire know better than anyone. America is in trouble; our people are really hurting. In the '80s, the rich got richer, the middle class declined, poverty exploded. Politicians in Washington raised their pay and pointed fingers. But no one took responsibility. It's time we had a president who cares, who takes responsibility, who has a plan for change. I'm Bill Clinton and I believe you deserve more than 30-second ads or vague promises. That's why I've offered a comprehensive plan to get our economy moving again, to take care of our own people, and regain our economic leadership. It starts with a tax cut for the middle class and asks the rich to pay their fair share again. It includes national health insurance, a major investment in education, training for our workers, tough trade laws, and no more tax breaks for corporations to move our jobs overseas. Take a look at our plan and let me know what you think. I hope you'll join us in this crusade for change. Together we can put government back on the side of the forgotten middle class and restore the American Dream." [5]

Clinton, "How're You Doing?" 1992

A voice-over says, "Remember President Bush saying, 'And if you elect me President, you will be better off four years from now than you are today.'" The announcer responds: "Average family income down $1,600 in two years" (Commerce Department Bureau of Census 9/1/92). A voice-over says, "President Bush says, 'You will be better off four years from now than you are today.'" The announcer responds, "Family health care costs up $1,800 in four years" (Health Insurance Association of America, 1988; KPMG Peat Marwick 1992). A voice-over says, "President Bush says, 'You will be better off in four years.'" The announcer responds, "The second biggest tax increase in history" (Congressional Budget Office Study 1/30/92; *New York Times* 8/7/92). A voice-over says, "President Bush says, 'If you elect me President, you will be better off four years from now than you are today.'" The announcer asks, "Well, it's four years later. How're you doing?"[6]

Bush on Clinton Economics, 1992

An announcer says: "Bill Clinton says he'll only tax the rich to pay for his campaign promises. But here's what Clinton economics could mean to you. (Picture of male steamfitter) $1,088 more in taxes. (Picture of female scientist) $2,072 more in taxes. 100 leading economists say his plan means higher taxes and bigger deficits. (Picture of professional couple) $1,191 more in taxes. (Picture of black housing lender) $2,072 more in taxes. You can't trust Clinton economics. It's wrong for you. It's wrong for America."[7]

Perot on Job Creation, 1992

(Background of ticking clock; text scrolling up screen) "It is a time when the threat of unemployment is greater than the threat of war. It is a time that the national debt demands as much attention as the national security. It is a time when the barriers to a better life are rising and the barriers between nations are falling. The issue is the economy. And it is a time that demands a candidate who is not a business-as-usual politician, but a business leader with the know-how to balance the budget, rebuild the job base and restore the meaning of 'Made in the U.S.A.' In this election, we can choose a candidate who has made the free enterprise system work, who has created thousands of jobs by building successful businesses. The candidate is Ross Perot. The election is November 3. The choice is yours."[8]

Perot on National Debt and Children, 1992

(Background of children's faces; text scrolling up screen) "Our children dream of the world that we promised them as parents, a world of unlimited opportunity. What would they say to us if they knew that by the year 2000, we will have left them with a national debt of $8 trillion? What would they say to us if they knew that we are making them the first generation of Americans with a standard of living below the generation before them? We cannot do this to our children. In this election, we have the opportunity to choose a candidate who is not a career politician, but a proven business leader with the ability to take on the tasks at hand, to balance the budget, to expand the tax base, to give our children back their American dream. The candidate is Ross Perot. The issue is our children. The choice is yours." [9]

Clinton, "Wrong in the Past, Wrong for Our Future," 1996

(Scenes of calendar flipping backward) "Let's go back in time." The 60s. "Bob Dole's in Congress. Votes against creating Medicare. Against creating student loans." The 70s. "Against the Department of Education. Against a higher minimum wage." The 80s. "Still there. Against creating a drug czar. Against the Brady Bill." The 90s. "Against the Brady Bill. Against Family and Medical Leave. Against vaccines for children. Against Medicare, again. Dole-Gingrich tried to cut $270 billion. Bob Dole. Wrong in the past. Wrong for our future." [10]

Dole, "MTV Drug Use," 1996

(Scenes of school children inspecting a plastic bag filled with marijuana and then passing around a marijuana cigarette) "We send them off to school. And we worry. Teenage drug use has doubled since 1992. And Bill Clinton? He cut the White House Drug Office 83 percent. His own surgeon general considered legalizing drugs. And in front of our children, on MTV, the President himself." (scene switches to black-and-white clip of MTV audience member asking a question) "If you had it to do over again, would you inhale?" (Mr. Clinton) "Sure, if I could. I tried before." (Announcer) "Bill Clinton doesn't get it. But we do." (Screen graphic: "Clinton's liberal drug policy has failed.") [11]

Perot, "Where's Ross?" 1996

"He's put together a bona fide campaign. (Woman) Where's Ross? (Narrator) He won the debates in '92. (Woman) Where's Ross? (Narrator) Set the campaign agenda and won 19 percent of the vote. (Woman) Where's Ross? (Narrator) He's been allocated $30 million of federal funds. (Woman) Where's Ross? (Narrator) 76 percent of Americans want him in the debate. But a Washington commission with no legal standing, headed by career politicians and meeting behind closed doors, said no. (Woman) Where's Ross? (Narrator) He's on the ballot in all 50 states. Vote for a change. Vote for Perot." [12]

Republican National Committee, "Talk Is Cheap," 1996

(Footage of Bill Clinton offering different projections for when he would balance the federal budget) (Announcer) "For four years you've heard a lot of talk from Bill Clinton about balancing the budget." (President Clinton) "I would present a five-year plan to balance the budget." ". . . we could do it in seven years." ". . . I think we can reach it in nine years." ". . . balance the budget in 10 years." ". . . I think we could reach it in eight years." ". . . so we're between seven and nine now." (Announcer) "No wonder Bill Clinton opposes a Constitutional amendment to balance the budget." (President Clinton) "7 . . . 9 . . . 10 . . . 8 . . . 5 . . ." (Announcer) "Talk is cheap. Double talk is expensive. Tell Mr. Clinton to support the balanced budget amendment." [13]

AFL-CIO, "Cutting Medicare," 1996

(Black-and-white pictures of the sad and weathered faces of several elderly people) "Congressman George Nethercutt voted to cut our Medicare benefits. George Nethercutt knows it. And so do we. Fact: On November 17, 1995, Nethercutt voted with Newt Gingrich to cut 270 billion dollars from Medicare funding, while voting for tax breaks for the wealthy. Now he's trying to deny it. Tell George Nethercutt we know the truth about his vote to cut our Medicare benefits. Another vote is coming. This time we'll be watching." [14] (This was a cookie-cutter ad in which they filled in the blank with local candidates.)

TABLE A-1
Prominent Ads Used in Content Study: 1952–1996

	Republicans	Democrats	Independents	Total
1952				
General election	8	8	0	16
1956				
General election	4	4	0	8
1960				
General election	2	12	0	14
Kennedy nomination	0	2	0	2
1964				
General election	7	19	0	26
1968				
General election	2	11	1	14
McCarthy nomination	0	2	0	2
1972				
General election	21	13	0	34
McGovern nomination	0	1	0	1
Humphrey nomination	0	2	0	2
Lindsay nomination	0	1	0	1
Wallace nomination	0	1	0	1
1976				
General election	11	17	0	28
Ford nomination	2	0	0	2
Carter nomination	0	3	0	3
Udall nomination	0	2	0	2
Bayh nomination	0	1	0	1
1980				
General election	32	12	0	44
Reagan nomination	5	0	0	5
Bush nomination	1	0	0	1
Carter nomination	0	2	0	2
Kennedy nomination	0	10	0	10
1984				
General election	13	9	0	22
Hart nomination	0	1	0	1
1988				
General election	17	12	0	29
1992				
General election	8	2	6	16
Bush nomination	7	0	0	7

TABLE A-1
(Continued)

	Republicans	Democrats	Independents	Total
Buchanan nomination	2	0	0	2
General Republican nomination	3	0	0	3
Clinton nomination	0	6	0	6
Kerrey nomination	0	3	0	3
Tsongas nomination	0	2	0	2
General Democratic nomination	0	1	0	1
Proposition	0	0	5	5
General independent	0	0	8	8
1996				
General election	6	5	0	14
Other general election	7	0	1	5
Dole nomination	12	0	0	12
Buchanan nomination	3	0	0	3
Forbes nomination	14	0	0	14
Alexander nomination	2	0	0	2
Gramm nomination	2	0	0	2
Lugar nomination	1	0	0	1
Clinton nomination	0	0	0	0
Other	0	2	0	2
Total	**192**	**166**	**21**	**379**

Sources: For 1952–1988, Kathleen Jamieson, *Packaging the Presidency,* 2d ed. (New York: Oxford University Press, 1992); and for 1992 and 1996, "CBS Evening News" tapes.

Note: Entries indicate number of prominent ads each year for Republicans, Democrats, and Independents.

TABLE A-2
CBS Stories about Party Ads: 1972–1996

	Republican	Democrat	Both Rep. and Dem.	Independent	Total
1972	2	9	0	0	11
General election	2	2	0	0	4
Nominating campaign	0	7	0	0	7
1976	8	7	4	0	19
General election	2	1	2	0	5
Nominating campaign	6	6	2	0	14
1980	7	8	3	2	20
General election	4	2	1	1	8
Nominating campaign	3	6	2	1	12
1984	6	10	5	0	21
General election	2	0	3	0	5
Nominating campaign	4	10	2	0	16
1988	19	24	7	0	50
General election	10	5	6	0	21
Nominating campaign	9	19	1	0	29
1992	20	14	4	15	53
General election	8	2	3	11	24
Nominating campaign	12	12	1	4	29
1996	26	3	5	1	35
General election	5	3	5	1	14
Nominating campaign	21	0	0	0	21
Total	**88**	**75**	**28**	**18**	**209**

Sources: "CBS Evening News," *Vanderbilt Television News Index and Abstracts* (for campaigns 1972–1988); and "CBS Evening News" tapes (for 1992 and 1996 campaigns).

Note: Entries indicate number of "CBS Evening News" stories about ads each year for Republicans, Democrats, both parties, and Independents.

Notes

Preface

1. The 1990 elections alone generated $203 million in spending on ads, according to an estimate by the Television Bureau of Advertising, a nonprofit organization representing the television industry. See Kim Foltz, "$203 Million Was Spent on Political Ads in '90," *New York Times*, February 12, 1991, D17.
2. Two notable exceptions are Kathleen Jamieson, *Packaging the Presidency*, 2d ed. (New York: Oxford University Press, 1992); and Edwin Diamond and Stephen Bates, *The Spot* (Cambridge, Mass.: MIT Press, 1984).
3. Robert Dahl, *A Preface to Democratic Theory* (Chicago: University of Chicago Press, 1957); Joseph Schumpeter, *Capitalism, Socialism and Democracy* (New York: Harper and Row, 1942); and Norman Luttbeg, ed., *Public Opinion and Public Policy*, 3d ed. (Itasca, Ill.: Peacock, 1981). But for a different interpretation, which emphasizes the ability of voters to make reasoned decisions based on small bits of information, see Samuel Popkin, *The Reasoning Voter* (Chicago: University of Chicago Press, 1991).
4. Joe McGinniss, *The Selling of the President* (New York: Simon and Schuster, 1969); and Robert Spero, *The Duping of the American Voter* (New York: Lippincott and Crowell, 1980).
5. A classic illustration of psychological reasoning is found in Linda Alwitt and Andrew Mitchell, eds., *Psychological Processes and Advertising Effects* (Hillsdale, N.J.: Erlbaum, 1985). The best application of psychological models to the evening news is Shanto Iyengar and Donald Kinder, *News that Matters* (Chicago: University of Chicago Press, 1987). For another example, see Diana Owen, *Media Messages in American Presidential Elections* (Westport, Conn.: Greenwood Press, 1991).

Chapter 1: Rethinking Ads

1. Kathleen Jamieson, *Packaging the Presidency*, 2d ed. (New York: Oxford University Press, 1992), 6–7.
2. Jamieson, *Packaging the Presidency*, 50.

3. Quoted in Jamieson, 195. For a description of Johnson's strategy, see Edwin Diamond and Stephen Bates, *The Spot* (Cambridge, Mass.: MIT Press, 1984), 127–140.

4. "How Bush Won," *Newsweek*, November 21, 1988, 117. Also see Paul Taylor and David Broder, "Early Volley of Bush Ads Exceeded Expectations," *Washington Post*, October 28, 1988.

5. Elizabeth Kolbert, "Secrecy over TV Ads, or, The Peculiar Logic of Political Combat," *New York Times*, September 17, 1992, A21.

6. Martin Schram, *The Great American Video Game* (New York: William Morrow, 1987), 25–26. For a reassessment of the differential impact of radio and television viewers on the 1960 debates, see David Vancil and Sue Pendell, "The Myth of Viewer-Listener Disagreement in the First Kennedy-Nixon Debate," *Central States Speech Journal* 38 (Spring 1987): 16–27.

7. *New York Times*, "Dole Campaign Agrees to Change Its Tune," September 14, 1996, 9; and Michael Farquhar, "End Notes," *Washington Post*, September 14, 1996, C3.

8. Harry Berkowitz, "Campaigns Aim at Economy," *Newsday*, September 28, 1996, A13.

9. Marjorie Connelly, "A 'Conservative' Is (Fill in the Blank)," *New York Times*, November 3, 1996, E5.

10. Richard Berke, "Is Clinton One? Was Nixon?" *New York Times Week in Review*, 1.

11. The Media Studies Center poll is reported in *Providence Journal*, "Hype Swells as First Presidential Debate Approaches," September 29, 1996, A7. The CBS News/*New York Times* numbers come from Richard Berke, "Should Dole Risk Tough Image? Poll Says He Already Has One," *New York Times*, October 16, 1996, A1.

12. Kathleen Hall Jamieson, "Context and the Creation of Meaning in the Advertising of the 1988 Presidential Campaign," *American Behavioral Scientist* 32 (1989): 415–424. Also see Marion Just, Ann Crigler, Dean Alger, Timothy Cook, Montague Kern, and Darrell M. West, *Cross Talk: Citizens, Candidates, and the Media in a Presidential Campaign* (Chicago: University of Chicago Press, 1996).

13. It is hardly surprising, given these changes, that over the past two decades we have seen a series of dark-horse candidates do unexpectedly well in nomination politics. See Darrell M. West, *Making Campaigns Count* (Westport, Conn.: Greenwood Press, 1984); and James Ceaser, *Presidential Selection* (Princeton, N.J.: Princeton University Press, 1979).

14. The Tsongas quote comes from Karen DeWitt, "Tsongas Pitches Economic Austerity Mixed with Patriotism," *New York Times*, January 1, 1992, A10.

15. Thomas Patterson and Robert McClure, *The Unseeing Eye* (New York: Putnam's, 1976). Also see Martin Wattenberg, *The Rise of Candidate-Centered Politics* (Cambridge, Mass.: Harvard University Press, 1991); and Richard M. Perloff, *Political Communication: Press, Politics, and Policy in America* (Mahway, N.J.: Erlbaum, in press).

16. The Harold Mendelsohn and Irving Crespi quote comes from their book, *Polls, Television, and the New Politics* (Scranton, Penn.: Chandler, 1970), 248.

17. Montague Kern, *30-Second Politics: Political Advertising in the Eighties* (New York: Praeger, 1989); Dean Alger, *The Media and Politics*, 2d ed. (Belmont, Calif.: Wadsworth, 1996); Richard F. Fenno Jr., *Home Style* (Boston: Little, Brown, 1978); and Larry Sabato, *The Rise of Political Consultants* (New York: Basic Books, 1981). Also see Craig Leonard Brians and Martin Wattenberg, "Campaign Issue Knowledge and Salience: Comparing Reception from TV Commercials, TV News, and Newspapers," *American Journal of Political Science* 40 (February 1996): 172–193; and Xinshu Zhao and Steven Chaffee, "Campaign Advertisements versus Television News as Sources of Political Issue Information," *Public Opinion Quarterly* 59 (Spring 1995): 41–65.

18. Elizabeth Kolbert, "Test-Marketing a President: How Focus Groups Pervade Campaign Politics," *New York Times Magazine*, August 30, 1992, 18–21, 60, 68, 72.

19. Quoted in John Foley, Dennis Britton, and Eugene Everett Jr., eds., *Nominating a President: The Process and the Press* (New York: Praeger, 1980), 79.

20. William McGuire, "Persuasion, Resistance, and Attitude Change," in *Handbook of Communication*, ed. Ithiel de Sola Pool (Chicago: Rand McNally, 1973), 216–252; and "The Nature of Attitudes and Attitude Change," in *Handbook of Social Psychology*, 2d ed., vol. 3, ed. Gardner Lindzey and Elliot Aronson (Reading, Mass.: Addison-Wesley, 1969), 136–314.

21. Quote taken from David Runkel, ed., *Campaign for President: The Managers Look at '88* (Dover, Mass.: Auburn House, 1989), 142.

22. Michael Robinson, "Public Affairs Television and the Growth of Political Malaise," *American Political Science Review* 70 (1976): 409–432.

23. Seymour Martin Lipset and William Schneider, *The Confidence Gap* (New York: Free Press, 1983), 17. The 1990 figure is cited in Robin Toner, "Poll Finds Postwar Glow Dimmed by the Economy," *New York Times*, March 8, 1991, A14. Changes in party identification are summarized in Paul Abramson, John Aldrich, and David Rohde, *Change and Continuity in the 1988 Elections* (Washington, D.C.: CQ Press, 1990).

24. Alexis de Tocqueville, *Democracy in America*, trans. George Lawrence (Garden City, N.J.: Doubleday, 1969), 198.

Chapter 2: Buying Air Time

1. Darrell M. West, *Making Campaigns Count* (Westport, Conn.: Greenwood Press, 1984), 29, 45.

2. Marilyn Roberts, "Advertising Strategy, Recall and Effectiveness in the 1992 Presidential Campaign" (Paper delivered at the annual meeting of the American Political Science Association, Washington, D.C., September 1993), 5.
3. Data for Bush and Clinton were provided by Robin Roberts of National Media, Inc., a major ad buyer. Data on Perot's national ad buys were provided by Clay Mulford of the Perot campaign and David Lyon of the Temerlin McClain advertising agency, which handled the Perot account.
4. For additional details on this study, see Darrell M. West, Montague Kern, Dean Alger, and Janice Goggin, "Ad Buys in Presidential Campaigns," *Political Communication* 12 (July–September 1995): 275–290.
5. Howard Kurtz, "In Advertising Give and Take, Clinton Camp Took and Responded," *Washington Post*, November 6, 1992, A10.
6. Charles Franklin, "Ad Wars: A Dynamic Model of Television Advertising in Congressional Campaigns" (Paper presented at the annual meeting of the Midwest Political Science Association, Chicago, April 1994).
7. Eleanor Randolph, "Candidates Blanket Primary, Caucus States with Ad Avalanche," *Los Angeles Times*, January 27, 1996, A10.
8. Elizabeth Kolbert, "Forbes's Ads Credited for Role in Outcome but Not in Helping Him," *New York Times*, February 14, 1996, B8.
9. "Inside Politics," CNN, February 19, 1996.
10. Robert Shogan, "Dole-Forbes Clash Becomes GOP Main Event," *Los Angeles Times*, January 28, 1996, A1.
11. Ruth Marcus, Walter Pincus, and Ira Chinoy, "Dole's Aggressive Maneuver: Spend Early and Freely," *Washington Post*, April 18, 1996, A1.
12. Michael Kranish, "'Deliberate Feint': The Dole Turnaround," *Boston Globe*, March 26, 1996, A1.
13. Amy Keller, "Campaign Media Pros Fight Back against Overcharging by TV Stations," *Roll Call*, May 30, 1996, 9, 12. Also see James Bennet, "New Tool in Political Combat: Computers to Track TV Ads," *New York Times*, June 6, 1996, A1; and Graeme Browning, "Medium Cool," *National Journal*, October 19, 1996, 2223–2225.
14. James Bennet, "Aftermath of '96 Race: 1,397 Hours of TV Ads," *New York Times*, November 13, 1996, A16.
15. "Inside Politics," CNN, March 20, 1996.
16. Susan Garland with Richard Dunham and Sandra Dallas, "Bill's First-Strike TV Blitz," *Business Week*, July 8, 1996, 126–128. Also see *Newsweek*, Special Election Issue, November 18, 1996.
17. Ruth Marcus and Ira Chinoy, "Lack of Primary Season Foe Leaves Clinton in the Money," *Washington Post*, August 24, 1996, A1; and Alison Mitchell, "Clinton Campaign Finds Harmony after a Swift Exit by Morris," *New York Times*, October 15, 1996, A25. Also see Howard Kurtz, "Clinton TV Ad Targets Black Voters," *Washington Post*, October 4, 1996, A14; and Howard Kurtz, "Clinton Team's

Early Offensive Blunted Effect of Dole Ad Blitz," *Washington Post,* October 25, 1996, A19.

18. Reported by Brooks Jackson on "Inside Politics," CNN, September 26, 1996.

19. *Boston Globe,* "Perot Steps up Spending in Final Days," November 1, 1996, A24.

20. Todd Purdum, "Clinton Opens Hard Charge in Drive for Majority of Vote," *New York Times,* October 31, 1996, B13; and Martha Moore, "In Final Days, Ads Turning Positive," *USA Today,* November 1, 1996, 2A.

Chapter 3: Ad Messages

1. This quote is taken from Jonathan Moore, ed., *Campaign for President: The Managers Look at '84* (Dover, Mass.: Auburn House, 1986), 206. An example regarding the use of focus groups to influence Mondale's advertising themes against Hart is found on 78–79.

2. Anthony Downs, *An Economic Theory of Democracy* (New York: Harper, 1957).

3. Benjamin Page, *Choices and Echoes in Presidential Elections* (Chicago: University of Chicago Press, 1978), chap. 2.

4. This quote comes from Joe McGinniss, *The Selling of the President* (New York: Simon and Schuster, 1969), 34.

5. Robert Spero, *The Duping of the American Voter* (New York: Lippincott and Crowell, 1980). Also see Lawrence Grossman, "Reflections on Television's Role in American Presidential Elections" (Discussion Paper D-3, the Joan Shorenstein Barone Center on the Press, Politics and Public Policy, Harvard University, January 1990).

6. The 1988 results were taken from the October 21–24 CBS News/*New York Times* poll. This survey was a national random sample of 1,287 registered voters. The 1992 figures come from a poll of southern states undertaken by the *Atlanta Journal-Constitution,* October 24–27, with 976 likely voters. Pama Mitchell, polling director at the newspaper, kindly made the data available to me. The 1996 numbers were reported in Richard Berke, "Should Dole Risk Tough Image? Poll Says He Already Has One," *New York Times,* October 16, 1996, A1, based on an October 10–13, 1996, national survey of 1,438 adults.

7. See Leonard Shyles, "Defining 'Images' of Presidential Candidates from Televised Political Spot Advertisements," *Political Behavior* 6 (1984): 171–181; and "Defining the Issues of a Presidential Election from Televised Political Spot Advertisements," *Journal of Broadcasting* 27 (1983): 333–343.

8. Richard Joslyn, "The Content of Political Spot Ads," *Journalism Quarterly* 57 (1980): 97. Also see Margaret Latimer, "Political Advertising for Federal and State Elections: Images or Substance?" *Journalism Quarterly* 62 (1985): 861–868.

9. See C. Richard Hofstetter and Cliff Zukin, "TV Network News and Advertising in the Nixon and McGovern Campaigns," *Journalism Quarterly* 56 (1979): 106–115, 152; Thomas Patterson and Robert McClure, *The Unseeing Eye* (New York: Putnam's, 1976); and Michael Robinson and Margaret Sheehan, *Over the Wire and on TV* (New York: Russell Sage, 1983), 144–147.

10. Samuel Popkin argues that voters can take cues about more general matters from small bites of information. See Popkin, *The Reasoning Voter* (Chicago: University of Chicago Press, 1991). A similar argument appears in Thomas Byrne Edsall, "Willie Horton's Message," *New York Review of Books,* February 13, 1992, 7–11.

11. One of the most obvious ways in which the strategic behavior of campaigns is manifest in the advertising arena is through what are called *time buys,* the amount of air time actually purchased for particular ads. A complete analysis obviously would need to incorporate information on these time buys. Unfortunately, though, it is very difficult to reconstruct accurate time-buy information for all ads from 1952 to 1996.

12. Kathleen Jamieson, *Packaging the Presidency,* 2d ed. (New York: Oxford University Press, 1992). Presentations of more than five minutes were not included because of the multiple nature of the messages presented.

13. For example, 1960 is underrepresented by Jamieson. Only two Republican spot ads during that general election were mentioned by her, compared to twelve for Kennedy in the fall. In general, though, it still is preferable to rely on ad historians in 1960 than a list of ads discussed in newspapers and on television. As shown later, there has been a dramatic increase in news coverage of advertising since that time, which obviously would bias a newspaper or television list quite seriously.

14. Jamieson, *Packaging the Presidency,* 83.

15. Joslyn, "The Content of Political Spot Ads"; Hofstetter and Zukin, "TV Network News and Advertising in the Nixon and McGovern Campaigns."

16. Angus Campbell, Philip Converse, Warren Miller, and Donald Stokes, *The American Voter* (New York: Wiley, 1960).

17. Jamieson, *Packaging the Presidency,* 115.

18. Norman Nie, Sidney Verba, and John Petrocik, *The Changing American Voter,* enl. ed. (Cambridge, Mass.: Harvard University Press, 1979).

19. Jamieson, *Packaging the Presidency,* 242.

20. The prominent ad listing underrepresents commercials on women's issues because, according to Jamieson, a long historical section dealing with the subject in her book, *Packaging the Presidency,* was cut from the final manuscript. Among the ads not described in her book that did appeal to social issues were Ellen McCormick's ads on abortion in 1976, Mondale on Jerry Falwell in 1984, the Roslyn Carter ad in 1980, and several 1972 Florida primary ads on busing.

21. Jamieson, *Packaging the Presidency*, 411.
22. Wilder's strategy is described in Michael Oreskes, "Virginia Campaign Watched as Test on Abortion Rights," *New York Times*, October 29, 1989, A1; and Robin Toner, "The Selling of the First Black Governor, in the Seat of the Old Confederacy," *New York Times*, November 10, 1989, A10. The 1992 congressional advertising involving abortion is discussed by Keith Glover in "Campaigning Crusaders Air Graphic Anti-Abortion Ads," *Congressional Quarterly Weekly Report*, September 26, 1992, 2970–2972.
23. Quote taken from Kevin Sack, "Georgia Republican Takes Abortion Stand," *New York Times*, June 16, 1996, 18. The election results are cited in Kevin Sack, "Abortion Opponents Prevail in 3 Republican Primaries," *New York Times*, August 8, 1996, B8.
24. The quotes come from Jamieson, *Packaging the Presidency*, 342, 384. Diamond and Bates describe Carter's strategy in their book, *The Spot* (Cambridge, Mass.: MIT Press, 1984), 221–257.
25. Jamieson, *Packaging the Presidency*, 338, 386.
26. See David Gopoian, "Issue Preferences and Candidate Choice in Presidential Primaries," *American Journal of Political Science* 26 (1982): 523–546, and Larry Bartels, "Issue Voting under Uncertainty," *American Journal of Political Science* 30 (1986): 709–728.
27. Jamieson, *Packaging the Presidency*, 338, 386, 395.
28. Stephanie Schorow, "Net of Votes: Candidates Reach Out and Touch On-Line Electorate," *Boston Herald*, March 13, 1996, 39; and John Carey, "Virtually Kissing Babies," *Business Week*, March 25, 1996, 69–71. Also see Michael Margolis, David Resnick, and Chin-chang Tu, "Campaigning on the Internet" (Paper delivered at the annual meeting of the Midwest Political Science Association, Chicago, April 18–21, 1996).
29. Larry Sabato, *The 1988 Elections in America* (Glenview, Ill.: Scott, Foresman, 1989), 24.
30. L. Patrick Devlin, "Contrasts in Presidential Campaign Commercials of 1988," *American Behavioral Scientist* 32 (1989): 401.
31. This quote comes from the "CBS Evening News," February 26, 1992.
32. Quoted in Robert Lineberry with George Edwards, *Government in America*, 4th ed. (Glenview, Ill.: Scott, Foresman, 1989), 153.
33. William Riker, "Why Negative Campaigning Is Rational: The Rhetoric of the Ratification Campaign of 1787–1788" (Paper delivered at the annual meeting of the American Political Science Association, Atlanta, August 1989).
34. Jamieson finds lower levels of "opposition" ads from 1952 to 1988. But she restricts her analysis to presidential general elections and adopts a different definition from mine. According to her formulation, the ad is oppositional "if more than 50 percent of the ad focuses on the record of the opponent without providing comparative information about what the sponsoring candidate would have done or germane information about the sponsoring candidate's record."

My formulation classifies an ad as negative if unflattering, threatening, or pejorative statements are made, regardless of whether comparative information is provided. Often, candidates attack without telling what they would do about a particular problem. For information on Jamieson's approach, see her book, *Dirty Politics: Deception, Distraction, and Democracy* (New York: Oxford University Press, 1992), 270 (chart 4-3).

35. Jamieson, *Packaging the Presidency*, 197.
36. Jamieson, *Packaging the Presidency*, 232.
37. Diamond and Bates, *The Spot*, 179.
38. Jamieson, *Packaging the Presidency*, 245.
39. Jamieson, *Packaging the Presidency*, 407. Also see L. Patrick Devlin, "Contrasts in Presidential Campaign Commercials of 1980," *Political Communications Review* 7 (1982): 11–12.
40. L. Patrick Devlin, "Contrasts in Presidential Campaign Commercials of 1984," *Political Communications Review* 12 (1987): 26.
41. Devlin, "Contrasts in Presidential Campaign Commercials of 1988," 390.
42. Cited in Harry Berkowitz, "Accentuating the Negative," *Newsday*, June 10, 1996, A10.
43. Devlin, "Contrasts in Presidential Campaign Commercials of 1988," 389.
44. See Karen Johnson-Cartee and Gary Copeland, "Southern Voters' Reaction to Negative Political Ads in 1986 Election," *Journalism Quarterly* 66 (1989): 888–893, 986. Also see Brian Roddy and Gina Garramone, "Appeals and Strategies of Negative Political Advertising," *Journal of Broadcasting and Electronic Media* 32 (1988): 415–427; Gina Garramone, "Voter Responses to Negative Political Ads," *Journalism Quarterly* 61 (1984): 250–259; and Gina Garramone, "Effects of Negative Political Advertising," *Journal of Broadcasting and Electronic Media* 29 (1985): 147–159.
45. Steven Ansolabehere and Shanto Iyengar, *Going Negative* (New York: Free Press, 1995).
46. Richard Berke, "Polls: Social Issues Don't Define G.O.P. Vote," *New York Times*, March 31, 1996, 24.
47. This regression model was estimated by ordinary least squares. The constant in the model is 66.55 and the unstandardized regression coefficient for mistrust was $-.177$ with a standard error of .037 $(t = -4.74;$ significant at .001). The unstandardized regression coefficient for ad negativity was $-.034$ with a standard error of .038 $(t = -.908;$ not significant).

Chapter 4: Media Coverage of Ads

1. See Theodore White, *The Making of the President 1960* (New York: Atheneum, 1961), for an early example of White's style of analysis. For example, White shows how Nixon's paranoia about the press

pervaded his entire staff. One aide said in June 1960: "Stuff the bastards. They're all against Dick anyway. Make them work—we aren't going to hand out prepared remarks; let them get their pencils out and listen and take notes," 366.

2. There are a number of excellent reviews of changes in the presidential nominating process. See John Kessel, *Presidential Campaign Politics* (Homewood, Ill.: Dorsey Press, 1980); James Ceaser, *Presidential Selection* (Princeton, N.J.: Princeton University Press, 1979); Byron Shafer, *Quiet Revolution: The Struggle for the Democratic Party and the Shaping of Post-Reform Politics* (New York: Russell Sage, 1983); and Martin Wattenberg, *The Rise of Candidate-Centered Politics* (Cambridge, Mass.: Harvard University Press, 1991).

3. Henry Brady and Richard Johnston, "What's the Primary Message: Horse Race or Issue Journalism?" in *Media and Momentum,* ed. Gary Orren and Nelson Polsby (Chatham, N.J.: Chatham House, 1987), 162; and Doris Graber, *Mass Media and American Politics* (Washington, D.C.: CQ Press, 1996), 190. Also see Matthew Kerbel, "Coverage of the 1992 Primaries on Network and Cable Television through 'Super Tuesday.'" (Paper delivered at the annual meeting of the Midwest Political Science Association, Chicago, April 1992).

4. Michael Robinson and Margaret Sheehan, *Over the Wire and on TV* (New York: Russell Sage, 1983), 149.

5. Bernard Berelson, Paul Lazarsfeld, and William McPhee, *Voting* (Chicago: University of Chicago Press, 1954), 106. Also quoted in Thomas Patterson, *The Mass Media Election* (New York: Praeger, 1980), 105.

6. Patterson, *The Mass Media Election,* 105.

7. Hugh Winebrenner discusses how Iowa was turned into a "media event" in his book, *The Iowa Precinct Caucuses* (Ames: Iowa State University Press, 1987).

8. Research assistants went through the *Times* and *Post* indexes of presidential election years and located stories about advertising. Press coverage was divided between the nominating period, which was defined as January 1 to the time of the California primary in each election year, and the general election, which ran from September 1 to election day. Articles were reviewed to determine the nature of the coverage. The study of television news proceeded along similar lines. Using the *Vanderbilt Television News Index and Abstracts,* which summarizes news stories for each network, reviewers tabulated the number and content of stories about political commercials that appeared Monday through Friday for the nominating process and general election each presidential year. The CBS analysis starts in 1972 because that was the first full presidential election year for which the abstracting service at Vanderbilt University compiled transcripts for the network evening news. CBS is used as the network of record in order to maintain comparability with past studies.

9. Appendix Table A-2 presents a breakdown of the CBS stories about paid ads by party, campaign stage, and election year.

10. For similar results on the general election from 1972 to 1988 based on all three networks, see Lynda Lee Kaid, Rob Gobetz, Jane Garner, Chris Leland, and David Scott, "Television News and Presidential Campaigns: The Legitimization of Televised Political Advertising," *Social Science Quarterly* (in press).
11. The early 1960s, though, were an exception to the pattern just described. There was little coverage of ads during the close campaign of 1960 and during those of earlier years. Remember that advertising was in its infancy at that time. There was little attention paid to television advertising or to the way in which the media could alter campaign dynamics. Johnson's 1964 landslide, though, generated eighteen articles on advertising from September through election day. There was unusual interest in advertising that year as a result of the controversial "Daisy" ad, which provoked several stories itself. Furthermore, 1964 was when it became apparent that advertising was dominating the campaign and helping to define candidates' images. After that race and the subsequent publication of Joe McGinniss's book on Nixon's 1968 advertising campaign (*The Selling of the President* [New York: Simon and Schuster, 1969]), awareness of television advertising became much higher among reporters.
12. Robinson and Sheehan, *Over the Wire and on TV.*
13. Quote cited in David Runkel, ed., *Campaign for President: The Managers Look at '88* (Dover, Mass.: Auburn House, 1989), 136.
14. Kathleen Jamieson, *Packaging the Presidency,* 2d ed. (New York: Oxford University Press, 1992), 198.
15. Quoted in Jamieson, *Packaging the Presidency,* 200–201.
16. See Kiku Adatto, "Sound Bite Democracy: Network Evening News Presidential Campaign Coverage, 1968 and 1988" (Research Paper R-2, Joan Shorenstein Barone Center for Press, Politics, and Public Policy, June 1990); and Kiku Adatto, "The Incredible Shrinking Sound Bite," *New Republic*, May 29, 1990, 20–23. Jack White discusses Horton in "Bush's Most Valuable Player," *Time*, November 14, 1988, 20–21.
17. E. J. Dionne, Jr., "Buchanan TV Spot Assails Arts Agency," *Washington Post*, February 27, 1992, A11.
18. The ad watch column by Howard Kurtz is found in the *Washington Post*, February 28, 1992, A20, and by Renee Loth in the *Boston Globe*, February 28, 1992, 12. Also see Howard Kurtz, "Buchanan Ad Consultant Turns Tables on Bush," *Washington Post*, February 28, 1992, A1, A20; and the response of Marlon Riggs, a journalism professor at the University of California at Berkeley, in "Meet the New Willie Horton," *New York Times*, March 6, 1992, A33.
19. See Robin Toner, "Moving toward a Crucial Round, Presidential Contest Turns Rough," *New York Times*, February 28, 1992, A1, A17; Elizabeth Kolbert, "Bitter G.O.P. Air War Reflects Competitiveness of Georgia Race," *New York Times*, February 28, 1992, A16; and Alessandra Stanley, "Gay Groups React Coolly to Buchanan Commercials," *New York Times*, March 8, 1992, 26.

20. See ad watch column by Howard Kurtz in the *Washington Post*, February 28, 1992, A20; and Kurtz, "Buchanan Ad Consultant Turns Tables on Bush."
21. Renee Loth, "Ad Watch," *Boston Globe*, February 28, 1992, 12.
22. In a telephone interview with me on July 20, 1992, Brooks Jackson cited focus group research by Jamieson showing that 67 percent of Georgia Republicans who saw Buchanan's ad thought it was unfair. For a more general review of CNN's coverage, see Jerry Hagstrom, "Ad Attack," *National Journal*, May 4, 1992, 810–815.

Chapter 5: Ad Watches and Voluntary Codes

1. Kim Lawton, "Efforts Under Way to Stop Negative Campaigning," *Providence Journal*, May 19, 1996, B3.
2. Quoted in Stuart Elliott, "Advertising Agencies Make a Pitch to Politicians and Consultants, Urging Them to Clean up Their Act," *New York Times*, April 29, 1996, D27.
3. David Rosenbaum, "In Minnesota Race, Negative Ads Outnumber the Lakes," *New York Times*, October 23, 1996, A21.
4. Samuel Schreiber of the Committee for the Study of the American Electorate helped collect these data.
5. Susan Lederman and Gerald Pomper, *CampaignWatch* (Washington, D.C.: League of Women Voters Education Fund, 1993). Also see Howard Kurtz, "When News Media Go to Grass Roots, Candidates Often Don't Follow," *Washington Post*, June 4, 1996, A6.
6. Iver Peterson, "Civic-Minded Pursuits Gain Ground at Newspapers," *New York Times*, March 4, 1996, D5.
7. Peterson, "Civic-Minded Pursuits Gain Ground at Newspapers," D5.
8. Kurtz, "When News Media Go to Grass Roots,"A6.
9. James Bennet, "North Carolina Media Try to Lead Politics to Issues," *New York Times*, September 24, 1996, A1. Also see Elliot Krieger and Jody McPhillips, "Power to the People," *Providence Journal*, November 3, 1996, D1.
10. Jonathan Yardley, "Public Journalism: Bad News," *Washington Post*, September 30, 1996, C2.
11. Howard Kurtz, "Americans Tuning out Campaign '96," *Washington Post*, October 10, 1996, A1.
12. Ad in *New York Times*, October 1, 1996, A15.
13. Lawrie Mifflin, "Clinton and Dole Accept Plan for Campaign Time on Fox TV," *New York Times*, September 11, 1996, B8; and Lawrie Mifflin, "CBS to Give Clinton and Dole Free Air Time on Radio and TV," *New York Times*, September 28, 1996, 11. For an evaluation of these efforts, see Howard Kurtz, "Campaign for Free Air Time Falls Short of Organizers' Goals," *Washington Post*, October 31, 1996, A17.
14. Martha Moore, "A Minute of the Voters' Time," *USA Today*, September 18, 1996, 4A.

15. Lawrie Mifflin, "Time for Local Candidates," *New York Times,* September 25, 1996, C16; and "Belo to Offer Free Airtime to Candidates," *Providence Journal,* October 5, 1996, B10.

16. Kathleen Jamieson described the development of ad watches in a telephone conversation with me on January 30, 1992. Also see Michael Milburn and Justin Brown, "Busted by the Ad Police" (Research Paper R-15, Joan Shorenstein Barone Center for Press, Politics and Public Policy, July 1995).

17. Quoted in Kurtz, "In Advertising Give and Take," A10. For reviews, see John Tedesco, Lori Melton McKinnon, and Lynda Lee Kaid, "Advertising Watchdogs," *Harvard International Journal of Press/Politics* 1 (Fall 1996): 76–93; and Joseph Capella and Kathleen Hall Jamieson, "Broadcast Adwatch Effects," *Communication Research* 3 (1994): 342–365.

18. The question was, "How helpful to viewers would you say these stories about campaign ads have been? (1) very helpful, (2) somewhat helpful, or (3) not very helpful."

19. Telephone interview with Howard Kurtz, April 8, 1992; with Mara Liasson, April 27, 1992; and with Renee Loth, April 27, 1992.

20. Steven Ansolabehere and Shanto Iyengar, *Going Negative* (New York: Free Press, 1995); and Stephen Ansolabehere and Shanto Iyengar, "Can the Press Monitor Campaign Advertising? An Experimental Study," *Harvard International Journal of Press/Politics* 1 (Winter 1996): 72–86.

21. "Inside Politics," CNN, January 19, 1996; and Kathleen Jamieson, "Truth and Advertising," *New York Times,* January 27, 1996, 21.

22. Interview with Martha Moore, July 19, 1996.

23. Samuel Schreiber of the Committee for the Study of the American Electorate helped collect these data.

24. John Carroll, "Truth or Consequences," *Boston Globe,* August 4, 1996, D1.

25. Quoted in Darrell West, Montague Kern, and Dean Alger, "Political Advertising and Ad Watches in the 1992 Presidential Nominating Campaign" (Paper delivered at the annual meeting of the American Political Science Association, Chicago, September 1992). Several networks in 1992 also used focus groups after debates to evaluate candidates' performances.

26. Personal interview with Robert Shrum, May 26, 1996.

27. Personal interview with Robert Shrum, May 26, 1996.

28. Telephone interview with Mara Liasson, April 27, 1992.

Chapter 6: Learning about the Candidates

1. Thomas Patterson and Robert McClure, *The Unseeing Eye* (New York: Putnam's, 1976). Also see Robert Meadow and Lee Sigelman, "Some Effects and Noneffects of Campaign Commercials," *Political Behavior* 4 (1982): 163–174; and Donald Cundy, "Political Com-

mercials and Candidate Image," in *New Perspectives on Political Advertising*, ed. Lynda Lee Kaid, Dan Nimmo, and Keith Sanders (Carbondale: Southern Illinois University Press, 1986), 210–234.

2. Garramone, "Issue versus Image Orientation"; Ronald Mulder, "The Effects of Televised Political Ads in the 1975 Chicago Mayoral Election," *Journalism Quarterly* 56 (1979): 25–36; Atkin and Heald, "Effects of Political Advertising"; and Charles Atkin, Lawrence Bowen, Oguz Nayman, and Kenneth Sheinkopf, "Quality versus Quantity in Televised Political Ads," *Public Opinion Quarterly* 37 (1973): 209–224.

3. Kathleen Jamieson, *Packaging the Presidency*, 2d ed. (New York: Oxford University Press, 1992); Edwin Diamond and Stephen Bates, *The Spot* (Cambridge, Mass.: MIT Press, 1984); L. Patrick Devlin, "Contrasts in Presidential Campaign Commercials of 1988," *American Behavioral Scientist* 32 (1989): 389–414.

4. Larry Bartels, *Presidential Primaries and the Dynamics of Public Choice* (Princeton, N.J.: Princeton University Press, 1988); and Edie Goldenberg and Michael Traugott, *Campaigning for Congress* (Washington, D.C.: CQ Press, 1984), 85–91.

5. See Stanley Kelley Jr. and Thad Mirer, "The Simple Act of Voting," *American Political Science Review* 68 (1974): 572–591. However, National Election Study coding of likes and dislikes allows for issue-oriented material as well as affective qualities.

6. Quoted in Patterson and McClure, *The Unseeing Eye*, 130.

7. On hearing this story at a postelection campaign seminar, John Anderson quipped that Dole's fourteen seconds consisted of a news report about his car breaking down in New Hampshire. Both stories are taken from Jonathan Moore, ed., *Campaign for President: 1980 in Retrospect* (Cambridge, Mass.: Ballinger, 1981), 129–130.

8. In the 1974 National Election Study, candidate recognition was a dichotomous variable ("heard of" coded 1; "not heard of" coded 5) based on "Now let's talk about the campaign for Senator. Do you remember what the candidates' names were?" The 1976 Patterson survey used, "I am going to read the names of people who have been mentioned as possible candidates for the Democratic and Republican presidential nominations. As I read each name tell me if you have (1) never heard the name before, (2) if you have heard the name, but really don't know anything about him, or (3) if you know something about him. First, how about [candidate]?" In the 1984 and 1988 CBS, 1990 Rhode Island, and 1992 surveys, candidate recognition was based on the question, "Is your opinion of [candidate] favorable, not favorable, undecided, or haven't you heard enough about [candidate] yet to have an opinion?" Recognition was a two-category variable in which those saying they were favorable or unfavorable were coded 0 as recognizing the candidate, and those who were undecided or said they hadn't heard enough were classified 1 as not recognizing the candidate. The North Carolina question gauged citizen familiarity with the Senate race: "How much do you think you know about the

Gantt-Helms Senate race—(1) a lot, (2) some, (3) only a little, or (4) nothing at all?" The 1972 Patterson and McClure survey did not include a recognition question. For further details about this analysis, see Darrell M. West, *Air Wars*, 1st ed. (Washington, D.C.: Congressional Quarterly, 1993).

9. The favorability item in the 1974 National Election Study was based on the question, "Was there anything in particular about the Democratic/Republican candidate for Senator that made you want to vote for him?" (Coded 0 if yes and 1 if no.) The 1976 Patterson survey used, "Now I'd like to get your feelings on those candidates whom you know something about. Please look at Card 2. You can use this scale to give us an indication of your feelings toward the candidates. If you feel extremely favorable toward a candidate, you would give him the number 1. If you feel fairly favorable, you would give him the number 2. If you feel only slightly favorable, you would give him a 3. If your feelings are mixed between favorable and unfavorable, you would give him a 4. Suppose, however, that you feel unfavorable toward a candidate. You would give him a 7 if you feel extremely unfavorable, a 6 if fairly unfavorable, and a 5 if only slightly unfavorable. Which number on the scale best describes your feelings about [candidate]?" In the 1984 and 1988 CBS, 1990 Rhode Island, and 1992 surveys, candidate favorability was based on the question, "Is your opinion of [candidate] favorable, not favorable, undecided, or haven't you heard enough about [candidate] yet to have an opinion?" Favorability was measured as a three-category item (1 favorable, 2 undecided, 3 not favorable). The 1972 Patterson and McClure and 1990 North Carolina Senate surveys did not include questions on favorability.

10. Quoted in "How He Won," *Newsweek,* November/December 1992 (special issue), 64.

11. The question wording for electability in the 1972 Patterson and McClure study was, "Richard Nixon will win the presidential election: (1) extremely likely, (2) quite likely, (3) slightly likely, (4) not sure, (5) slightly unlikely, (6) quite unlikely, (7) extremely unlikely." The 1976 Patterson survey used the question, "Let's consider the Democratic/Republican candidates whom you know something about. We'd like to know what chance you think each candidate has of becoming his party's nominee for President. Look at Card 3. This scale is similar to the one we just worked with. If you think it likely that a candidate will get his party's nomination you would select a 1, 2, or 3; if unlikely, then a 5, 6, or 7. Select a 4 if you feel it is as likely to happen as not to happen. It is important to base your opinions only on whether you think a candidate will be the nominee, and not on whether you want him to be the nominee. Which number on the card best describes the likelihood that [candidate] will be the Democratic/Republican presidential nominee?" Electability in the 1988 CBS, 1990 Rhode Island, and 1992 surveys was measured as a dichotomous variable (1 if electable, 0 if not electable) by the ques-

tion: "Regardless of which candidate you support [for the nomination], which of these (Democratic/Republican) candidates do you think would have the best chance of winning the election in November [if he were nominated]?" No electability item was asked in the 1974 National Election Study, the 1984 CBS survey, or the 1990 North Carolina survey.

12. The question wordings in the 1972 Patterson and McClure study were, "Richard Nixon favors honoring our commitments to other nations: (1) extremely likely, (2) quite likely, (3) slightly likely, (4) not sure, (5) slightly unlikely, (6) quite unlikely, (7) extremely unlikely"; "George McGovern favors an immediate pull-out of all U.S. troops from Vietnam: (1) extremely likely, (2) quite likely, (3) slightly likely, (4) not sure, (5) slightly unlikely, (6) quite unlikely, (7) extremely unlikely"; and "Richard Nixon/George McGovern is experienced in government: (1) extremely likely, (2) quite likely, (3) slightly likely, (4) not sure, (5) slightly unlikely, (6) quite unlikely, (7) extremely unlikely."

13. The 1976 Patterson survey used scales of 1 through 7 for candidates' positions and character traits: "There is a lot of talk these days about the level of spending by the federal government for social welfare programs. Some people feel that the current level of social welfare spending is necessary because almost everyone receiving this government help really needs it. Others feel a great deal of this social welfare spending is wasted because a lot of people receiving this government help don't deserve it. Where would you place [candidate] on this scale or don't you know about his position? 1 is current level of social welfare is necessary and 7 is a great deal of current social welfare spending is wasted"; "Some people think our military strength has diminished in comparison to Russia and that much more must be spent on planes, ships, and weapons to build a stronger defense. Others feel that our military defense is adequate and that no increase in military spending is currently necessary. Where would you place [candidate] on this scale, or don't you know about his position? 1 is spend much more on military defense and 7 is no increase in military defense spending"; "Now, we'd like to discuss a few of the presidential candidates with you. People have different opinions about the specific qualities of individual candidates. Look at Card 4. Some people think that a certain candidate is very trustworthy, that is, they feel he is completely sincere, truthful, straightforward, and honest. Others might think that the same candidate is very untrustworthy. Which number best describes your feeling about [candidate] or don't you know how trustworthy or untrustworthy he is? 1 is very trustworthy and 7 is very untrustworthy"; and "Next, whether or not a candidate has a great deal of ability, that is, competent, capable, and skillful. Which number best describes your feeling about [candidate] or don't you know about him? 1 is great deal of ability and 7 is almost no ability."

14. Questions in the 1988 CBS nominating study included, "Right now, would you say the United States (1) is superior in military strength

to the Soviet Union, (2) is about equal in strength, or (3) is not as strong as the Soviet Union?" "(1) Are imports of Japanese goods creating unfair competition for U.S. industries, or (2) are Japanese imports really being blamed for U.S. industrial problems?" "In order to reduce the size of the federal budget deficit, would you be (1) willing, or (2) not willing to pay more in federal taxes?" "Do you think that [candidate] (1) says what he really believes most of the time, or (2) says what he thinks people want to hear?" "Regardless of which candidate you support for the nomination, which of these Democratic/Republican candidates do you think cares the most about the needs and problems of people like yourself?" (coded 1 for mention of each candidate and 0 if not), and "Do you think that [candidate] has strong qualities of leadership?" (coded 1 if yes and 2 if no).

15. Michael Kelly, "Clinton, after Raising Hopes, Tries to Lower Expectations," *New York Times*, November 9, 1992, A1.

16. The 1992 nominating questions were based on the question, "Regardless of which candidate you support for the nomination, which of these candidates do you think cares the most about the needs and problems of people like yourself?" (coded 1 for mention of each candidate and 0 if not); "Which of these candidates do you think can best handle the economy?" (coded 1 for mention of each candidate and 0 if not); and "We'd like to know your impressions of the candidates. Please tell us whether you (1) strongly agree, (2) agree, (3) disagree, or (4) strongly disagree with the following statement: [candidate] is honest and trustworthy." The 1992 general election questions included, "Now we would like to know something about the feelings you have toward [candidate]. Has [candidate]—because of the kind of person he is, or because of something he has done—ever made you feel hopeful/disgusted/excited? (yes or no)"; "If [candidate] were elected President, would he make the U.S. economy get better, get worse, or stay about the same?"; and "If [candidate] were elected President, would he improve America's standing in the world? (yes or no)."

17. The multivariate model for the 1990 Rhode Island Senate race controlled for party identification, education, age, and gender only. The 1990 North Carolina poll did not include a measure for political interest. The 1988 CBS Super Tuesday nominating study did not include a question on free media exposure.

18. Interview with Elizabeth Kolbert, July 20, 1992.

19. "How He Won," 40.

20. Quotes taken from Darrell West, Montague Kern, and Dean Alger, "Political Advertising and Ad Watches in the 1992 Presidential Nominating Campaign" (Paper delivered at the annual meeting of the American Political Science Association, Chicago, September 1992), 15–16. Also see Marion Just, Ann Crigler, Dean Alger, Timothy Cook, Montague Kern, and Darrell M. West, *Cross Talk* (Chicago: University of Chicago Press, 1996).

21. Candidate favorability was based on the question, "Is your opinion of [candidate] favorable, not favorable, undecided, or haven't you heard enough about [candidate] yet to have an opinion?" Favorability was measured as a three-category item (1 favorable, 2 undecided, 3 not favorable). The electability question was, "Regardless of which candidate you support, which of these candidates do you think would have the best chance of winning the election in November?"

22. Questions included, "Bill Clinton/Bob Dole provides strong leadership [strongly agree, agree, disagree, or strongly disagree]"; "Bill Clinton is honest and trustworthy [strongly agree, agree, disagree, or strongly disagree]"; "Which of these candidates do you think cares the most about the needs and problems of people like yourself [coded 1 for mentioning the candidate and 0 if not]"; "Which candidate do you feel would do a better job of protecting Medicare [coded 1 for mentioning the candidate and 0 if not]"; "Which candidate do you feel would bring fiscal discipline to the federal government [coded 1 for mentioning the candidate and 0 if not]"; and "Which candidate do you feel would do a better job of protecting the environment [coded 1 for mentioning the candidate and 0 if not]?"

23. For more details, see West, *Air Wars*, 1st ed.

24. Jack Germond and Jules Witcover, *Whose Broad Stripes and Bright Stars?* (New York: Warner, 1989), 283–286.

25. Germond and Witcover, *Whose Broad Stripes and Bright Stars?* 290.

26. Another example of two-stage models can be found in Benjamin Page and Calvin Jones, "Reciprocal Effects of Policy Preferences, Party Loyalties and the Vote," *American Political Science Review* 73 (1979): 1071–1089.

27. The direct effect of electability on the vote in this two-stage analysis was .47 ($p<.001$). Other coefficients that were significant included race (.13; $p<.001$), party identification (–.05; $p<.01$), and gender (–.11; $p<.01$).

28. The best predictors of views regarding electability were exposure to Dukakis ads (.18; $p<.01$) and party (.06; $p<.01$). The significant relationship for advertisements remains even after preferred candidate choice is included in the model as a control factor.

29. The direct effect of electability on the vote in this two-stage analysis was .47 ($p<.001$). The effect on electability from exposure to Dukakis ads was .20 ($p<.001$) and from exposure to Gore ads was .06 (not significant). The following variables were included as control variables: party identification, education, age, gender, race, ideology, political interest, and media exposure.

30. This quote and those that follow come from an interview with the author conducted May 13, 1992. Bob Woodward documents the massive bureaucratic infighting that preceded the insertion of the "read my lips" line in Bush's 1988 convention speech in "Origin of the Tax Pledge," *Washington Post*, October 4, 1992, A1.

31. The direct effect of electability on the vote in this two-stage analysis was .40 ($p<.001$). People who saw Bush ads were less likely to say they would vote for him ($-.02$; $p<.05$). Exposure to Buchanan ads had no significant impact on the vote. The effect on electability from exposure to Bush ads was $-.02$ ($p<.10$) and from exposure to Buchanan ads was .01 (not significant). The following variables were included in the analysis as control variables: party identification, education, age, gender, race, ideology, political interest, and media exposure.

32. This information on Bush's ads comes from an interview of Montague Kern with Robin Roberts on April 10, 1992.

Chapter 7: Setting the Agenda

1. The classics in this area are E. E. Schattschneider, *The Semisovereign People* (Hinsdale, Ill.: Dryden Press, 1960); Roger Cobb and Charles Elder, *Participation in American Politics: The Dynamics of Agenda-Building*, 2d ed. (Baltimore: Johns Hopkins University Press, 1983); and John Kingdon, *Agendas, Alternatives, and Public Policies* (Boston: Little, Brown, 1984).

2. Good examples include Maxwell McCombs and Donald Shaw, "The Agenda-Setting Function of Mass Media," *Public Opinion Quarterly* 36 (1972): 176–187; Ray Funkhouser, "The Issues of the Sixties: An Exploratory Study in the Dynamics of Public Opinion," *Public Opinion Quarterly* 37 (1973): 62–75; Jack McLeod, Lee Becker, and James Byrnes, "Another Look at the Agenda-Setting Function of the Press," *Communication Research* 1 (1974): 131–166; Lutz Erbring, Edie Goldenberg, and Arthur Miller, "Front-Page News and Real-World Cues: A New Look at Agenda-Setting by the Media," *American Journal of Political Science* 24 (1980): 16–49; and David Weaver, *Media Agenda-Setting in a Presidential Election* (New York: Praeger, 1981).

3. Shanto Iyengar and Donald Kinder, *News that Matters* (Chicago: University of Chicago Press, 1987), 112; and Samuel Kernell, *Going Public*, 2d ed. (Washington, D.C.: CQ Press, 1993). Also see Benjamin Page, Robert Shapiro, and Glenn Dempsey, "What Moves Public Opinion?" *American Political Science Review* 81 (1987): 23–44.

4. Stanley Feldman, "Economic Self-Interest and Political Behavior," *American Journal of Political Science* 26 (1982): 446–466. Also see Euel Elliott, *Issues and Elections* (Boulder, Colo.: Westview Press, 1989).

5. Paul Light, *The President's Agenda* (Baltimore: Johns Hopkins University Press, 1982).

6. Cobb and Elder, *Participation in American Politics*, 91–92. Also see Arthur Miller, Edie Goldenberg, and Lutz Erbring, "Type-Set Politics: Impact of Newspapers on Public Confidence," *American Polit-*

ical Science Review 73 (1979): 67–84; Michael MacKuen, "Exposure to Information, Belief Integration, and Individual Responsiveness to Agenda Change," *American Political Science Review* 78 (1984): 372–391; and Michael MacKuen, "Political Drama, Economic Conditions, and the Dynamics of Presidential Popularity," *American Journal of Political Science* 27 (1983): 165–192.

7. Good examples include McCombs and Shaw, "The Agenda-Setting Function of Mass Media"; and McLeod, Becker, and Byrnes, "Another Look at the Agenda-Setting Function of the Press."

8. Gladys Lang and Kurt Lang, *The Battle for Public Opinion* (New York: Columbia University Press, 1983).

9. Kingdon, *Agendas, Alternatives, and Public Policies,* 61–64.

10. Kingdon, *Agendas, Alternatives, and Public Policies,* 63.

11. Quoted in Light, *The President's Agenda,* 96. For congressional studies, see Barbara Sinclair, "The Role of Committees in Agenda Setting in the U.S. Congress," *Legislative Studies Quarterly* 11 (1986): 35–45; Roberta Herzberg and Rick Wilson, "Results on Sophisticated Voting in an Experimental Setting," *Journal of Politics* 50 (1988): 471–486; and Darrell M. West, *Congress and Economic Policymaking* (Pittsburgh, Pa.: University of Pittsburgh Press, 1987).

12. Charles Atkin and Gary Heald, "Effects of Political Advertising," *Public Opinion Quarterly* 40 (1976): 216–228.

13. Thomas Bowers, "Issue and Personality Information in Newspaper Political Advertising," *Journalism Quarterly* 49 (1972): 446–452; and Bowers, "Newspaper Political Advertising and the Agenda-Setting Function," *Journalism Quarterly* 50 (1973): 552–556.

14. For a review of the character issue, see Peter Goldman, Tom Mathews, and Tony Fuller, *The Quest for the Presidency 1988* (New York: Simon and Schuster, 1989); and Jack Germond and Jules Witcover, *Whose Broad Stripes and Bright Stars?* (New York: Warner, 1989).

15. Nelson Polsby also discusses this quality of press coverage in "The News Media as an Alternative to Party in the Presidential Selection Process," in *Political Parties in the Eighties,* ed. Robert Goldwin (Washington, D.C.: American Enterprise Institute, 1980), 50–66.

16. Each of these open-ended questions was coded 1 for mention of a particular problem and 0 if no mention. The 1972 Patterson and McClure survey question was, "There are many problems of concern to people today. Based on your own everyday experiences, what one political problem matters most to you personally?" The 1974 National Election Study used, "Tell me the letter of the issue which is most important to you" (from ten cards—list of issues—provided). The 1976 Patterson survey was based on the questions, "Please think for a moment of the problems that face this country today. In your mind, what do you feel is the one most important problem that the national government in Washington should do

something about?" and "So far during the presidential campaign, what do you think is the one most important thing that has happened?" In 1984, the CBS News/*New York Times* poll asked, "What is the single most important thing you would like to see Ronald Reagan accomplish in the next four years as President?" and "What was the best/worst thing Ronald Reagan/Walter Mondale did in this campaign?" The 1988 CBS News/*New York Times* poll asked, "As far as you are concerned, what should be the single most important issue in this election?" and "What is the best/worst thing George Bush/Michael Dukakis did in this campaign?" The 1990 Rhode Island survey asked, "As far as you are concerned, what is the single most important policy issue in the Senate election?" and "What is the most important event that has occurred in the Senate campaign?" The 1992 surveys asked, "As far as you are concerned, what is the most important problem facing the country today?" and "What do you think is the most important event that has happened so far in this presidential campaign?" The 1990 North Carolina survey did not ask about the most important problem facing the state.

17. For the text of this speech, see "Bush's Presidential Nomination Acceptance Address," *Congressional Quarterly Weekly Report* 46 (1988), 2353–2356.

18. See Eric Uslaner and Margaret Conway, "The Responsible Electorate: Watergate, the Economy, and Vote Choice in 1974," *American Political Science Review* 79 (1985): 788–803.

19. The CBS News/*New York Times* post-general-election surveys run in 1984 and 1988 did not include measures for free media exposure.

20. The 1984 analysis of individual ads does not include a measure of media exposure; the October 1988 CBS News/*New York Times* survey regarding Bush's "Revolving Door" and Dukakis's family/education commercials does incorporate media exposure as a control factor.

21. There often has been confusion between the Bush-produced "Revolving Door" ad, which did not mention Horton directly by name, and the Horton ad aired by an independent political action committee, which used his name and picture. It is not clear whether viewers actually distinguished the two, because both dealt with crime.

22. Marjorie Hershey, "The Campaign and the Media," in *The Election of 1988*, ed. Gerald M. Pomper (Chatham, N.J.: Chatham House, 1989), 95–96.

23. Criticisms about Dukakis's failure to respond to Bush, however, were influenced by personal circumstances. People in the Northeast, those aged forty-five years of age or older, and women were most likely after viewing Dukakis advertising to conclude Dukakis had erred in not responding to Bush's attacks. For more general discussions of the impact of personal predicaments, see Erbring, Goldenberg, and

Miller, "Front-Page News and Real-World Cues," 16–49; Tom Tyler, "Impact of Directly and Indirectly Experienced Events: The Origins of Crime-Related Judgments and Behaviors," *Journal of Personality and Social Psychology* 39 (1980): 13–28; and David Sears, Tom Tyler, T. Citrin, and Donald Kinder, "Political System Support and Public Response to the Energy Crisis," *American Journal of Political Science* 22 (1978): 56–82.

24. "How He Won," *Newsweek*, November/December 1992 (special issue), 78.

25. I also confirmed this result through a logistic regression analysis that included an interaction term for gender and exposure to Bush's "Revolving Door" ad. The coefficient for the interaction term was 1.39 with a standard error of .62 ($p<.05$), indicating a strong relationship in the expected direction.

26. Quote taken from David Runkel, ed., *Campaign for President: The Managers Look at '88* (Dover, Mass.: Auburn House, 1989), 113–114.

27. For a related argument, see Darrell M. West, "Television and Presidential Popularity in America," *British Journal of Political Science* 21 (1991): 199–214.

28. Stephen Ansolabehere and Shanto Iyengar, "The Electoral Effects of Issues and Attacks in Campaign Advertising" (Paper delivered at the annual meeting of the American Political Science Association, Washington, D.C., August 1991).

29. Quote taken from Runkel, *Campaign for President*, 110. In anticipation of similar treatment, Clinton in 1992 hired someone to do opposition research on himself. See Sonni Efron and David Lauter, "Spy vs. Spy: Campaign Dirt Game," *Los Angeles Times*, March 28, 1992, 1.

30. Following the election, Atwater claimed that it was Gore, during the Democratic nominating process, who first criticized Dukakis on the Horton furlough issue. See Runkel, *Campaign for President*, 115.

31. Runkel, *Campaign for President*, 221.

32. Runkel, *Campaign for President*, 9.

33. In this two-stage analysis of the 1988 CBS News/*New York Times* survey data, the direct effect on the vote of citing crime as the most important problem was .70 ($p<.05$). People who saw Bush's "Revolving Door" ad were more likely to cite crime (.10; $p<.01$), whereas those who saw Dukakis's family education ad were less likely to name crime (–.06; $p<.05$). The following variables were included in the analysis as control variables: party identification, education, age, gender, race, ideology, political interest, and media exposure. Neither ad had a direct effect on the vote, so those links were removed from the path model. Other agenda items displaying significant correlations with the vote included social welfare problems and jobs.

34. Quote taken from Runkel, *Campaign for President*, 9.

35. See Kiku Adatto, "Sound Bite Democracy: Network Evening News Presidential Campaign Coverage, 1968 and 1988" (Research Paper R-2, Joan Shorenstein Barone Center for Press, Politics and Public Policy, June 1990), 9, 26–27. On October 25, 1988, CBS reporter Lesley Stahl corrected the revolving-door claim that "268 escaped" by pointing out that four first-degree murderers escaped while on parole. Other reporting on the furlough ad can be found on ABC on September 22, CBS on October 28, "Meet the Press" and "Face the Nation" the last weekend in October, and "Good Morning America" in early October.
36. "How He Won," 84.
37. Richard Berke, "The Ad Campaign: Mixing Harshness with Warmth," *New York Times,* October 22, 1992, A20; and Leslie Phillips, "Bush Ads Revive 'Man on the Street,' " *USA Today,* October 23, 1992, A2.
38. Robin Toner, "Clinton Retains Significant Lead in Latest Survey," *New York Times,* September 16, 1992, A1.
39. Robin Toner, "Clinton Fending off Assaults, Retains Sizable Lead, Poll Finds," *New York Times,* October 15, 1992, A1.
40. "How He Won," 81.
41. Toner, "Clinton Fending Off Assaults." After the election, it was revealed that searches had been made of Perot's passport file, too.
42. Quoted in Howard Kurtz, "In Advertising Give and Take, Clinton Camp Took and Responded," *Washington Post,* November 6, 1992, A10.
43. "How He Won," 84.

Chapter 8: Changing the Standards

1. See Herbert Simon, *Models of Thought* (New Haven: Yale University Press, 1979); S. E. Asch, "Forming Impressions of Personality," *Journal of Abnormal and Social Psychology* 41 (1946): 258–290; and B. Fischhoff, P. Slovic, and S. Lichtenstein, "Knowing What You Want," in *Cognitive Processes in Choice and Decision Behavior,* ed. T. Wallsten (Hillsdale, N.J.: Erlbaum, 1980).
2. A number of studies have investigated this relationship. See George Bishop, Robert Oldendick, and Alfred Tuchfarber, "Political Information Processing: Question Order and Context Effects," *Political Behavior* 4 (1982): 177–200; C. Turner and E. Krauss, "Fallible Indicators of the Subjective State of the Nation," *American Psychologist* 33 (1978): 456–470; and Amos Tversky and Daniel Kahneman, "The Framing of Decisions and the Psychology of Choice," *Science* 211 (1981): 453–458.
3. Peter Goldman, Tom Mathews, and Tony Fuller, *The Quest for the Presidency, 1988* (New York: Simon and Schuster, 1989); Jack Germond and Jules Witcover, *Whose Broad Stripes and Bright Stars?* (New York: Warner, 1989).

4. Daniel Kahneman, Paul Slovic, and Amos Tversky, *Judgment under Uncertainty: Heuristics and Biases* (New York: Cambridge University Press, 1982).

5. Goldman, Mathews, and Fuller, *The Quest for the Presidency, 1988;* and Germond and Witcover, *Whose Broad Stripes and Bright Stars?*

6. Shanto Iyengar and Donald Kinder, *News that Matters* (Chicago: University of Chicago Press, 1987), 63–64. Also see Jon Krosnick and Donald Kinder, "Altering the Foundations of Popular Support for the President through Priming: Reagan and the Iran-Contra Affair," *American Political Science Review* 84 (1990): 497–512.

7. Iyengar and Kinder, *News that Matters,* 63.

8. Krosnick and Kinder, "Altering the Foundations of Popular Support."

9. Lawrence Jacobs and Robert Shapiro, "Issues, Candidate Image, and Priming: The Use of Private Polls in Kennedy's 1960 Presidential Campaign" (Unpublished paper, Columbia University, 1992).

10. Michael Robinson and Margaret Sheehan, *Over the Wire and on TV* (New York: Russell Sage, 1983); and F. Christopher Arterton, "Campaign Organizations Confront the Media-Political Environment," in *Race for the Presidency,* ed. James David Barber (Englewood Cliffs, N.J.: Prentice Hall, 1978), 3–24.

11. Richard Brody and Catherine Shapiro, "Policy Failure and Public Support," *Political Behavior 11* (1989): 353–369. A more general discussion of this argument can be found in Richard Brody, *Assessing the President: The Media, Elite Opinion, and Public Support* (Stanford, Calif.: Stanford University Press, 1991).

12. Jeff Fishel, *Presidents and Promises* (Washington, D.C.: CQ Press, 1985); and Gerald Pomper with Susan Lederman, *Elections in America,* 2d ed. (New York: Longman, 1980).

13. Iyengar and Kinder, *News that Matters,* 66–68.

14. Krosnick and Kinder, "Altering the Foundations of Popular Support."

15. Descriptions of the 1972 presidential campaign can be found in Thomas Patterson and Robert McClure, *The Unseeing Eye* (New York: Putnam's, 1976); and Warren Miller and J. Merrill Shanks, "Policy Directions and Presidential Leadership: Alternative Interpretations of the 1980 Presidential Election," *British Journal of Political Science* 12 (1982): 299–356.

16. Theodore White, *The Making of the President, 1972* (New York: Atheneum, 1973).

17. Goldman, Mathews, and Fuller, *The Quest for the Presidency, 1988;* and Germond and Witcover, *Whose Broad Stripes and Bright Stars?*

18. The questions used in this analysis were based on an October 1988 CBS News/*New York Times* survey. The items used were, "If George Bush were elected President, do you think he would make U.S. defenses stronger, make them weaker, or would he keep defenses at the present level?" "Regardless of who you intend to vote for, do you think 1) George Bush or 2) Michael Dukakis would do a better job

of protecting the environment?" "Regardless of who you intend to vote for, do you think 1) George Bush or 2) Michael Dukakis cares more about the needs and problems of people like yourself?" and [The death penalty for people convicted of controlling large drug dealing operations]: "Does George Bush agree with your position on this issue, or doesn't he? (1) yes or (2) no."

19. Dave Kaplan, "Early Readings on '90 Elections," *Congressional Quarterly Weekly Report*, February 17, 1990, 488–489. A discussion of the 1990 contest can be found in Montague Kern and Marion Just, "Constructing Candidate Images: Focus Group Discourse about Campaign News and Advertising" (Paper delivered at the annual meeting of the New England Political Science Association, Providence, R.I., April 1992).

20. Bob Benenson, "Republicans' Net Loss: One Seat and Many Expectations," *Congressional Quarterly Weekly Report*, November 10, 1990, 3824–3829.

21. Thomas Edsall, "Carolina Senate Contest Shows Voters' Age Gap," *Washington Post*, November 4, 1990, A16.

22. Thomas Edsall, "Helms Makes Race an Issue," *Washington Post*, November 1, 1990, A1, 6.

23. These questions were asked in the following way: "Do you (1) support or (2) oppose drilling for gas and oil off the coast of North Carolina?" "Do you think abortions should (1) be legal under any circumstances, (2) be legal only under certain circumstances, or (3) never be legal under any circumstances?" "Do you think it will be best for the future of this country (1) if we take an active part in world affairs, or (2) if we stay out of world affairs?" and "Do you (1) favor or (2) oppose the death penalty for persons convicted of murder?"

24. Robin Toner, "An Underdog Forces Helms into a Surprisingly Tight Race," *New York Times*, October 31, 1990, A1, D25.

25. This and the following description of the Clinton strategy can be found in "How He Won," *Newsweek*, November/December 1992 (special issue), 40–56. Also see Michael Kelly, "The Making of a First Family: A Blueprint," *New York Times*, November 14, 1992, 1.

26. This analysis was based on the questions, "As far as you are concerned, what is the most important problem facing the country today?" (open-ended responses coded for mentioning or not mentioning the economy); "If Bill Clinton were elected president, would he make the U.S. economy get better, get worse, or stay about the same?"; and "Bill Clinton is honest and trustworthy: strongly agree, agree, disagree, or strongly disagree." The vote was support or non-support for Clinton. Controls were included for party identification, education, age, gender, race, ideology, political interest, and media exposure.

27. For example, Yale economist Ray Fair's model, based on national economic growth, boldly predicted a big Bush reelection. What he failed to recognize, though, was the cumulative nature of economic fears and the ability of candidates to influence attributions of respon-

sibility. A discussion of 1992 forecasting models is found in Richard Morin, "For Political Forecasters, Key Variable Is the Winner," *Washington Post*, September 5, 1992, A1. Only two of the five forecasters cited in this article anticipated a Clinton victory.

Chapter 9: Playing the Blame Game

1. Panel data from before and after the election show 58 percent felt in both the pre- and postelection surveys that Bush was responsible for negative campaigning. Among low ad viewers, 46 percent consistently cited Bush as the culprit, whereas among high viewers, 67 percent named him.
2. Discussions of voter backlash against Bush can be found in Howard Kurtz, "Bush's Negative Ads Appear to Be Backfiring," *Washington Post*, October 10, 1992, A12; Renee Loth, "Ads Afford View of Camps' Strong, Weak Spots," *Boston Globe*, October 22, 1992, 19; Howard Kurtz, "Negative Ads Appear to Lose Potency," *Washington Post*, October 26, 1992, A1; Howard Kurtz, "Perot Escalates Costly TV Ad Blitz Targeting Media, Parties, Pundits," *Washington Post*, October 27, 1992, A1; and Leslie Phillips, "Hopefuls May Spend Record $300 Million," *USA Today*, October 23–25, 1992, A1.
3. The Clinton quote comes from the text of his acceptance speech printed in *Congressional Quarterly Weekly Report*, July 18, 1992, 2130. Quinn's quote is cited in Phil Duncan, "Unease about Party's Chances Underlies Week of Glitz," *Congressional Quarterly Weekly Report*, July 18, 1992, 2091.
4. Text shown in Howard Kurtz, "In Advertising Give and Take, Clinton Camp Took and Responded," *Washington Post*, November 6, 1992, A10.
5. The first quote comes from Michael Kelly with David Johnston, "Campaign Renews Disputes of the Vietnam War Years," *New York Times*, October 9, 1992, 1. The second quote is taken from Michael Isikoff, "Clinton Denounces Attacks by Bush," *Washington Post*, October 9, 1992, A1.
6. In this two-stage analysis of the September 1992 Winston-Salem, North Carolina, data, the direct effect on the vote of attributions of responsibility for negative campaigning was −.24 ($p<.001$). People who saw Bush as attacking were more likely to attribute responsibility to him (.31; $p<.001$), whereas those who saw Clinton as attacking were more likely to attribute responsibility to him (.32; $p<.001$). The following variables were included in the analysis as control variables: party identification, education, age, gender, race, ideology, political interest, and media exposure.
7. Quote cited in David Hilzenrath, "GOP Aide Slams Administration," *Washington Post*, November 6, 1992, A18.
8. See Kurtz, "Advertising Give and Take," A10; and Ross Perot, *United We Stand* (New York: Hyperion, 1992).

9. Personal interview, May 25, 1996.

10. Michael Crowley, "Forbes' Henchmen," *Pittsburgh Post-Gazette,* January 14, 1996, B4.

11. The June numbers were reported in Richard Berke, "Voter Ratings for President Change Little," *New York Times,* June 5, 1996, A1, B7. The early October numbers come from Richard Berke, "Should Dole Risk Tough Image? Poll Says He Already Has One," *New York Times,* October 16, 1996, A1. For September numbers, see Richard Berke, "Some Images Stick. Some Don't. Why?" *New York Times Week in Review,* September 15, 1996, 1.

12. Richard Berke, "Aggressive Turn by Dole Appears to be Backfiring," *New York Times,* October 22, 1996, A1. Also see interview with the author by Mara Liasson, "Clinton Attacks Dole, Too, but Subtly," National Public Radio Morning Edition, October 22, 1996.

13. Hillary Clinton is quoted in Francis Clines, "1,000 Friends Help Cheer Up A Beleaguered Mrs. Clinton," *New York Times,* April 27, 1996, 10. The Stephanopoulos quote comes from Berke, "Should Dole Risk Tough Image? Poll Says He Already Has One," *New York Times,* October 16, 1996, A1.

14. Helen Dewar and David Maraniss, "Morphing and Bashing in Madison," *Washington Post,* October 11, 1996, A14; and Robin Toner, "In Final Rounds, Both Sides Whip out Bare-Knuckle Ads," *New York Times,* October 21, 1996, A1. Also see Howard Kurtz, "Clinton Team's Early Offensive Blunted Effect of Dole Ad Blitz," *Washington Post,* October 25, 1996, A19.

15. Scott MacKay, "Reed Counterattacks GOP's Negative TV Ad," *Providence Journal,* May 17, 1996, B1; and M. Charles Bakst, "Saying It Straight: Political Attack Ads Fill Air with Garbage," *Providence Journal,* May 16, 1996, B1. Also see Eliza Carney, "Party Time," *National Journal,* October 19, 1996, 2214–2218; and Adam Nagourney, "For G.O.P., Northeast Is Becoming Foreign Turf," *New York Times,* November 14, 1996, B12.

16. Interview with Reed campaign manager J. B. Poersch on October 30, 1996.

Chapter 10: Advertising and Democratic Elections

1. John Dryzek, *Discursive Democracy* (Cambridge: Cambridge University Press, 1990); Christopher Arterton, *Teledemocracy: Can Technology Protect Democracy?* (Newbury Park, Calif.: Sage, 1987); Jeffrey Abramson, Christopher Arterton, and Gary Orren, *The Electronic Commonwealth: The Impact of New Media Technologies on Democratic Politics* (New York: Basic Books, 1988); and Robert Entman, *Democracy without Citizens* (New York: Oxford University Press, 1989). General analyses of the impact of the media can be found in W. Russell Neuman, *The Paradox of Mass Politics* (Cambridge, Mass.: Harvard University Press, 1986); and Theodore

Lowi, *The Personal President* (Ithaca, N.Y.: Cornell University Press, 1985).

2. Joseph Schumpeter, *Capitalism, Socialism and Democracy* (New York: Harper and Row, 1942), 250–268.

3. Nelson Polsby, *Consequences of Party Reform* (New York: Oxford University Press, 1983).

4. Morris Fiorina, *Retrospective Evaluations in American National Elections* (New Haven, Conn.: Yale University Press, 1981).

5. Richard Merelman, *Making Something of Ourselves: On Culture and Politics in the United States* (Berkeley: University of California Press, 1984). Nancy Rosenblum also has made this point in a personal communication to me.

6. Benjamin Barber has made a useful distinction between strong and thin democracy in *Strong Democracy: Participatory Politics for a New Age* (Berkeley: University of California Press, 1984). *Thin democracy* makes relatively few demands of the electorate. This formulation sees the major activity of citizens as choosing leaders. Candidates are expected to facilitate voters' decisions by avoiding information that is misleading or incorrect. This view of democracy obviously places little emphasis on the general civic education of voters (other than that required for electoral choice), and therefore requires that little detailed information be presented in campaign ads. *Strong democracy*, however, rests on a more fully involved electorate. Candidates are expected to avoid misinformation, and they are required to transmit material to the electorate that will aid voters' judgments as well as facilitate political education beyond the immediate choice between candidates. This formulation clearly places a much heavier burden on campaign advertising than does thin democracy.

7. Diana Mutz, "Mass Media and the Depoliticization of Personal Experience," *American Journal of Political Science* 36 (1992): 483–508.

8. The emphasis placed on brevity today often leads consultants to advise candidates not to communicate an idea that is too lengthy to fit on a bumper sticker! This bumper-sticker standard is illustrated in Paul Magnusson, "Bush Just Might Buy This Plan—If No One Calls It 'Industrial Policy,' " *Business Week*, April 1, 1991, 27.

9. Barbara Hinckley, Richard Hofstetter, and John Kessel, "Information and the Vote: A Comparative Election Study," *American Politics Quarterly* 2 (1974): 131–158; Kim Kahn, "Senate Elections in the News," *Legislative Studies Quarterly* 16 (1991): 349–374; and Kim Kahn, "Does Being Male Help? An Investigation of the Effects of Candidate Gender and Campaign Coverage on Evaluations of U.S. Senate Candidates," *Journal of Politics* 54 (1992): 497–517.

10. Benjamin Page and Robert Shapiro, "Educating and Manipulating the Public," in *Manipulating Public Opinion,* ed. Michael Margolis and Gary Mauser (Belmont, Calif.: Brooks/Cole, 1989), 307–308. Also see Benjamin Page, *Choices and Echoes in Presidential Elections* (Chicago: University of Chicago Press, 1978), 266–277;

Schumpeter, *Capitalism, Socialism and Democracy,* 250–268; and Kathleen Jamieson, *Dirty Politics: Deception, Distraction, and Democracy* (New York: Oxford University Press, 1992).

11. Floyd Brown's fakery is described in Mike Robinson, "Clinton Camp Denounces TV Ad," *Providence Journal,* October 24, 1992, A1.

12. Spencer Hsu and Ellen Nakashima, "J. Warner's Ad Alters Photo to Cast Democrat as Insider," *Washington Post,* October 10, 1996, A1; and Spencer Hsu, "John Warner Fires Consultant Who Altered Challenger's Photo in Ad," *Washington Post,* October 11, 1996, B1.

13. Joe McGinniss, *The Selling of the President* (New York: Simon and Schuster, 1969); and Robert Spero, *The Duping of the American Voter* (New York: Lippincott and Crowell, 1980).

14. J. Gregory Payne, John Marlier, and Robert Baukus, "Polispots in the 1988 Presidential Primaries," *American Behavioral Scientist* 32 (1989): 375.

15. Where strong prior beliefs are present, the danger of advertising goes down dramatically. But, of course, in a rapidly changing world in which traditional moorings are disappearing—witness the collapse of communism on the world scene—even prior assumptions are being challenged. For a discussion of constraints on ad influence, see Elizabeth Kolbert, "Ad Effect on Vote Slipping," *New York Times,* March 22, 1992, "Week in Review," 4.

16. The Clinton quote comes from the text of his acceptance speech as printed in *Congressional Quarterly Weekly Report,* July 18, 1992, 2130.

17. Critics have also complained about the effectiveness of ad targeting on underage youths by tobacco companies. Research reported in the December 11, 1991, issue of the *Journal of the American Medical Association* has shown that the cartoon figure Old Joe Camel, used to advertise Camel cigarettes, has been a huge hit among youths aged twelve to nineteen years. Compared with adults in general, students were much more likely to indicate that they recognized Old Joe, liked him as a friend, and thought the ads looked cool. See Walecia Konrad, "I'd Toddle a Mile for a Camel," *Business Week,* December 23, 1991, 34.

18. The classic Supreme Court ruling in the campaign area was *Buckley v. Valeo* in 1976 (424 U.S. 1 1976). This case struck down a number of finance regulations as unconstitutional encroachments. See Clarke Caywood and Ivan Preston, "The Continuing Debate on Political Advertising: Toward a Jeopardy Theory of Political Advertising as Regulated Speech," *Journal of Public Policy and Marketing* 8 (1989): 204–226. For other reviews of newly emerging technologies, see Jeffrey Abramson, Christopher Arterton, and Gary Orren, *The Electronic Commonwealth* (New York: Basic Books, 1988); and Erwin Krasnow, Lawrence Longley, and Herbert Terry, *The Politics of Broadcast Regulation,* 3d ed. (New York: St. Martin's, 1982).

19. A more extended discussion of reform proposals can be found in Darrell West, "Reforming Campaign Ads," *PS: Political Science and Politics* 24 (1992): 74–77.
20. Laurence Parisot, "Attitudes about the Media: A Five-Country Comparison," *Public Opinion* 10 (1988): 18–19, 60. However, viewers do see differences in the helpfulness of television and newspapers. A May 1992 survey of Los Angeles residents revealed that those who followed ad watches in newspapers were much more likely (35 percent) to see them as being very helpful than those who relied on television (16 percent).
21. Kathleen Hall Jamieson, "For Televised Mendacity, This Year Is the Worst Ever," *Washington Post,* October 30, 1988, C1; and David Broder, "Five Ways to Put Some Sanity Back in Elections," *Washington Post,* January 14, 1990, B1.
22. Media scholar Jamieson has been instrumental in encouraging these ad watch efforts. According to personal correspondence from her, forty-two campaigns in 1990 were subjected to detailed critiques. For example, television stations airing discussions of particular ads included WFAA in Dallas, KVUE in Austin, WCVB in Boston, KRON in San Francisco, WBBM in Chicago, and WCCO in Minneapolis. Newspapers that followed ad campaigns closely were the *New York Times, Washington Post, Los Angeles Times, Chicago Sun-Times, Dallas Morning News, Houston Chronicle, Cleveland Plain-Dealer, Akron Beacon-Journal,* and *Louisville Courier-Journal.*
23. Race, of course, has been a controversial subject in many areas of American life. See Edward Carmines and James Stimson, *Issue Evolution: Race and the Transformation of American Politics* (Princeton: Princeton University Press, 1989).
24. Quoted by Kathleen Jamieson and Karlyn Kohrs Campbell in *The Interplay of Influence,* 2d ed. (Belmont, Calif.: Wadsworth, 1988), 55.
25. For an example of this thinking, see L. Brent Bozell and Brent Baker, eds., *And That's the Way It Isn't* (Alexandria, Va.: Media Research Center, 1990). Also see Lynda Lee Kaid, Rob Gobetz, Jane Garner, Chris Leland, and David Scott, "Television News and Presidential Campaigns: The Legitimization of Televised Political Advertising," *Social Science Quarterly* (in press); and Elizabeth Kolbert, "As Political Campaigns Turn Negative, the Press Is Given a Negative Rating," *New York Times,* May 1, 1992, A18.
26. Text is quoted from Roberto Suro, "In Louisiana, Both Edwards and Duke Are Sending a Message of Fear," *New York Times,* November 15, 1991, A20.
27. The media rating was in response to an October 1992 question in our Los Angeles County survey: "So far this year, would you say the news media have done an excellent, good, fair, or poor job of covering this presidential campaign?" The press bias question also was asked in the October survey: "In your opinion, has news coverage of

this year's fall presidential campaign been biased against any individual candidate? If so, which candidate received the most biased coverage?" The figures on television coverage come from Howard Kurtz, "Networks Stressed the Negative in Comments about Bush, Study Finds," *Washington Post*, November 15, 1992, A7. The longitudinal evidence on the party leanings of reporters is discussed by William Glaberson in "More Reporters Leaning Democratic, Study Says," *New York Times*, November 18, 1992, A20. Also see Elizabeth Kolbert, "Maybe the Media Did Treat Bush a Bit Harshly," *New York Times*, November 22, 1992, "Week in Review," 3.

28. Jeffrey Tulis, *The Rhetorical Presidency* (Princeton, N.J.: Princeton University Press, 1987).

29. Fox Butterfield, "Dukakis Says Race Was Harmed by TV," *New York Times*, April 22, 1990, 31.

30. 424 U.S. 1 (1976).

31. Eliza Carney, "Air Strikes," *National Journal* 28 (June 15, 1996): 1313–1317. Also see Ruth Marcus, "Taking 'Voter Guides' to the TV Audience," *Washington Post*, October 17, 1996, A16.

32. "Inside Politics," CNN, October 25, 1996.

33. John H. Cushman Jr., "Environmentalists Ante Up To Sway a Number of Races," *New York Times*, October 23, 1996, A21.

Appendix

1. L. Patrick Devlin, "Contrasts in Presidential Campaign Commercials of 1984," *Political Communications Review* 12 (1987): 26.

2. Devlin, "Contrasts in Presidential Campaign Commericals of 1984."

3. L. Patrick Devlin, "Contrasts in Presidential Campaign Commercials of 1988," *American Behavioral Scientist* 32 (1989): 390.

4. Ed McCabe, "The Campaign You Never Saw," *New York Times*, December 12, 1988, 32.

5. Author's transcription from 1992 Clinton primary ad tapes.

6. Author's transcription from 1992 general election ad tapes.

7. Author's transcription from 1992 general election ad tapes.

8. Author's transcription from 1992 general election ad tapes.

9. Author's transcription from 1992 general election ad tapes.

10. *New York Times*, "Clinton Unleashes a Fierce Attack on Dole," September 25, 1996, A18.

11. Adam Nagourney, "An Attack in Black and White on Clinton's Drug Policy," *New York Times*, September 21, 1996, 8.

12. Howard Kurtz, "Ad Watch," *Washington Post*, September 28, 1996, A12.

13. James Bennet, "Republicans Return to a Tested Weapon," *New York Times*, May 18, 1996, 8.

14. Kevin Sack, "Organized Labor Fires Back on Medicare," *New York Times*, August 30, 1996, A16.

Index

Abortion, 49–50, 152, 153
Action statements, 43
Adams, John Quincy, 2
Adatto, Kiku, 138
Advertisements. *See also* Election-year
  advertisements; Negative advertise-
  ments; Prominent advertisements;
  Television advertisements
  ad buys
    Connally, John, and, 17–18, 20
    explanation of, 17
    by geographic area, 34, 45
    local, 25–26
    national, 22–25
    in 1992 general election, 20–22
    in 1996 general election, 31–36
    in 1996 primaries, 28–31
    problems incurred in, 20
    strategies of, 18–20
    in Winston-Salem, North Caroli-
      na, 26–28
  ad watches. *See also* Media coverage
    American Association of Adver-
      tising Agencies, by, 83–84
    development of, 88–91, 96
    function of, 82, 95–96
    impact of, 97–98, 104–105
    importance of, 182–183
    during 1996 campaign, 102
    nonpresidential campaign, 99,
      102–104
    organizations conducting, 83–84
    types of, 101–102
  audiotape voice-overs in, 8
  campaign. *See* Election-year adver-
    tisements, *specific years*
  code words in, 8–9

  codes of conduct for, 83–88
  color in, 7
  credibility of, 98
  editing of, 7–8
  effectiveness of, 9–11
  election-year. *See* Election-year
    advertisements, *specific years*
  exposure
    agenda setting and, 129–131,
      133–134
    voter perceptions and, 114–119
  government regulation of, 182–184
  history of, 2–4
  legal remedies for, 185–188
  manipulation by, 176–179
  media coverage of, 68–72. *See also*
    Media coverage
  messages. *See also* Negative adver-
    tisements
    campaign stages and, 50–52
    elements in choosing, 37–39
    Internet use for, 53–57
    objects of negativity in, 62–64
    policy appeals as, 43–45
    rise in negative, 39, 57–61
    shifts in, 45–47, 49–50
    studies of, 39–41
    study of prominent, 41–43, 48
  music and sounds in, 6–7
  news coverage of, 14–15
  print, 2
  prior beliefs and, 114–119
  proposed remedies for, 82–83
  public opinion regarding, 39
  sponsorship, 185, 188
  television coverage of, 68–71
  visual aspects of, 4–6